This book brings together the results of fresh scholarly research to present a unique overview of the financial history of The Netherlands from the sixteenth century to the present day. The Netherlands has always occupied a role in international finance way out of proportion with its geographical size. Since the eighteenth century the country has been one of the largest exporters of capital in the world. In addition, several important financial innovations were pioneered in The Netherlands, such as funded public debt, the famous Amsterdam Wisselbank, large public limited companies with transferable shares and securitised international loans. The authors show the evolution of the Dutch financial system during nearly four and a half centuries, and explain this evolution by detailing the close interrelationship between currency policy, public finance and banking.

The book should be of great interest to economic historians in particular and international economists in general. It provides invaluable insights into the financial history of a country which, in many respects, paved the way for others in modern finance.

A financial history of The Netherlands

A financial history of
The Netherlands

edited by

MARJOLEIN 'T HART, JOOST JONKER AND
JAN LUITEN VAN ZANDEN

CAMBRIDGE
UNIVERSITY PRESS

Published by the Press Syndicate of the University of Cambridge
The Pitt Building, Trumpington Street, Cambridge CB2 1RP
40 West 20th Street, New York, NY 10011-4211, USA
10 Stamford Road, Oakleigh, Melbourne 3166, Australia

First published 1997

Printed in Great Britain at the University Press, Cambridge

Typeset in 10/12pt Monotype Times   [SE]

A catalogue record for this book is available from the British Library

Library of Congress cataloguing in publication data

A financial history of The Netherlands / edited by Marjolein 't Hart,
   Joost Jonker, and Jan Luiten van Zanden.
      p.   cm.
   Includes bibliographical references and index.
   ISBN 0 521 58161 3 (hardcover)
   1. Finance, Public – Netherlands – History.   2. Finance –
Netherlands – History.   I. Hart, Marjolein C. 't.   II. Jonker,
Joost, 1955–   .   III. Zanden, J. L. van.
HJ1201.F56   1997
336.492–dc20   96–26313
                                                            CIP

ISBN 0 521 58161 3 hardback

Contents

Figures

Tables

The Republic of the Seven United Provinces

The Kingdom of the Netherlands

1   Introduction

MARJOLEIN 'T HART, JOOST JONKER AND
JAN LUITEN VAN ZANDEN

The study of the financial and monetary history of The Netherlands shows
a vacuum between about 1965 and 1985. Silence ruled for almost 20 years
after J.G. van Dillen, the most important historian of the financial history
of the Dutch Republic, laid his pen aside and A.M. de Jong completed his
history of the Nederlandsche Bank (the Dutch central bank). M.G. Buist's
history of the banking house of Hope & Co. proved for long the only exception among Dutch scholarship. The field was left to British and American
historians who conducted pioneering research into government finance in
Holland in the sixteenth century (J.D. Tracy) and the Amsterdam capital
market in the eighteenth century (A.C. Carter and J.C. Riley). However,
new outlooks of Dutch origin arose in the slipstream of an international
boom in monetary and financial history. W. Fritschy (1988), M. 't Hart
(1989a), E.H.M. Dormans (1991), J. Barendregt (1993) and R. van der
Voort (1994) obtained their doctorate on studies of government finance in
the seventeenth to the twentieth centuries. The first volume of Joh. de Vries'
history of the Nederlandsche Bank in the period 1914–48 appeared in 1989.
In the meantime the discussion about monetary policy in the 1930s was
revived by contributions of Den Bakker and Bochove 1988, Van Zanden
1988c and J.W. Drukker 1990. Finally, this period witnessed the start of
research into the Bank of Amsterdam (P. Dehing in progress) and into
Amsterdam banking during the nineteenth century (J. Jonker 1996b). The
work in progress shows that these studies have provided important new
insights into Dutch financial history. In short, in the range of a couple of
years time a moribund specialism revived.

   Such considerations induced the editors to compile this book. Its main
aim is to unlock the new findings of recent research to an international audi-
ence. By allowing the specialists of the new wave to contribute a chapter on
their subject, a new overview is established of the financial history of The
Netherlands. An important part of these results has not yet appeared in
print. An even larger share of the contributions is published in English for
the first time.

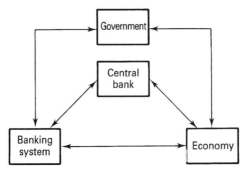

Figure 1.1 The actors in the financial system

This financial history of The Netherlands describes and analyses developments in three closely related fields, viz. the monetary system (such as currency and the gold standard), banking and public finance. Three groups of actors interact on this historical stage: the agents of the government, the governors of the banks and the other members of the financial elite – entrepreneurs, speculators, stockbrokers, (institutional) investors and more. Such interactions are only partly regulated by operations of the central bank, which acts in modern economies as the bank of the government, as the regulator of the monetary system, as the guardian of the value of money and as lender of last resort (see figure 1.1).

A lead in this book concerns the impact of public institutions upon the development of the financial and monetary system. Governments affect monetary developments in various ways. Rulers define the currency system, manipulate the value of money or create money to finance their expenditure. To mention yet another example, the creation of a funded debt is one of the most crucial moments in the financial history of a nation.

The close relationship between political–institutional and financial developments define the periodisation of Dutch financial history. The following periods can be discerned: from c. 1550 until the Revolt of 1572; the period of the Republic (1572–1795); the transition to a nation state (1795–1848); and The Netherlands as a nation state (1848 until today). This periodisation will be elaborated in more detail.

Around 1550, the starting point of this book, the northern Netherlands constituted a loose conglomeration of some well-developed provinces (Zeeland and Holland) and some fairly marginal parts of the large Habsburg Empire during the reign of Charles V (1515–55). The economy of the Low Countries was dominated by the commercial and financial metropolis of Antwerp. In a monetary field the maritime regions of The Netherlands were already fairly uniform due to the reforms of the fifteenth-century Burgundian princes and of Charles V. The currency system was unified and well-guarded in particular. However, the various provinces (*gewesten*) were characterised by a high degree of fiscal autonomy, which was carried by their striving to preserve urban and provincial privileges. The Provincial Councils and the States General at Brussels were in almost continuous negotiation with the monarch (Charles V, later Philip II) about the incidence and structure of taxation. In comparison with Antwerp and Bruges banking had made relatively little progress in the northern Netherlands.

The Revolt of 1572 and the successful war against the legitimate author-ities – a war, fuelled by the broad resistance to plans for a highly centralised system of taxation schemed up by Philip II and his governor Alva – resulted in an institutional structure in which the various provinces and cities of the northern Netherlands were bestowed a high degree of autonomy. The States General of the Republic of the United Provinces constituted a comparatively weak party, most certainly in financial respect, that did not succeed in levying national taxes (see chapter 2). This highly fragmented institutional structure remained until 1795, despite some moves of *Stadhouders* of the House of Orange (Prince and King William III and Prince William IV) towards the centralisation of power. In connection with this framework the provinces developed their own financial and banking system to a significant extent. The well-known exchange banks of Amsterdam, Rotterdam and Middelburg were essentially local banks that regulated payments within the city. Generally, almost every city pursued its own economic policy: to encourage the establishment of exchange brokers and industrial entrepreneurs, or to forbid their settlement as in the case of the Amsterdam cashiers; to raise local taxes; to protect the local industry by prohibiting the importation of certain products; and so on and so forth. Due to the Burgundian legacy the currency system was less fragmented. Yet, every province had its own mint that was to some degree autonomous (see chapter 3). Each province administered its own public finances. However, the dominance of the wealthy Holland, which accounted for c. 60 per cent of the government expenditure of the Republic, parried the worst of early modern fiscal problems, like bankruptcies. Moreover, the loose institutional structure allowed for the development of Amsterdam as the world's most important capital market of the time. Its network was sus-tained by the joint settlement of a multitude of leading merchants and banking houses.

It has long been debated whether or not this fragmented political–institu-tional and financial structure contributed to the decline of the Republic in the eighteenth century. In any case, the discontent about the rapidly growing burden of the public debt of Holland after 1780 did play a portentous part in the efforts of representatives of the Holland patriot bourgeoisie to create a nation state. Such schemes became ultimately possible through the occupation of The Netherlands by French troops in 1795, which put an end to the Republic. The subsequent 53 years – between the end of the Republic in 1795 and the liberal constitution of 1848 – were characterised by a gradual and intermittent construction of the institutional structure of a centralised nation state. After the defeat of Napoleon the merging of The Netherlands and Belgium was designed. Although these plans were ended by the Belgian revolt of 1830, the transition to a national financial and monetary system moved firmly ahead. Several determining events can be mentioned here: the amalgamation of the public debt in 1798, the creation of a national system of taxation in 1806, the centralisation of the mint in 1806/7, the currency reform of 1843, the reorganisation of government debt in 1844/5, the establishment of the Nederlandsche Bank in 1814, and the remodelling of this bank from a strictly local, Amsterdam bank to a (more or less) national bank in the 1860s.

The next hundred years or so, up to the creation of the EEC in 1958, was dominated by the maturation of the bonds within the financial system. The nationwide interaction between government, the central bank, bankers, and entrepreneurs increasingly determined the ups and downs of Dutch finance. Whereas the early nineteenth-century state had been geared to primary tasks – defence and servicing the public debt were by far the most important items of expenditure – after 1850 it gradually developed a policy aimed at stimulating the wealth of the nation. More attention was devoted to education, poor relief, and infrastructural works. After 1900 a wide range of policies was added to encourage house construction, to provide social services, to protect the weaker economic sectors (such as agriculture after 1929), or to prevent unemployment.

Through trial and error, the Nederlandsche Bank gradually acquired a role as the bankers' bank and came to exert a significant sway on banking in all parts of the economy. The Dutch private banks, although later as compared with neighbouring countries, increasingly expanded their financial services to entrepreneurs, (institutional) investors and, in the long run, also to households.

With the Treaty of Rome in 1958 another turning point was set. This time the transformation headed towards a united Europe. As for these last 35 years it is still unclear what the final outcome will be like, and when the transformation process will be completed. The complexity can be compared with the earlier phase in Dutch history when the provinces strove into the effort of a nation-state during 1795–1848. Without doubt the recent transition to a new institutional structure will be a long process with many ups and downs. Following the so-called snake arrangement (1973–9) and the

European Monetary System (since 1979) cooperation in the sphere of international monetary policy stuck, despite (or because of) the ambitious plans adopted in Maastricht in 1991. The attempts to accomplish institutional collaboration should be regarded in the context of a strong internationalisation of economic life in the after war period, also due to the success of the European Community in liberalising intra-European trade. While capital and product markets are increasingly tied together, the internationalisation has considerably limited the margins of national government policies. A national economic policy to stimulate the economy by means of lowering exchange rates or increasing government expenditure is hardly feasible and virtually ineffective. A national financial and monetary system no longer exists. Neither can the international political institutions shoulder the tasks of the nation-state.

The development of the political–institutional structure, outlined above, provides the framework of the financial history of The Netherlands. Another significant ingredient is the specific economic development of this region that was characterised by a relatively modern economic structure at an early stage. Already in the fifteenth and sixteenth centuries the provinces of Holland and Zeeland (and future Noord-Brabant) experienced an economic boom, based on the rise of export-oriented industries, fisheries, trade and shipping. Yet the region was outstripped by the expansion of the economy of the southern Netherlands where the centres of merchant capitalism (Bruges, later Antwerp) dominated economics. After the southern Netherlands were recaptured by the Spanish and the port of Antwerp was blocked by the Dutch in 1585, the economic centre of the Low Countries shifted towards Holland, in particular to the large industrial centres (Leiden, Haarlem) and to Amsterdam which then became the centre of world trade. In financial respects the establishment of the Bank of Amsterdam in 1609 added significantly to the key role of Amsterdam in the world economy. In addition, the abundance of capital that was amassed after 1585 allowed an enormous increase in government expenditure and debt, without the need for the creation of a powerful central tax authority.

At some time between 1650 and 1700 the remarkable expansion of the economy of Holland came to a standstill. After 1700 Holland was surpassed by Great Britain (Israel 1989). Yet the abundant wealth remained. Due to the high ratio of savings of the Dutch bourgeoisie this wealth even increased during the eighteenth century. However, because of the lack of domestic investment opportunities, funds were invested more and more in foreign countries. With the absence of a powerful central authority this flight of capital could not be prevented. Furthermore, the political crises of the 1780s and 1790s discouraged a large section of the bourgeoisie from buying the new government bonds, leaving the Dutch state an easy prey to foreign troops.

The economic stagnation that started in Holland around 1670 wore on until about 1825 (Van Zanden 1993). The years during which the country was part of the French Empire (1809–13) constituted a break in this extended period of economic stagnation. In the periphery of the Republic – in Groningen, Drenthe, Overijssel, Limburg, and Brabant – there may have been some degree of economic growth during the eighteenth century, a process that continued after 1825. Still, the economic (and political) centre remained in Holland. In 1850, on the eve of a new phase of expansion, Dutch wealth was still concentrated in this province. Between 1830 and 1914 economic growth gradually accelerated. After 1860 stagnation belonged definitely to a distant past and the rate of growth was more or less consistent with (northwestern) European standards. But the economic lead over western Europe, dating from the former Golden Age, was indisputably lost by about 1850. The secondary role of Dutch finance in an international respect coincided with the weakness of the Dutch state with regard to political connections.

In the twentieth century, the economy of The Netherlands was much less exceptional in a European respect as compared with the seventeenth and eighteenth centuries. Several features were characteristic of Dutch development, though. Demographic growth was unique. While the populations of the neighbouring countries increased at a slow rate, the population of The Netherlands doubled between 1900 and 1950. As a result, the growth of total GDP was higher than in neighbouring countries, although the rate of growth of GDP per capita was average. Also, the depression of the 1930s lasted longer in The Netherlands than anywhere else – the peak in unemployment was not reached until 1935! – which is generally attributed to the exchange rate policy (Van Zanden and Griffiths 1989). The Netherlands was the last country to abandon the gold standard. On the other hand, the economic expansion in the 1950s and 1960s seems to be in line with developments of the surrounding economies.

Summing up, in the period prior to 1850 the economic development of The Netherlands deviated considerably from the European pattern. The economy had relatively modern features as early as the sixteenth century. During the first half of the seventeenth century, the Dutch economy expanded, whereas most other countries faced economic crises. Subsequently, growth in Holland stagnated between 1670 and 1825, when economic development gained momentum elsewhere. After 1850 the economic advancement of The Netherlands was well on course with the rest of Western Europe.

These two ingredients, the specific political–institutional development and the early economic modernity of The Netherlands, constitute the framework for Dutch financial history. Despite several turning points and structural changes, several constant ingredients form fundamental threads in the development of the financial system. Some of these threads, i.e., the abundance of capital, the high degree of capital exports, a stable currency, and a comparatively high tax burden, are highlighted below.

A remarkable continuous element in the financial history of The Netherlands is the wealth of capital. Due to the relatively high profits that were earned in international trade from the sixteenth century on, and as a result of the high savings ratio of the bourgeoisie, whether or not arising from a Calvinist way of life, the private sector continuously had a large (net) surplus of savings. The funds were diverted to two major, alternating destinations: foreign investments (predominant between 1720 and 1790 and between 1850 and 1940) and the public debt. There is no exact information or even an educated guess of the size of capital imports and exports in the sixteenth and early seventeenth centuries, but presumably The Netherlands was a capital-importing country until the first decades of the seventeenth century. Such can primarily be ascribed to the migration of numerous merchants from the southern Netherlands into Holland between 1580 and 1620. During the seventeenth century, direct investments in other countries became increasingly more important. The activities of the Dutch East India Company in Asia and of the Dutch West India Company in America and Africa can be interpreted as a kind of direct foreign investment in production and transportation on the spot. Entrepreneurs such as De Geer and Trip were involved in the expansion and modernisation of the Swedish iron industry. Others invested in various activities ranging from wine improvements around Bordeaux to the production of marble in Italy. During the phase of stagnation after 1670 investments in the public debt were the first to increase rapidly. In the eighteenth century, investments in foreign government bonds gained the upper hand. Direct investments were concentrated in one colony, Surinam, particularly in the period 1760–75 (Van Stipriaan 1993). After the French financial crisis following the French Revolution of 1789 the Dutch state absorbed the surplus savings of the private sector again. Liquidations during the Napoleonic Wars diminished their value significantly and investments abroad stagnated until 1850. However, after 1845 the spectacular growth of public debt came to a halt (see chapter 4) and the government began to redeem part of its debt, aided by the net revenue (*batig slot*) of the colonies in Dutch East India. Consequently indirect foreign investments increased tremendously between 1850 and 1875. After 1875 (when large losses were incurred on American railway companies) the growth of Dutch investments abroad slowed down, while opportunities to invest in domestic trade and industry expanded. In the twentieth century, direct foreign investments once again dominated, as they did in the period 1600–70. Around 1900 only 20 per cent of capital invested in other countries consisted of direct investments and 90 per cent of this amount was tied up in Indonesia. The former proportion would rise to more than 50 per cent in 1985, due to the ascent of major multinational corporations such as Shell, Philips, Akzo and Unilever. The expansion of foreign direct investments was violently interrupted by World War II. The war caused, among other things, forcible liquidations of foreign investments as well as the loss of Indonesia. During these years the surplus savings of the private sector were entirely absorbed by the increase in government debt. Nevertheless, throughout the twentieth century, The Netherlands remained one of the world's major investors in other countries, despite the small size of the country. Between 1920 and 1985 The Netherlands was recurrently the third or fourth international investor after Great Britain and the United States, at a level comparable to Germany and France. It was not until 1973 that it had to yield the third place to Japan (Gales and Sluyterman 1993). In per capita terms it has always ranked at the top of the list, a position that actually dates back to the seventeenth century.

The abundance of capital in Holland had major consequences for its financial development. Interest rates were generally lower than those in most other European countries; between 1670 and 1780 Holland was the leading nation in this respect. The ample supply on the capital market enabled government to finance its rapidly rising expenditure in times of war by increasing the public debt. Elsewhere in early modern Europe, governments had to resort to a devaluation of their currency in order to generate sufficient revenue. State bankruptcies were no exception for much of Europe up to the nineteenth century; for the Dutch, such crises were limited in scope. In the twentieth century, manipulation of several foreign currencies was performed by the printing press. The Dutch government managed to avoid such monetary financing and the value of the coin remained virtually intact. Since the early seventeenth century, the guilder had a well-nigh unchanging intrinsic value. Up to 1931 this stability was only equalled by that of the pound sterling. Thereafter, their ways parted: the pound was the first to be devalued in September 1931, the guilder was the last in September 1936. After 1945 and especially since the fall of the pound in 1967 the ratio between the guilder and the pound changed drastically. In the entire twentieth century, the stability of the guilder was matched only by the Swiss franc and by the post-1923 German mark.

But the fact that the Dutch guilder has been such stable currency since the seventeenth century cannot be ascribed only to the abundance of above-mentioned capital. As will be shown in chapter 3 other factors also played a part. In the seventeenth and eighteenth centuries coins struck in The Netherlands were export products, destined for circulation in Asia or the Baltic. The demand for this product was partly determined by its quality, i.e., its stability. Strong economic interests prohibited the weakening of the currency. In the main, the stability of the coin reflects the stability of the economic and political system of The Netherlands. Since 1572, when the urban bourgeoisie seized power, the political–economic structure remained basically the same. Even the 'break' of 1795 was less radical than it seemed at first sight: after 1795 the Holland bourgeoisie still ran the show. The comparatively stable socio-economic and political relations, and the absence of major social conflicts, contributed significantly to the stability of the monetary system (and vice versa). The emergence of social movements, the process of pillarisation (*verzuiling*), and the spread of political democracy were gradual – they did not disrupt the calm of Dutch economic life. The political elite continued to adhere to a fairly conservative economic ideology. Prominent politicians of the left and right, such as Colijn, Lieftinck, Drees and Zijlstra, were models of the proverbial Dutch frugality. Experiments with a more expansive economic policy were shunned. Only in cases of *force majeure* – in World War I and during the occupation by Nazi Germany between 1940 and 1945 – did government resort to the printing of new money, which affected the value of the currency. But after both wars the path of financial orthodoxy was soon recaptured.

In the light of the legacy of parsimony the immense expansion of government expenditure, in particular the spending on social services after 1960, is all the more peculiar. In a rather short period The Netherlands developed from a country with a tiny government apparatus into one with a disproportionately large collective sector. This u-turn was marked above all in social security. In the first half of the twentieth century, The Netherlands lagged behind its neighbouring countries in this field, but after 1960 the lag was quickly turned into a considerable lead (Van Zanden and Griffiths 1989). Still, the traditional conservative monetary policy of the Dutch government did remain in place, partly due to the enormous power of the central bank. The exchange rate of the guilder was therefore hardly affected by the expansive policies, the more so since a similar course was pursued in most of the surrounding countries. After 1980 economic policy returned to the mainstream of Dutch history. An explanation for this almost un-Dutch period from 1960 to 1980 is still lacking. The heritage of the years 1960–80, i.e., a high tax burden and a big government, claimed its toll on economic developments after 1980.

The high burden of taxation, which confronted entrepreneurs and households alike after 1960, had historical precedents. In the seventeenth and eighteenth centuries the tax burden was more elevated in The Netherlands, and especially in Holland, than in the rest of Europe. After the Revolt the Dutch provinces raised considerably the burden of taxation, a pursuit in which the Habsburgs had not been very successful before 1572. The wealth of capital in Holland and the high degree of commercialisation allowed an increase in taxes to such an extent that the small population of the Republic could compete with the great powers until 1713. Despite a more passive role in international politics after 1713 the tax burden remained high throughout the eighteenth century. The load even increased, forced by the large expenses needed to pay the interest on the public debt. In most countries around 1800 the tax burden probably amounted to no more than 5 or 10 per cent of national income, but in The Netherlands this percentage had reached 12 per cent (Fritschy 1990). In relation to a hodman's wage the incidence of taxation was raised fivefold in the early modern period in Holland. Around 1510 this burden did not exceed c. 7 working days; this augmented to about 20 days in 1700 and more than 33 days in 1790. In other provinces this rise can also be observed, although it was less extreme. Data on Overijssel show a rise from c. 3 working days in 1578 to 14 in 1720, followed by a decline to 11 working days for a hodman in 1790 (Van Zanden 1985).

In this regard the nineteenth century is a unique period: the burden of taxation gradually decreased from c. 12 per cent to almost 7 per cent of national income. In the first half of the nineteenth century this was mainly a result of cut-backs in expenditure. Above all, the army was strongly reduced in accordance with its marginal role in international politics. In the second half of the nineteenth century, the decline in the tax burden was enabled by a revival of economic growth that allowed the concurrence of a modest increase in government expenditure per capita and a continuous lowering of the tax burden. World War I and its aftermath suddenly ended this trend. From 1914 on the ratio of taxes to national income once more shows an upward tendency, in particular during 1960–80. At the end of the twentieth century, The Netherlands became again what it had been in the seventeenth and eighteenth centuries: a country with a high tax burden, large surplus savings, a sizable export of capital, and a strong currency. Above all, the interactions between government, banks, and the financial elite had created and preserved a highly stable, conservative financial–economic climate.

Note

The editors wish to thank Mrs. L. van Roosmalen of the Universiteit Utrecht for her great efforts to shape the manuscript towards publication.

2 The merits of a financial revolution: public finance, 1550–1700

MARJOLEIN 'T HART

2.1 Introduction

In the early modern era, the system of public finance of the northern Netherlands constituted a most singular type among its neighbouring countries. This tiny nation, without large resources of its own, was extremely successful in raising sizable quantities of funds for public purposes, in particular for warfare. Various larger monarchies experienced enormous difficulties in making both ends meet. Powerful princes went bankrupt, but not this conglomeration of sovereign provinces. Distinguished ambassadors of foreign authorities reported home on how the Dutch managed their astonishingly high levels of public debt.

Within this state, the commercial and financial strength of the province of Holland constituted the major backbone. In the course of the sixteenth century, Holland had developed a system of provincial public finance which enabled the ascent of a secured public debt against relatively low rates of interest. This so-called 'financial revolution' (Tracy 1985a, p. 3; Dickson 1967) acted as a most welcome safety-valve for unforeseen and exorbitant military expenses.

The reverse side of the coin was an enormous incidence of taxation. Loans, after all, had to be serviced by duties that had to be paid by the populace. In 1595, a young English traveller by the name of Fynes Moryson noted the paradox of this burden:

The Tributes, Taxes, and Customes, of all kinds imposed by mutuall consent – so great is the love of liberty or freedome – are very burthensome, and they willingly beare them, though for much lesse exactions imposed by the King of *Spaine* ... they had the boldnesse to make warre against a Prince of such great power. (Quoted by Jacobsen Jensen 1918, p. 267)

Indeed, the imposition of new taxes by the Habsburg overlord had sparked off the Dutch struggle for independence in the 1570s. Yet, by the end of the seventeenth century, the Dutch were widely known as being the most heavily taxed people in Europe. Figures drafted by the contemporary

11

statistician Gregory King confirmed this impression. Per capita, the English paid £1 4s. 0d. in taxes, the French £1 5s. 0d., but the inhabitants of The Netherlands stood out with £3 1s. 7d. (Wilson 1963, p. 120).

The conditions of this peculiar system of public finance are traced in this chapter. First, the situation is sketched in the later sixteenth century. The circumstances are described just before the outbreak of the Revolt against Spain, emphasising the centralising reforms of the Habsburgs. Then, the regulations of the newly established state are delineated. Although the institutions were meant to be temporary only, they proved to be quite durable, lasting up to the end of the eighteenth century. Next, the increase in expenditure and subsequent rise in the public debt are dealt with. Several sections follow on the revenues marked for expenses: the funds controlled by the central state and those managed by the provinces. The elasticity of the tax system in the maritime western part of the country deserves a special note. The chapter concludes on the political and socio-economic conditions which enabled the development of this relatively modern system of public credit.

2.2 The centralisation of finances under the Habsburgs

The ability of the Dutch to mobilise such considerable resources during the Eighty Years' War (1568–1648) was the more surprising as their territories were only weakly integrated. The Dutch Republic had become a nation almost by accident. Only by the 1550s had the 17 Netherlands been united under one single overlord, the Habsburg Charles V (1515–55). His Burgundian heritage counted several possessions to which new *gewesten* (provinces and counties) were added. The independent traditions of the separate regions were strong. Old rivalries and hostilities among the *gewesten* were not yet forgotten. Gelderland had even sacked The Hague as late as 1528. Charles V tried to overcome these differences by establishing a single political unit in 1548. This act liberated The Netherlands from the legislation of the Holy Roman Empire.

At the same time, these 1,548 statutes enhanced the power of the respective governments of the *gewesten*, the Provincial Estates. Aspirations for differing interests and perspectives were boosted. A most strong dividing line existed between the maritime western part and the inland provinces. The provinces in the west: Holland, Zeeland and Utrecht, were highly urbanised and commercialised. Their finances, even the revenues of the cities, had long stood under close supervision of their overlords, the Burgundian princes. The contributions for the Habsburgs, Charles V and his son Philip II, went under the heading of *bede*. Literally, this word means request, and these funds had indeed to be negotiated for. In the main, the

Table 2.1. *Revenue from domains, ca. 1550 (in guilders)*

Holland	330,000
Zeeland	186,000
Friesland, Utrecht, Drenthe, Overijssel, Groningen	504,000
Total	1,120,000

Source: Baelde 1963, p. 21.

bede constituted a tax on property, mainly on land. Gradually, the *bede* evolved into a loan from the provinces. For the service thereof provincial taxes were levied. Since 1542, next to the land tax, excise duties (taxes on consumption) were imposed, such as on wine, beer, milling grain, meat, and salt. In Holland, the revenue was considerable: from the *beden* for 1550–66 234,377 guilders annually on average (Tracy 1985b, p. 109; Bos-Rops 1993, p. 41). The two other provinces of the core region in the west, Zeeland and Utrecht, traditionally paid sums amounting to one-quarter and one-tenth of that of Holland respectively.

The fiscal structure of the *gewesten* that had not belonged to the Burgundian patrimony was far less developed. There, ancient privileges overshadowed and hampered public funds. As for the cities, their power structure was traditionally independent of any overlord or any provincial government, a major difference from the urban centres in the west. Even 20 years after the unification of 1548 neither the inland cities, nor the rural quarters, nor their landlords were subjected to a unified financial system at the provincial level. The relatively modernised fiscal system of Holland, Zeeland, or Utrecht contrasted sharply with these eastern and northern areas.

Although exact figures are still lacking, the revenue from taxation in the inland communities must have been negligible. Next to taxes, the overlord could dispose of funds from domains, the customary lordly possessions. These resources were quite significant, as can be seen from table 2.1. In Holland and Zeeland, the amounts even surpassed the level of ordinary taxation. However, in the years following the succession of Philip II in 1557, these sums diminished rapidly. Many domains were pawned or sold in order to pay for the rising costs of war.

With the expansive policies of the Habsburg king, the only solution left for the authorities was to raise taxes. The Duke of Alva, the governor for the Spanish Habsburgs in The Netherlands, introduced a system of unified taxation in 1569. According to his plans, three sorts of taxes were to be introduced: a 1 per cent tax (hundredth) upon all property, a 5 per cent tax (twentieth) upon all transfers of real estate, and a 10 per cent tax (tenth) that was to become a general sales tax.

The hundredth was not designed to become a permanent duty. Being a single levy, almost all provinces proved willing to accept the tax. The yield amounted to 3,628,507 guilders. As such, the tax constituted already a considerable success for the Spanish Habsburg government. Yet more was foreseen with the twentieth and the tenth, which were both to become permanent levies. Their expected yield ranged from 4 million guilders for the tenth to 13 million guilders for both (Grapperhaus 1982, p. 120; Parker 1977, p. 115).

The fact that the tenth and the twentieth were to become lasting duties rendered them much more controversial. Above all, the tenth was highly contested. The provinces feared the impact upon commerce and sales. Shipping and trade constituted a most rewarding business for the mercantile communities. The Habsburg government allowed exemptions for overseas trade and for consumption of primary produce. Lower tariffs were conceded for bread and meat, whereas exports were to be taxed at a rate of 3.3 per cent only. Still, the provinces were not willing to accept the perpetual character of the tax. In the end, a compromise was found by having the taxes bought off by a lump sum (redemption), which was to yield 574,750 guilders annually.

In the distribution of these funds the sheer domination among the northern *gewesten* by the province of Holland was obvious: they paid almost half of the contribution. Such was consistent with the wealth of the area. Second came Gelderland, the largest inland province, paying more than one-fifth of the total (Grapperhaus 1982, p. 114). Of all the areas that had not belonged to the Burgundian heritage, this was definitely the most important province in financial terms (Van de Pas 1995). Third came Zeeland, the second major maritime *gewest*.

With the above solution, the fiscal autonomy of the provinces was preserved. Yet the central government was at a disadvantage because the sums were much lower than was expected. Moreover, such settlements would prove to be less rewarding in the future, as additional levies were precluded. Therefore, even before the monies were handed over to the Habsburg government, the Spanish governor decided to impose the taxes after all in 1571. This step washed out all possible compromises and surely precipitated the outbreak of the Revolt – a war that was to last almost 80 years followed.

2.3 Early fiscal structures during the Revolt

In the first decades the southern provinces (such as Flanders and Brabant) were the more outspoken and rebellious as compared with the north. Yet, after the fall of Antwerp in 1585, they came under strict Spanish control. The northern provinces (Holland, Zeeland, Utrecht, Friesland, Groningen,

Gelderland, Overijssel and Drenthe) managed to remain free, albeit at the cost of a protracted war. As a result of pressing needs, former fiscal structures in the north were reinforced. *Ad hoc* measures became permanent. Due to the hatred of the Habsburg measures, the process of centralisation that had begun under the Burgundian dukes was reversed into a diverging trend. The new Republic became a confederation, in which each of the United Provinces were sovereign. They agreed to a common effort, in particular for waging war against Spain. A new States General was constituted, with representatives of the provinces along with a new Council of State, the executive body. Both came to be located in The Hague. Prince William of Orange, the former *Stadhouder* (substitute for the king), was elected as the new *Stadhouder* (highest dignitary) of the provinces. The nation was characterised by a highly fragmented political constitution. The political centre at The Hague commanded only a couple of hundred civil servants ('t Hart 1993). These basic traits of the Dutch state endured until 1795, when French troops invaded the country and put an end to the old regime.

Of direct significance was the fact that no unified tax system was implemented, apart from the customs duties (taxes on imports and exports) and some minor levies. Efforts to create a larger degree of financial unanimity among the federated provinces failed. Opposition to the central policies from The Hague was manifest and strong. Most recalcitrance against the attempts to impose central fiscal measures was demonstrated in the east. For example, Overijssel's hesitance to join the Union was strongly motivated by its unwillingness to make the new financial sacrifices demanded. The province, in fact, never formally signed the treaty of Union, although it was always regarded as an integral part of the Republic (Reitsma 1982, p. 165). Gelderland as a province never signed the Union either, yet its regions joined the confederation separately. The highly decentralised constitution of this province hampered several future efforts to improve central control.

The only solution for the greater part of the Union's expenses was a traditional device to share the costs. The latter were listed in a kind of budget called *Staat van Oorlog*. This war establishment was presented by the Council of State in a petition to the States General. Each province was to promise in a *consent* to pay a certain allotted part (under the name of *quota*) to the costs of warfare and administration. To facilitate ratification, these *quotas* were fixed. The distribution of 1616 (see figure 2.1) remained in force for most of the time up to the 1790s.[1]

Obviously, Holland was responsible for the bulk of the burden. Its quota ran at about 58 per cent. Although its share of the population was less (approximately 48 per cent of the northern Netherlands), such a contribution was not surprising in view of its prosperous development. Friesland's agriculture was apparently thriving, as this northern maritime province

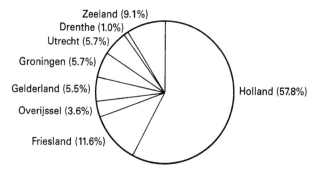

Figure 2.1 Contribution by province, 1616–1792
Source: Zwitzer 1991, p. 69.

now came second as compared with a couple of decades earlier. Third came, again, seabound Zeeland. Most striking was a downfall in the contribution of Gelderland from almost 20 per cent to a mere 5.5 per cent. A significant part of its territory, the Upper Quarter of Gelderland, was lost to the enemy. Yet this fact could not excuse the whole reduction. And although commercialisation proceeded less favourably as compared with the maritime regions, political resentment must have counted significantly too.

2.4 The burden of war in the republican expenses

In the meantime, expenses rose. Years of warfare were recurrent for almost all early modern states (Körner 1995a, p. 416; Tilly 1990). The Eighty Years' War against the former Spanish–Habsburg overlord pressed heavily upon the Union's budget. By 1586, the sums of the petitions in the States General amounted to a modest 2.9 million. As can be seen in figure 2.2, they gradually increased up to the Truce of 1609–21. After a stagnation of costs during the armistice, they climbed as high as 22 million guilders annually in the 1630s. They were to fall drastically after peace was signed in 1648, yet a rise was noticeable during the First Anglo-Dutch War of 1652–4, and yet again due to the naval expedition to the Baltic in 1658. Peaks followed with the Second Anglo-Dutch War (over 30 million guilders in 1665) and the Third Anglo-Dutch War (over 40 million guilders in 1672). Military costs were reduced thereafter, but they rose again during the Nine Years' War of 1688–97 with France. A temporary low was recorded in the last three years of the seventeenth century, with annual expenses even below the 2 million guilders. They rose again in the early eighteenth century, due to the War of the Austrian Succession (1702–13). The financial consequences of this last war were to weigh heavily (see chapter 4).

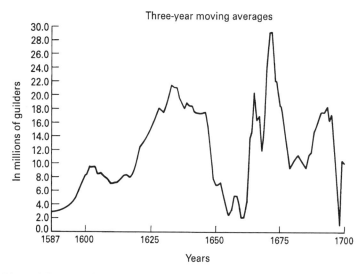

Figure 2.2 Expenditure Dutch Republic, 1587–1700
Source: ARA Generaliteitsrekenkamer, Staat van Petitiën.

Warfare, thus, affected the overall expenditure of the Union in a most direct way. The peace establishment came to a modest amount only. From a reconstructed budget around 1641 it was found that almost 90 per cent of the near 24 million guilders was directly related to war, namely spent on the army, the navy, army pensions and fortifications ('t Hart 1993, p. 61). The debt service absorbed by then slightly over 4 per cent: such sums were to increase significantly after the steep rise of the public debt (see below). The costs of administration (almost 5 per cent in the 1640s) were contained in general. In this respect, the Dutch differed from several larger monarchies as no costly court had to be supported. The court of the Princes of Orange, who acted as *Stadhouders* and representatives of the republican government, was financed by their private funds. In the meantime, many tasks of the public administration were left to the regional and local governments. The revenues thereof came from local taxes and domains. By all accounts, the largest recurrent problem for the Dutch state constituted the costs for warfare.

2.5 The safety-valve of the public debt

Having a fragmented fiscal structure, it proved of tremendous advantage that those military costs could be provided for by loans. A mature money market stood at the disposal of the Dutch and economic prosperity allowed the accumulation of major private funds. Moreover, after 1585 the centre of international lending activity had shifted from Antwerp to Amsterdam. During most of the seventeenth century, the substantial assets of native Dutch citizens allowed the government to tap from these riches for public purposes (see chapter 3).

However, loans could be very costly as interest rates tended to be quite elevated, particularly during times of war. In early modern Europe, the costs of debts caused several bankruptcies of states (Webber 1986, p. 252). In the maritime Netherlands though, a smooth functioning system of (provincial) public debt unfolded in the sixteenth century that was vested upon the steady tradition of city finances. Public loans tended to become long term instead of short term; a large proportion was even never repaid at all. This process was described by Tracy (1985a) for the province of Holland. Debt charges were reduced as the payment thereof was secured (*funded*) by regular provincial taxation. In this respect, the imposition of excises (duties upon popular consumption) in the larger urban centres proved of distinctive bearing.

Such a development in public finance has been labelled a *financial revolution*. It allowed, above all, the contracts of long-term loans and the development of a consolidated debt, guaranteed by the authorities. The introduction of provincial excises in 1542 and the abolishment of forced loans in 1555 proved conducive. As a consequence of these measures, the rates of interest upon government loans tended to be reasonable up to 1560. The outbreak of the Eighty Years' War led temporarily to a sharp escalation of interest rates, even to 20 per cent in the 1570s (see figure 2.3). In this decade, interest payments were postponed. For a while, the credit of Holland was weak. A large-scale conversion of former loans was necessary to restore faith in public finances. The confiscation of the possessions and assets of catholic institutions, related to the introduction of the Dutch Reformed Church, was helpful as well. Rates of interest could drop again, lowering to slightly over 8 per cent in the 1580s. By the beginning of the seventeenth century they decreased further to 6.25 per cent, which had been the level of the early sixteenth-century loans. Around 1650 they attained the level of 5 per cent. Thereafter the rate stabilised at 4 per cent, although it dropped even to 3 per cent for a short period of time. The eighteenth century witnessed another low, a trend which was only reversed in the late 1780s. Above all, the abundance of credit and the low interest rates resulted in the admiration of the Dutch by competing regimes, as most other countries were handicapped by much higher rates of interest (Homer 1963, p. 174; Parker 1974, p. 573).

A solid money market was of major relevance for the soundness of the Dutch financial system. Although its main threats are the subject of chapter

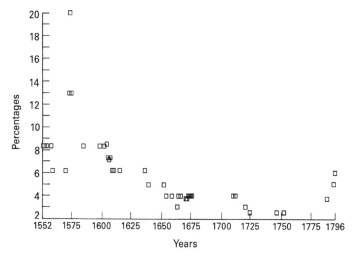

Figure 2.3 Rates of interest upon Holland's loans, 1552–1796
Source: Dormans 1991, pp. 26, 47, 71, 87; Homer 1963, p. 120.

3, mention should be made in this section about the stability of the currency. Frequent debasements by many a monarchical state as to their currencies disrupted the stability of interest rates elsewhere. Such abuses were avoided in this republican state, although the crisis of the 1570s did invite the authorities to adopt such practices also. Coins in circulation obtained an imprint by the provincial authorities of Holland which increased their nominal value by 12.5 per cent in 1573. The additional revenue was intended as a public loan, yet the funds were never repaid to the owners. The yield must have been approximately 250,000 guilders. Another time around 1575–7 the mint was used as a fiscal measure as the States of Holland issued the *leeuwedaalder* at 32 stuivers, three stuivers above their intrinsic value, the extra revenue to be used for warfare, with a yield of 1,000,000 guilders. Even the States General issued new coins (*statenmunten*) with so-called *opgeld* (a specific imprint) in 1577 (Grapperhaus 1982, p. 278; Korthals Altes 1996, pp. 60–2).

But such attacks on the currency did not recur. The strong backing of the financial structures allowed for recurrent lending, which put the actual payments of sailors and soldiers on a firm footing in the 1590s. As a consequence, mutinies were restricted, despite the fact that the Dutch commanded one of the largest armies in Europe. This was a major achievement for the new-born state, that stood in contrast with most of its larger competitors in this respect (Howard 1978, p. 37).

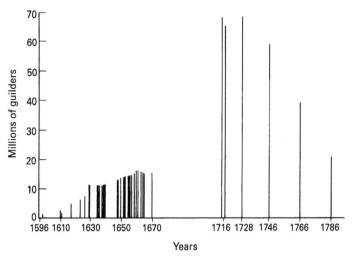

Figure 2.4 Public debt of the Union, 1596–1796
Source: Up to 1650 ARA 1.01.06 12548–188; after 1650 Dormans 1991, pp. 140, 156, 165.

At first, most loans were short term, policy demanding their repayment as quickly as possible. But long-term arrangements resulted in a public debt of the Union since 1596. In that year, a Union debt of 92,300 guilders was recorded, which had increased to almost 14 million guilders in 1650. By the turn of the century, it was registered at about 19 million guilders (figure 2.4). Due to the enormous expenses of the War of the Austrian Succession, the debt soared in the early eighteenth century (see chapter 4).

But provincial debts rose too, above all in Holland. The debt of this province, which was relatively contained up to 1618, came to exceed the Union obligations ten-fold (see figure 2.5).[2] By 1700, the outstanding capital almost reached 200 million guilders. Debt service therefore, despite the low rate of interest, became a growing item on the provincial budget. While after the Eighty Years' War the military costs were suppressed and administration was restrained, debt charges rose. In Holland, they even amounted to over 61 per cent of the expenses during most of the second half of the seventeenth century (Dormans 1991, p. 72, see also figure 4.1). Because of the enormous burden of the debt, the famous statesman John de Witt introduced a policy of *sinking fund* in the 1650s: the yield on the interest reduction was used to redeem part of the debt. Indeed, for a couple of years, due to limited involvement in wars, this scheme resulted indeed in a temporary lowering of the debt burden.

Most striking was the fact that no central public bank took care of the

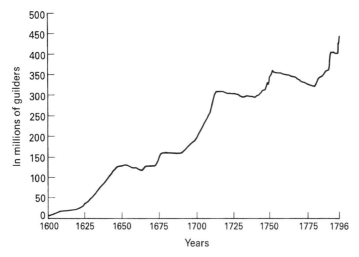

Figure 2.5 Public debt of Holland, 1600–1796
Source: Dormans 1991, pp. 65–6, 80–1, 110–11.

issue and regulation of the numerous loans. The Bank of Amsterdam (see chapter 3) was not designed for these purposes. Instead, the republican bonds were issued by several public authorities: the Union, the provinces, the major cities, and the boards of admiralty. Mostly, the respective receivers of taxes (the Receiver General of the Union, the Receivers General of the seven provinces, the Receivers of the larger cities, the Receivers General of the five navy boards) took care for the placement and management of the loans, as well as for the payment of interest. Actually, they acted like semi-private bankers for the state. Their bonds were worded differently and could not be exchanged easily for one another, yet they made a good price on the market, being a favoured kind of investment. Forced loans did appear incidentally in the late sixteenth century, in 1747–8 and again in the last decades of the eighteenth century, yet voluntary contracts constituted the rule. Most bonds were perpetual annuities (under the name of *losrenten*) or short-term annuities of six months renewed repeatedly (called *obligaties*). Another important category was constituted by life annuities (*lijfrenten*). The latter carried more interest – generally twice the rate for perpetual annuities – yet payments halted after the death of the person named in the contract.

Life annuities were extremely popular among the investors, but in fact quite expensive for the government. No distinction was made as to the age of the stipulated individuals. John de Witt, spurred by the enormous debt burden of the province, wrote a treatise in 1671 on the relationship between longevity and profitability of the life annuities, pointing to the need for low rates for the young and higher rates for the elderly. Although the rates were lowered from 8.33 per cent to 7.15 per cent, they remained unrelated to age.

Among the investors in public debt during the sixteenth century, (semi-)public institutes like orphanages figured prominently. Yet since 1620 the debt came to be widely spread among numerous domestic and private investors. The relatively well-off were eager to buy one or more public bonds, which were offered by the local tax receivers in coupons of various sizes. In this respect the Dutch Republic differed again from most other states, where public debts were held mainly by officials (such as in France), by bankers (as in London) or by foreign merchants (as in Sweden). Women were counted among the financiers too: estimations run at about two-fifths of the total. The purchase of Dutch public bonds brought grist to the mills of the investors: in the second half of the seventeenth century, 8 to 10 million guilders were paid in interest to the multitude of debt holders annually (De Vries and Van der Woude 1995, p. 150).

The province of Holland proved unquestionably more solvent than the whole Union, owing to the traditional loan system of the city governments. Part of Holland's debt was made up of loans that were contracted first by the confederation and then transferred to the province because the Union itself lacked the cornerstone of sufficient taxation (Union debts proved difficult to fund, see next section). The reason for the enormous increase in the public debt was first and foremost warfare. All other items of expenditure constituted a mere fraction thereof. The mushrooming of the debt did not seem to harm the limited area of the Republic, at least not during the seventeenth century. No other state, except perhaps some city states, could raise so much in funds respective to its population (Körner 1995b, p. 532). Also, whereas many city states still harked back to the system of forced loans, Holland's flotations were predominantly voluntary. The province of Holland was a most welcome intermediary to the Union, as the central republican state had only a few fiscal instruments to secure the repayments and debt charges of the sums contracted. The financial revolution, thus, remained strictly a provincial affair in The Netherlands. In this respect, the financial revolution of England of the 1690s proved much more flexible, as it was based upon nationwide, centrally controlled taxes (Dickson 1967). These limits to the Dutch fiscal system started to count in the eighteenth century.

2.6 The limited fiscal instruments of the central state

The central state (the colleges of the States General and the Council of State) commanded only a fraction of public resources directly. In comparison with other European countries, a number of revenue categories were

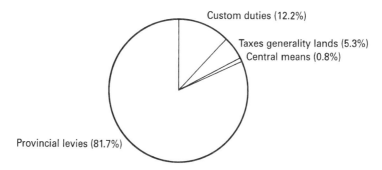

Custom duties (12.2%)

Taxes generality lands (5.3%)
Central means (0.8%)

Provincial levies (81.7%)

Figure 2.6 Revenues of the Union by four categories (ca. 1640s)
Source: 't Hart 1993, p. 86.

clearly absent. No major central tax was imposed at all, such as a levy on land and houses or hearths, despite the fact that the treaty of the Union (1579) had commanded the levy of uniform taxation. Most taxes were levied and administered by the provinces themselves in varied styles. Domains did not yield funds to the central government either, contrary to for example the crown lands in Denmark, England or Prussia (Ladewig Petersen 1983, p. 34; Aylmer 1987, p. 6; Bonney 1995, p. 462). The domains that were left after the sales of the sixteenth century supplied means for provincial administrations only, such as in Overijssel and Utrecht. Furthermore, no offices and titles were sold at a central level, contrary to for example the system of *venalité* in France (Bosher 1970, p. 6). Exceptions were found among some navy boards, whereas some provinces (in particular Friesland and Gelderland) engaged in selling offices to a limited degree too. And, finally, the colonies did not bring in monies directly, such as Spanish America did for Spain (Thompson 1976, p. 68). Colonial possessions and their trade were practically owned by the semi-private East and West India Companies, and funds accrued only indirectly to the state by way of customs duties.

About four-fifths of all public funds was provided by the *quota*-system and managed by the provinces themselves. Under control of the colleges in The Hague stood some minor central taxes, the customs duties, and the taxes levied in the reconquered regions (see figure 2.6). These items constituted the regular, *ordinary*, part of the revenue. Some extraordinary revenues existed, that came in irregularly, such as foreign subsidies, a hearth tax in 1606, and prizes and confiscations from enemy property.

As for the central Union taxes, they consisted of the following: some minor temporary duties (such as an excise on soap and beer in the sixteenth century), a stamp duty (levied since 1635), the revenue from items like

Table 2.2. *Yield of customs duties in Dutch Republic, 1601–1700, by the five navy boards (in percentages)*

Navy board	1601/25	1626/50	1651/75	1676/1700
Amsterdam	42.7	47.1	53.1	64.5
Rotterdam	24.3	21.1	19.6	19.5
North Holland	6.9	6.4	7.6	6.0
Zeeland	21.8	22.7	17.3	7.6
Friesland	4.4	2.7	2.5	2.3
Total	100.0	100.0	100.0	100.0

Source: Becht 1908, table III; 't Hart 1993, p. 103.

passports and safe-conducts, an excise duty on salt (levied up to 1680), and a lottery of the Union in the later eighteenth century. Their combined yield was probably never more than 1 per cent of the total revenue ('t Hart 1993, p. 86).

Customs duties were more considerable, making up approximately one tenth of all Union revenue in the seventeenth century. The Union of Utrecht (1579) had specified that no customs were to be levied among the provinces henceforth, a rule that was followed in the main. Since 1582, the customs were collected for the confederation by the five navy boards as import and export duties under the heading of *convooien* and *licenten*, levied respectively for the protection of vessels at sea and upon trade with enemy regions. Among the five navy boards (located in Amsterdam, Rotterdam, North Holland, Zeeland and Friesland) the one in Amsterdam gradually gained a dominant position, due to the commercial power of this entrepot (see table 2.2). By comparison, the Rotterdam board declined in importance. Most dramatic was the reduced importance of the Zeeland board, situated in Middelburg, with its proportion declining from 22 per cent to only 8 per cent, due to an overall shift of trade routes from the southern Netherlands to the northern regions. The North Holland college managed to maintain its share in trade, but the Friesland board dwindled.

The revenue fluctuated according to the overall trends of trade and the repercussions of war (cf. Westermann 1948; De Vries 1958). Customs were extremely vulnerable to warfare conditions. Figure 2.7 displays the revenue from ordinary customs duties. Up to 1650, the tendency was rather advantageous. Then, the positive trend was halted. Trade was severely disrupted due to the wars with Britain in the 1650s, 1660s and 1670s. Towards the end of the century the development stabilised again. All in all, the Amsterdam navy board continued to gain from the terms of trade to the disadvantage of other boards.

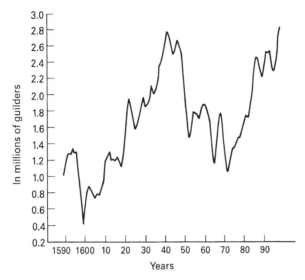

Figure 2.7 Ordinary revenue from customs, 1590–1700 (three-year moving averages)
Sources: Becht 1908, table III; 't Hart 1993, p. 103.

The rates were increased only modestly. A first overall augmentation in customs rates dated from 1584. The general list was revised in 1603, which raised most of the duties. Another modification during 1651–5, increased most customs duties to 22 per cent. These increases did not always yield higher revenues for the navy boards, as trade routes may have been severely disrupted. Next to ordinary customs, extraordinary (mostly temporary) duties existed too, under the name of *veilgeld* and *lastgeld*. Some trade routes were charged as extras to account for the specific convoys for the vessels.

In general though, customs rates were moderate throughout the period of the Republic. In comparison with neighbouring countries (Davis 1966, p. 310), they were quite low, varying usually around 3 per cent. In all probability, they hardly ever exceeded the 5 per cent level, although particular items could be charged at higher rates. High duties were levied, for example, upon the export of Dutch cheese (8–11 per cent) and butter (12 per cent). Wool imports were exempt from customs duties, but cloth imports were charged high duties. Cloth exports carried extremely low duties of 0.1 or 0.2 per cent. Grain paid a low duty upon arrival in the Republic, yet exports paid 4–6 per cent (Voorthuysen 1965, pp. 67, 72).

All in all, when considering the budget of the Union, the contribution from the trading communities was constrained, despite the fact that the

Dutch held the 'primacy in world trade' (Israel 1989). To increase revenues from these resources proved extremely difficult. In the course of the eighteenth century, the relative proportion of customs was even declining *vis-à-vis* the seventeenth century. The directors of the navy boards, having associated themselves with the local oligarchy, were rather reluctant to impose the tariffs strictly. Indeed, a rebate on rates was always beneficial to attract cargoes to their harbours! Complaints about frauds were frequent. And not only through the navy boards did merchants exert significant pressures upon decision making. Owing to the decentralised political structure, they held a major voice in the body politic, mainly through the governments of the maritime cities, which tended to keep the rates low (Meijer 1995, p. 113).

Customs duties, then, were difficult to control for the central state because of the powerful oligarchies in the five seats of the admiralty. There was yet another item of revenue in addition to the central Union taxes and the customs duties. The areas reconquered from Spain were put under the direct administration of the Council of State in The Hague. For the sake of convenience, they were labelled *generaliteitslanden* (generality lands) although this term came into official use only after 1648. These included northern parts of Brabant and Flanders together with parts of Limburg in the south. In the north, a border region under the name of Wedde and Westerwolde was a generality land too.

Unlike the provinces, the generality lands did not have financial autonomy. Yet the central state could not impose taxes at will. In particular during the Eighty Years' War, much of the region paid so-called contributions rather than regular taxes. Even after the peace of 1648 some excises were never imposed in reality but were redeemed by villages and cities, which implied weak control by the Council of State.

The peace of 1648 allowed the introduction of a new fiscal system in the reconquered areas. The land tax was specified at approximately 20 per cent of the land rent. New stamp duties and excises were introduced. The keeping of cattle and the tilling of crops bore significant additional burdens. In the 1660s, duties upon transfers and wills were added. Extraordinary increases upon the land tax were imposed, such as in 1665 and 1676–80. Moreover, most duties were raised by 10 per cent in the 1690s (Kappelhof 1986, pp. 97, 113). Of all the duties, the taxes on land yielded the largest portion.

Despite these additions, funds from the generality lands remained modest in view of total public revenues (see figure 2.6). They hardly exceeded 5 per cent of the Republican funds. The overall yield from ordinary taxation in these areas averaged approximately 1 million guilders in the seventeenth century. Lows were recorded in the 1660s, despite the fact that some duties were increased. A downward economic trend was partly responsible. The 1680s signalled a recovery in the yield again (Kappelhof 1986, pp. 263, 286).

Yet little of these monies found their way to the central state. Most of the yield was needed for the expenses of the local administration. In addition, major impediments existed for the Council of State to render these reconquered areas into truly gainful assets. The nearness of enemy territory and fear of political separation prevented more increases. One should note also the emphasis on land taxes and on agricultural produce, which was always a harder way to levy taxes as compared with duties upon consumption and trade (Ardant 1975). Likewise, the revenue from customs duties was spent directly upon the war vessels of the navy boards. Subsequently, only a fraction of the total central tax burden in the Union was channelled through the Union institutions at all.

2.7 General patterns in taxation

Thus most funds, ranging from 80 to 90 per cent, were furnished by the autonomous fiscal structures of the provinces. Although each province was free to select the appropriate instruments, some characteristics were shared over the whole territory (Engels 1862; Sickenga 1864; Vrankrijker 1969). For example, in contrast to France (Mousnier 1980, p. 415), exemptions in taxation were few. Only a couple of dignitaries were privileged: the *Stadhouder* and foreign notables did not have to pay taxes. In The Hague, the central colleges were exonerated from some of the excises too. In the inland provinces, the nobles were exempt from some taxes for their own manors. Examples are found in Overijssel, Gelderland, Zeeland and Drenthe for the *hofsteden, vrije heerlijkheden* and *havezathen* of the order of the nobility (the *Ridderschap*). Yet overall, the tax base was broad, in particular for an early modern state.

Invariably, all provinces imposed a land tax, either under the name of *verponding, floreen, morgengeld* or *oldschildgeld*. The rate was generally at 20 per cent of the rental value after deduction of dike duties and similar local taxes. Also, all provincial governments imposed a house tax, generally at 12.5 per cent. This rate was lower than the land tax because maintenance charges were not deducted beforehand. The differences among the provinces were to be found in augmentations to the existing house and land taxes. In some cases, taxes on hearths existed too.

The excises, the duties upon consumption, were designated as *generale* or *gemene middelen* (general or common means). The highest income from such duties came invariably from the tax on milling grain (*gemaal*) and on beers. Beer, after all, was not a luxury product, but the main popular drink.

Furthermore, taxes were levied on wine, meat and spirits. Apart from these universal impositions, most provinces levied a duty upon woollen cloth, soap, tobacco, salt, peat and – of all interesting things – vinegar. And at all major markets (except in Nijmegen) a poundage duty existed for goods sold on the market. Again, the provincial variance in these duties was to be noted in the rates applied.

In addition, three duties were imposed upon agricultural produce. They were included under the heading of general means, although they were not excises. Cattle were to pay a certain tax per beast, varying according to district and age. Fields under crop were charged too, with differing arrangements for district and produce. A third duty concerned the keeping of a horse, which was taxed in general at 1.20 guilders. These charges actually assumed the character of a tax upon property, or to be more specific, as a tax upon the use of land.

Duties on the transfer of real estate existed in all provinces. Death duties and stamp duties were almost universal, Overijssel and Drenthe were the only exceptions. Passengers in coaches, ferries and tow-boats were mostly taxed by some sort of duty as well, although at times in an indirect way, in a charge upon the owner of the vessel or coach.

Methods of collection were quite universal as well. Most of the land taxes and other duties upon property were gathered by provincial and local officials. The common means, however, including all excises and the duties upon agriculture, were farmed out. Farming was a method of selling a tax to the highest bidder. The tax farmers, who acted as semi-private entrepreneurs, collected the funds for a certain period of time. Most contracts lasted for six months or a year, and for a specified district only. The farmers employed their own personnel. All surplus yields (above the sum specified in the contract) were theirs, but so also were the losses (Boone 1989, p. 117). An advantage for the authorities was constituted by the fact that the sums for revenue were known ahead of collection. No civil servants had to be appointed either, and no costs of collection had to be accounted for. Disadvantages for the state were the deprivation of direct control and misfortune when tax farmers went bankrupt. But tax farming was also a way to circumvent the power of local oligarchies whose collectors were likely to spare the privileged (Thompson 1976, p. 285). For this reason, in an attempt to avoid the impact of the local oligarchies in the navy boards, in order to increase the revenue from customs, the import and export duties were temporarily farmed out as well during 1625–38 and 1687–90 (Meijer 1995, pp. 102–3; 't Hart 1990, p. 78). Yet these attempts foundered on the opposition by the navy oligarchies, particularly in Amsterdam. Taxes could be sold to a monopoly also. Monopolies existed above all in the inland provinces, often concerning luxury articles like spirits, wine or tobacco. The wholesale rights were controlled by the monopolist. Farming and monopolies were in all probability quite effective for early modern states with a weak bureaucracy.

One serious disadvantage of the farming system entailed the danger that the semi-private entrepreneurs would try to squeeze as much as possible from their taxes. In addition, tax farmers could plot among themselves in keeping the bids low. As a result, in case of popular discontent, the hatred was directed against the tax farmers. Such revolts remained localised in most cases, except for the tax revolt in 1748 which spread out over a larger territory. The dislike of tax farmers was shared with other states. Nevertheless, the Dutch tax farmers never developed into a powerful caste of officers in contrast to, for instance, the French *fermiers* (Durand 1971). Districts were rather small, and contracts were renewed on a seasonal basis. As a result, they tended to be men of moderate means, like shoemakers, carpenters or knifemakers (Van Deursen 1979, pp. 27–8; Brood 1991, p. 115).

2.8 The varying burden of taxation in the provinces

Despite the common traits in the provincial fiscal systems mentioned above, the actual incidence of taxation varied widely per province. The major reason was due to the rates applied. The land tax was more burdensome in Zeeland, Groningen and Friesland, whereas Overijssel, Gelderland and Drenthe had lower rates. The house tax was quite high in Utrecht due to its additional hearth tax. The tax on milling grain was five times higher in Utrecht as compared with Overijssel. Beers paid 23 per cent for the cheaper kinds to 240 per cent for the most expensive ones. As for the duties on cattle, the lowest tariffs (at 0.30 guilders) were recorded in several parts of Drenthe and Gelderland, the highest in some districts of Holland (at 2.70), Groningen (at 2.93) and Overijssel (at three guilders). The lowest duties for spirits were apparently levied in Holland, and the highest in Utrecht. In the provinces of Gelderland and Overijssel the duty was collected by a monopolist, the sale being concentrated in the hands of a single entrepreneur. In Groningen and Friesland, no tax on spirits was paid, as the distilleries had it redeemed directly. Death duties ranged from 2 per cent in Gelderland to 10 per cent in Holland (Kappelhof 1986, pp. 396–402). In addition, each province levied its own *extraordinary*, temporary taxes.

A major contrast was the fact that the core provinces in the west imposed more excises as compared with the inland regions. Examples were an addition to the poundage on the market (the *ronde maat*), excises upon fish (with different rates for herring, salmon and sturgeon), coal and firewood, building materials such as chalk, tiles, and bricks, fruits, candles, butter, printed paper, coffee and tea. A tax on the keeping of servants was levied in

Table 2.3. *Percentage distribution of the ordinary tax burden in two provinces, seventeenth century*

item/year	Holland		Overijssel	
	1599	1671/7	1601/3	1683
Land and property taxes	27	31	42	51
Taxes on cattle and crops		7	55	46
Excises	58	50	3	
Stamp duties	15	12		2
Total	100	100	100	100
In guilders	4,000,000	22,302,000	198,475	371,900

Source: Reitsma 1982, p. 270; Dormans 1991, p. 25; Fritschy 1996, table III.2.1.

Holland, Zeeland, Utrecht and Groningen. The latter even imposed a rudimentary income tax in three categories. But in all, the range of taxes, above all excises, was highest in Holland. The number of duties was so large that rewards were promised in case one could think of another item to be taxed. Holland was followed closely by Zeeland and Utrecht. In the 1570s these three provinces had adopted a long list of general means, next to their ordinary land taxes, to which several supplements were added in the following decades. For them, these fiscal measures were a continuation of the period before the revolt against Spain, the time of being a part of the Burgundian heritage under Habsburg rule. High yields had not been uncommon: for example in Holland the unprecedented sum of 500,000 guilders had been voted already in 1572 (Grapperhaus 1982, p. 262).

By contrast, the inland provinces counted only some minor duties that did not exist in the maritime areas, such as a small duty upon the keeping of bees and sheep. With a lower degree of commerce and trade, funds were harder to get. In Overijssel, for example, the annual revenue averaged only 18,500 guilders in 1571–4. The major cities – Zwolle, Deventer and Kampen – staunchly blocked the introduction of general means. By the turn of the century, some new Overijssel taxes were introduced. Yet excises remained limited: most taxes still pressed on agriculture, such as the taxes on cattle and sown lands (see table 2.3). The overall picture of the distributions was always affected by the imposition of *extraordinary*, temporary taxes. In table 2.3 (see also figures 4.3 and 4.4) they were excluded for the sake of comparison of the regular, recurrent (*ordinary*) burden. On the whole, it is obvious that Holland drew considerably more resources from taxes upon consumption and stamp duties as compared with Overijssel.

In Overijssel, duties on consumption finally arrived with a major revision in 1623. Yet consent was achieved only under the conditions that the IJssel cities were allowed to keep one-third of the excises for their own administration. The nobility was allowed to redeem the excises (*Tegenwoordige Staat* 1739, p. 218). The other inland provinces showed a similar reluctance to introduce the general means, which had much to do with the fact that their tax tradition had been based upon taxation of landed revenue, and much less upon commercial flows (cf. Ardant 1975).

In all, the emphasis on indirect taxes in the province of Holland was remarkable. It was one of the conditions which allowed the public debt to increase. Figure 2.8 depicts the revenues received from tax on farmers, which included the excises and the taxes on cattle and crops. They had yielded 540,000 guilders by 1574. But in the following decade, this sum more than doubled, due to higher rates and new taxes, confirming the observation of Fynes Moryson quoted earlier. The revenues rose to over two million by the end of the sixteenth century, although few additions were voted for. Major increases were enacted in 1604–6, resulting in an amount of 4,344,000 guilders in 1608.

The Truce (1609–21) offered an opportunity to decrease taxation. However, expenses remained high, in particular for the payment of the debt charges. As a result, only a couple of minor taxes were abolished. With the resumption of war, taxation was stepped up again in the 1620s through new duties and increases upon previous taxes. In 1625–9, the farmed taxes contributed 6,301,000 annually. After this round of tax raises, few new taxes were introduced, apart from an increase in the duty on milling and a new tax on the keeping of servants. In 1635–9 this sum had climbed up to 7,630,000. The farmed taxes were to reach a first peak around 1645: 8,777,000 on average annually, due mainly to the increase in trade (figure 2.8).

Apart from a small duty on wagons no taxes were abolished with the signing of the peace in 1648. Thereafter, a downward economic trend affected revenues. A minor improvement occurred in the 1660s. But this was nullified by a drop in revenue in the 1670s, due to warfare conditions, despite a doubling of the beer and milling duties and the reintroduction of some minor taxes.

The negative economic conditions led to an apparent ceiling on the excise system in the 1670s and called for a shift towards more taxes upon property. In 1678/9 a major reform was brought about in the general means. Several excises were abolished: on candles, shoes, woollen cloth, fish, oils, pitch and tar, salt and soap. They were replaced by a heavier semi-direct tax system in which people had to pay according to their possessions listed in the registers of the property tax. The previous duties on those commodities were replaced by the so-called *zout-, zeep-, heere-, en redemptiegeld*, levied along

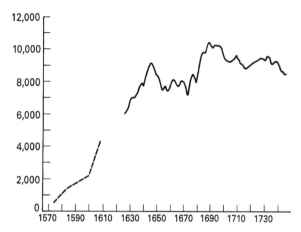

Figure 2.8 Revenue of farmed taxes in Holland, 1574–1747 (three-year moving averages after 1624)
Source: 't Hart 1993, p. 137; Dormans 1991, pp. 56, 73, 96.

with the rates on property. The keeping of servants was taxed accordingly. The result was overwhelming: the revenue from these duties increased by 36 per cent. In the decade following, the revenue mounted, which was partly due to a 10 per cent increase on all taxes, voted for in 1683. New increases followed in 1687–8. The yield from the farmed taxes even reached 10,000,000 guilders. By 1700 the semi-direct taxes, including the taxes on agriculture, contributed 18 per cent of the farmed duties. By then, the ceiling on the farmed taxes seemed to have been reached. A revolt in the later 1740s was to result in a system of collection of these duties; but the yield would not exceed the seventeenth-century peaks any more.

Not only were semi-direct taxes stepped up in the last quarter of the seventeenth century, the direct taxes were increased as well. The higher burden of direct taxation in Holland was achieved by having a regular extraordinary tax upon property introduced. This duty was to become recurrent in the eighteenth century, although the tax was still regarded as an extraordinary measure. A new register with the respective contributions for this property tax was introduced in 1654. Bonds and obligations were included as well. Up to 1661, the rate had been generally 0.1 per cent. The registers of this property tax was divided in three categories: capitalists (owning more than 2,000 guilders), semi-capitalists (owning between 1,000 and 2,000 guilders) and a third class with less than 1,000 guilders worth. The first class paid the full rate, the second half, and the third one was exempted. Since 1654, with the new registers of the property taxes, additional revenue could be had by imposing a 0.1, 0.2 or 0.5 per cent tax. The flexibility of the tax

Table 2.4. *Incidence of ordinary taxation in Holland, 1600 and 1700*

	1600	1700
Population	550,000	850,000
Excises/farmed taxes	ƒ 2,500,000	f 9,300,000
Land/property taxes	ƒ 1,500,000	f 4,800,000
Total tax burden	ƒ 4,000,000	f 14,100,000
Burden per capita	ƒ 7.27	f 16.59
Avg. daily wage	ƒ 0.70	f 0.92

Source: Fritschy 1988, pp. 51, 54.

system, then, came to rest more and more upon the direct impositions and less upon the indirect ones. Such trends were to continue in the eighteenth century (see chapter 4).

The land tax of Holland was occasionally burdened with an extra levy. For a long time, the basis of this tax remained the same, and was collected in fixed quotas. The proportions were adjusted for the first time in 1632, putting a more just levy upon the wealthier communities and sparing the poorer ones. The result was an increase in the yield of 50 per cent, which was considerable, although much more had been expected from this move. Thereafter, the 1632 quotas remained fixed for over a hundred years, as the second revision of the land tax registers had to wait until 1734. Obviously, communities that experienced expansion during this time span, like Amsterdam, were at an advantage, paying less per capita as compared with cities that were on the decline, such as Delft or Gouda. Meanwhile, if necessary as a result of soaring war expenses, additional revenues from the land tax were found by putting an extraordinary 50 per cent increase upon the existing quotas under the heading of a *halve verponding*. With the outbreak of the First Anglo-Dutch War in 1652 this additional charge was even increased by levying another 50 per cent, which in fact doubled the inequitable land tax.

As could be expected, the total burden of taxation rose (see table 2.4). Excluded from table 2.4 were the local taxes (such as duties for drainage boards, town taxes and tolls), the extraordinary impositions, and the costs of perception of the tax farmers, which could increase the actual burden considerably. Yet the overall trend is clear. Whereas the general wage level increased only by 30 per cent, the tax burden more than doubled. A wage labourer had to work ten days for taxation in 1600, but approximately eighteen days in 1700. With such a large degree of indirect taxes upon necessities, the burden tended to be regressive.

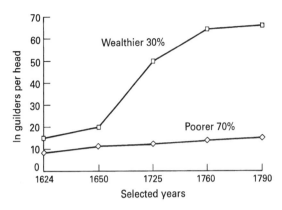

Figure 2.9 Estimated development of tax burden upon the 30 per cent wealthier households and upon the 70 per cent poorer households in Holland, 1600–1790
Source: De Vries and Van der Woude 1995, p. 143.

However, the regressive character was diminished by the introduction of heavier semi-direct and direct taxes. As such, the *per capita* burden (table 2.4) could be evaluated further. Figure 2.9 shows the estimated development of the tax burden for the wealthier 30 per cent of the society, as well as for the poorer 70 per cent. Apparently, Holland managed to focus a relatively larger proportion of the burden upon the rich.

In all, the diverse structure of taxation allowed the authorities to increase one tax permanently, another temporarily, and to introduce a third one. On the whole, the tax system of Holland was clearly fostered by the commercialisation and urbanisation of the region. Such a flexible and broad tax base was extremely important with regard to the enormous increase in public debt. The loans remained secured, in this way, by the regularity of taxation. Yet the lower classes in the cities paid a disproportionate amount of the tax yield, above all through the excises upon beer and grain, although their burden seemed to have increased less as compared with the wealthier classes. On the other hand, the higher and middle classes in Holland received principal back in the form of charges on their debts.

2.9 The financial success of the Dutch Republic

Undoubtedly, the late sixteenth century was a time of severe crisis in the northern Netherlands. But the solutions found for the pressing financial problems, despite the archaic structure of *quotas*, proved sufficient for most of the seventeenth century. The rising expenses were well managed as compared with other early modern nation-states. The public debt was spread

widely among savers, and the interest rates were among the lowest in
Europe. Yet there was an obvious disparity between the maritime west and
the inland provinces. Holland, Zeeland and Utrecht profited from socio-
economic structures that were advantageous for the imposition of excises
and dependable property registers. The high level of urbanisation and
commercialisation allowed for elastic fiscal structures. Moreover, a strong
urban tradition of representation rendered the local elites willing to support
state fiscal policies. Among those paying property taxes, it proved beneficial
to be included in the highest category of capitalists, for the sake of obtaining
credit. The local oligarchies did exert a significant say in the Dutch body
politic, but they also profited from the rise in the public debt. The expansion
of the state yielded major revenues in the way of interest payments to the
buyers of the government bonds. Most regents had invested themselves in
state obligations, which linked their private benefits to public pursuits in a
most direct way (Blockmans 1988; Burke 1974, pp. 56–7; 't Hart 1995a).

The commercial expansion permitted the state to derive significant
revenue from indirect taxation on transactions, even though taxes were
levied on consumption rather than on trade. Debasements of currency, so
disastrous for the economies of many another state, were avoided by permanent indirect levies and extraordinary taxes upon property. In this setting,
the financial structure proved of tremendous advantage for merchants and
bankers. The customs rates were extremely low and few taxes bothered
invested capital. The hindrances of fragmentation were overcome by the
financial power of the maritime provinces, above all of Holland. By taking
over the bulk of the Union debt, this province exerted an increasing, albeit
semi-official, centralising tendency.

Although the burden of taxation increased obviously, war did not appear
disastrous for the Dutch. On the contrary, the young Fynes Moryson
observed in 1595:

One thing is hardly to be understood how these Provinces thus oppressed with tributes, and making warre against a most powerful King, yet at this time in the heate of
the warre – which useth to waste most flourishing Kingdomes, and make Provinces
desolate – had farre greater riches, than any most peaceable Countrey of their neighbours (Quoted by Jacobsen Jensen 1918, pp. 268–9).

Thus the long conflict with Spain tested Dutch resources but it did not
exhaust them. What was more, the struggle for independence even yielded
the Republic new resources – domestic as well as foreign. In that respect, the
Union of Provinces was indeed a living paradox. The public finances that
emerged stood out for their modernity among European powers.

However, the fragmented power structure dominated by the *gewesten*
proved an impediment for renewals. The oligarchies tended to revert to the

successful methods of the early seventeenth century. Yet, by the end of the Golden Age, the French and above all the British managed to overtake the Dutch financial system. Their systems of public finance, although in certain respects not as modern as the Dutch, proved much more effective in mobil-ising resources on a nationwide scale (cf. chapter 4). By then, the shortcom-ings of the Dutch Republic (its limited area and population, and its fragmented political structure) came to overshadow its initial advantages in urbanisation and commercialisation ('t Hart 1995b, p. 85). That the Dutch continued for another century to safeguard their independence and power was mostly due to the enormous reserve of accumulated funds.

Notes

1 Both Gelderland and Overijssel had their quotas temporarily reduced between 1622 and 1633. Also, a deviant distribution was in force during 1673–4 at the time of the war with England and France.
2 The data in figure 2.5 should be used with great caution. Dormans constructed these numbers based upon estimations for over 95 per cent. The figures cannot be used for any year separately to establish the amount; but put together they do give an overall impression of the development.

3 Linking the fortunes: currency and banking, 1550–1800

PIT DEHING AND MARJOLEIN 'T HART

3.1 Introduction

In the course of the seventeenth century, Dutch finance became intricately connected to the world economic system. Its development was bolstered by favourable developments in international trade, which allowed the Dutch to exploit their geographic position and their harbours to the full, and by an economic boom which lasted long enough for considerable capital accumulation. The political and social structures were well suited to the preservation of wealth and allowed for high propensities to save. The accumulated funds in The Netherlands are estimated to have grown enormously since approximately 1500, even during the less favourable eighteenth century. Van Zanden calculated for Holland alone a rise in capital wealth from ten to twelve million guilders around 1500 to approximately 1,750 million guilders around 1790 (Van Zanden 1993, p. 23).

In the beginning, the swell of capital was mainly diverted to domestic investments and trade. Increasingly, the Dutch funds came to be invested in public loans and foreign assets. The demand by public authorities, in particular for government loans, had increased considerably (cf. previous chapter). But during the eighteenth century, foreign governments came to attract Dutch capital too, specifically for the underwriting of warfare loans. As such, the Amsterdam capital market served to link varied networks of funds and fortunes, both of domestic and of foreign origin.

The development was the more remarkable as the Dutch financial institutions did not excel in innovation. On the contrary, the establishment remained basically oriented towards the past. Several Italian cities and also the English state, in the meantime, moved ahead of the Dutch. The confusion over currency, for example, was large, and no central public bank came to issue banknotes during the time of the Republic. The fragmented structure of politics must have been another impediment for further development. Nevertheless, Dutch finances seemed well-suited to perform crucial functions within the world capital market. This chapter discusses this intriguing paradox, looking at the issues of mint and currency, banking, the structure of the capital market and foreign assets.

3.2 The Revolt and its consequences for mint and currency

A striking example of the deficiency of a central policy during the time of the Republic concerned coinage and currency (Korthals Altes 1996, pp. 53–111). A solid coin system, after all, constituted a basic component for any financial policy. Such was perceived by the overlords of The Netherlands in the early sixteenth century. Standard coins like the *stuiver* (stiver) or *patard* were introduced by the Dukes of Burgundy. These coins were administered by 11 or 12 mint masters, whose mints were comparable with large industrial complexes. They produced coins out of bullion according to market requirements and to the rules set out by the general mint officers, who were appointed in all the dukal dominions of the Low Countries. Charles V, the Burgundian–Habsburg overlord, introduced several regulations, such as fixing the guilder, in order to halt monetary depreciation (Van der Wee 1983, p. 13). The golden *carolusgulden* of 1521 and the silver *carolusgulden* of 1544 tried to combine currency and money of account in one. His son Philip II continued the policy of centralisation, for which he introduced a comprehensive new silver coin: the *philipsdaalder* in 1557. Although the guilder virtually disappeared from currency, it remained the main unit of account.

But the Revolt in The Netherlands in 1572 discarded all centralised policies. The western maritime provinces, Holland and Zeeland, tried to solve the acute financial problems caused by warfare on their own. The government of Holland took control of the mint in Dordrecht and were bent on a devaluation of 15 per cent in 1573. Two years later this province lowered the mint ratio. It was to reduce the profit on the export of silver but stimulated the inflow too. This unexpected monetary move raised its silver stock. At the same time, the other provinces of The Netherlands noticed the backlash of this policy. There, the opposite occurred: an outflow and shortage of silver, which led to substantial objections of the inland provincial governments.

The Pacification of Ghent in 1576, an agreement between the provinces of the Low Countries, offered an opportunity to reorganise the disrupted monetary system. It was agreed that for the preservation of unity and mutual commerce a common rate had to be maintained. A few years later, in 1579, a similar intention was confirmed in the Union of Utrecht (Fruin 1980, pp. 396–7). This act was to become a kind of constitution for the United Netherlands (1579–1795).

However, such agreements were only worded in vague terms. All attempts for monetary unity broke down as the separate provincial governments were granted the licence and privilege of mint. Obviously, provincial sovereignty triumphed over unity. As a result, 14 official mints existed in the newborn Republic: eight provincial and six municipal ones. Many different (under)valued imitations of official coins came into circulation. As local and provincial interests determined the monetary decision making, the States General were unable to execute the rather vague intention in the Union of Utrecht to impose monetary accord. An excessive production of small coins dismantled the domestic money circulation.

The continued absence of any general valuation or regulation prompted the province of Holland to action as commerce suffered from the monetary confusion. In May 1583 this province introduced a series of new coins that were imitations of reliable foreign examples. The golden *dukaat* at 68 *stuiver*, after the successful coin in the German Empire, was chosen because of the important trade relations with the Baltic and the German hinterland. Next, the *gehelmde rijksdaalder* or *prinsendaalder* was introduced. Temporarily at least, such coins served to sustain the transfers in international trade relations. Due to Holland's prominent role in trade, in most of the northern provinces the guilder of twenty *stuivers* became subsequently the dominant money of account.[1] This imaginary money performed the duties of a common denominator, in which prices, balance sheets and exchange rates were usually quoted. Thus any currency could be translated in terms of the money of account in order to facilitate commerce.

But the failed centralisation of the mint continued to hamper policies. A consequence was the gradual debasement of the large silver coins during the Eighty Years' War (1568–1648). The provinces with their sovereign right of coinage allowed their mint masters to act as private entrepreneurs. Often they were tempted to mint low valued coins for domestic circulation. In these years, only one lasting central measure was decided upon: the General Masters of the Mint were reestablished in 1586. Appointed as supervisors of the currency and the mints, this move did imply some improvement in suppressing illegal minting.

Nevertheless, the variety of coins in circulation was startling. The situation worsened as mintage in the southern (Habsburg) provinces rose in a spectacular fashion (Janssens 1955). Large quantities of silver were received there through the official *Asiento* contracts, which were used to finance the Spanish army. In particular the Spanish–English peace treaty of 1630 allowed large Spanish silver shipments via England to Antwerp. Golden *albertijnen*, silver *ducatons*, *kruisdaalders*, *patacons*, gold guilders, silver florins, *daalders* of 30 *stuiver* and *schellingen* struck in the official mints penetrated the northern Netherlands. Coins of the numerous small, fraudulent mints just over the borders of the territory of the States General joined the stream. The inflow was furthered even more by the higher official rate in Holland for some major southern coins. This situation caused an additional deterioration of the monetary conditions. At the end of the sixteenth century, nearly 800 foreign coins were officially permitted in the Dutch Republic. In 1610 contemporary money changers had to handle almost a thousand golden and silver coins (Van Gelder 1978/9, p. 62).

3.3 Reforms and improvements in the currency system

To ease the transfers, all money in circulation was tariffed and valued in manuals. The Republic could only adjust its currency by adaptation to the penetration of southern coins, thus by allowing the lower valued coins an official status. An additional problem was the general increase in the value of gold relative to silver, due to the rapid increase of silver inflow as compared with gold. It endangered, among others, stability in the value of the guilder, which had become in almost all provinces the central unit of account.

No central decision was reached, but steps by Amsterdam magistrates proved decisive. In 1638 the city council settled its silver currency, in particular the ratio of the current guilder *vis-à-vis* the guilder of account. As a result, the bank guilder was officially disentangled from its current counterpart. In 1659 the States General followed suit. A major consequence was extreme stability in the value of the guilder. These reforms brought about a long-lasting improvement. The silver alloy remained in fact unaltered up to the crisis of the 1930s (Korthals Altes 1996, p. 89; see figure 3.1). The lifting of the Spanish silver embargo for Holland and the prohibition of Spanish silver consignments to the southern Netherlands were very helpful as well. As liquidity multiplied, Amsterdam grew into a major centre for the redistribution of commercial silver flows. Foreign rulers became committed to the Dutch silver entrepot. Such was furthered in particular after the beginning of the Civil War in England in 1640 when the English king confiscated the Spanish silver deposits in London and stopped their intermediation.

The government of Holland pushed their policy based on local sovereignty. For instance, they forbade Zeeland's small coins to circulate in Holland because of their poor alloy. A low degree of fineness was also recurrent in the coins of Zwolle, Kampen, Deventer, Zutphen, Nijmegen and Groningen. Holland introduced new small coins in 1670, followed by a new silver guilder in September 1681 and the *duit* in 1702. The other provinces were obliged to do the same because of the sheer economic domination of Amsterdam in the bullion market. Also, Amsterdam's policy was supported by *Stadhouder* William III. As King of Great Britain he had noted the negative effects of the monetary confusion upon soldier's pay. In 1686 the

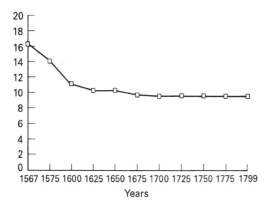

Figure 3.1 Grams of fine silver in guilder, 1567–1799
Source: Korthals Altes 1996, p. 8.

provinces of Gelderland, Utrecht and Overijssel followed the 1681 guilder example and the States General agreed upon this move in May 1694. The municipal mints conceded to refrain from minting in exchange for annual compensation, and the General Masters of the Mint obtained increased powers of control. In 1798, the new revolutionary regime decided to abolish all provincial mints but the Utrecht one. It took up to 1807 before this resolution was put into effect. Henceforth, only one national mint remained.

Despite the low degree of official centralisation during the time of the Republic a consolidated equilibrium existed after the second half of the seventeenth century, even though old coins did not disappear totally out of circulation throughout the eighteenth century. An advantage for the Republic was that government engineered inflation, a problem for many centralised states, was avoided (Klein 1980, pp. 181–2). No repetition occurred of the initial debasement policies of the 1570s. Furthermore, the monetary confusion was reduced by the duality of the Dutch currency system. Most troubles existed on the domestic market with its great variety in coins minted from gold, silver and copper. For foreign trade purposes, The Netherlands mints produced three great coins, the *negotiepenningen*, with fixed prices as to the bank guilder. There was the *leeuwendaalder* (1606) for trade with the Levant; the silver *dukaat* (1659) for trade with the Baltic, where it gradually assumed the older name of *rijksdaalder* or *rixdaalder*; and the silver *rijder* or *ducaton* (1659) for trade with the Far East (Glamann 1958, pp. 50–72). This international dimension was held apart from the domestic economy.

The trade coins stood next to the *standpenningen* of silver *gulden* and gold *rijder* for use in domestic payments and assets. Although silver coins dominated, the standard was in fact bi-metallic. The *negotiepenningen* maintained internationally an unequalled status of solidity and reliance, which bolstered the trade position of the Dutch. Despite the fragmented political structure of the Republic, Dutch money was the key currency in many international transfers for most of the seventeenth and eighteenth centuries. Due to the careful policy of the Bank of Amsterdam (see below) the currency system of the Dutch provinces experienced no severe crises up to the end of the eighteenth century. Moreover, inflation was contained. Characteristic of the Dutch situation was that local policies, notably influenced by merchants' interests, managed to fix the monetary system, in a way that was highly satisfactory for the Dutch trade network. In fact, monetary reform was the by-product of particularistic interests. The result was a wide-ranging international monetary system, in which Dutch institutions imposed control upon its liquidity.

3.4 Money changers, cashiers and pawnbrokers

Monetary equilibrium, despite the currency confusion, served the development of Dutch banking. Domestic banks were further underpinned by other factors. The northern Netherlands were less affected by civil strife and local revolts as compared with many other contemporary states. Even wars seemed to have been less disruptive for the Dutch. Apparently, the principals of the provinces managed to make the best out of the strife of others. In particular since the fall of Antwerp in 1585 Amsterdam had grown at the cost of this former metropolis.

Moreover, much of Europe experienced a downward economic trend in the early seventeenth century. As northwestern Europe escaped these negative developments for at least several decades, these circumstances were surely a boon for the Dutch (J. de Vries 1976, p. 21). In addition, the northern Netherlands benefited from the international trade movement, which favoured maritime oriented trade.

Soon after the shift of economic gravity from Antwerp to Amsterdam, all kinds of currency, bills of exchange,[2] assignments, promissory notes, annuities and other securities were circulated in order to make extensive trade possible. It was obvious that Dutch banking and its instruments had matured in Flanders and Brabant. The larger commercial cities in the northern Netherlands applied the exchange laws and financial techniques of Antwerp. For example, Amsterdam published the Antwerpse Costuymen in 1597 and 1613. Innovations were little, but of major relevance was the perfection of the negotiability of foreign bills of exchange in Amsterdam (Neal 1990, p. 7).

Banking functions were performed by a diverse set of institutions and persons: money changers, cashiers, merchants, public banks, brokers, insurance agents, pawnshops, receivers of taxes and commercial agents. Above all, money changers and cashiers were very important in preventing liquidity shortage in the era of expanding trade. A limited number of money changers had been licensed by the provincial government since mediaeval times. Appointment occurred by the General Masters of the Mint, who gave instructions to these sworn semi-official functionaries. In 1602, however, the provincial government decided that towns in Holland were allowed to appoint money changers themselves. They were also no longer obliged to pass their gold and silver purchases to the provincial mints only, but could furnish these coins to merchants in urgent need of cash. This move allowed money changers to become cashiers with depositing businesses (Van der Wee 1977, pp. 322–32).

The business of private cashkeeping by cashiers or *kassiers* had originated in Antwerp. Formally, a cashier was under a merchants' order to pay creditors and collect from debtors. The system progressed fully in Amsterdam. The number of merchant clients rapidly increased, and the cashiers facilitated payments by simple book assignments. Their written *orderbriefjes* or *assignaties* acted as cheques. Like bills of exchange, they were endorsable and thus might pass, as means of payment, from hand to hand. Their *kassierskwitantiën* (goldsmithnotes), receipts to their depositors, equally became negotiable by endorsement. They could take the form of promises to (re)pay the sum deposited. Such promises became gradually payable to bearer. These instruments effectively raised the money supply (Jonker 1992; Spufford 1995, p. 306).

At first, the Amsterdam municipality tried to limit the number of cashiers and money changers because of the dangers of overtrading and consequential financial distress. Good specie was allowed to be sold at a premium of no more than 1.25 per cent, but premiums regularly exceeded this maximum. A project of the magistrates to curb the number of money changers and cashiers failed, however. The merchants were in such need of the private cashkeepers that they were outraged. The burgomasters were induced to revise their policy (Van Dillen 1925 I, no. 14).

Problems continued, however, as the large number of money changers and cashiers rendered control extremely difficult. As a compromise the municipal authorities of Amsterdam temporarily prohibited all money changers and cashiers and their paper money, and established in 1609 the Wisselbank (Exchange Bank or Bank of Amsterdam; see below). The ban was lifted in 1621, and the remaining money changers and cashiers became licensed officials. Their services were accessible for all who wished to use them, on the condition that the cashiers themselves held an account at the

Bank of Amsterdam. Still, cashiers were prohibited to keep the money received for longer than 24 hours.

Towards the end of the seventeenth century, the cashiers' influence rose again as their trade in bank money and bullion opened up opportunities for international credit facilities. In particular, after 1750, the expanding demand for commercial credit was directed towards the cashiers, and left the Bank of Amsterdam with an increasingly passive role. The maturation of the cashiers was complete with the removal of the obstacle to note circulation in 1776 and at the same time the beginning of mutual clearing.

Another source of credit besides the cashiers were the Lombards with their pawnshops. Since the thirteenth century, pawnbrokers had established themselves in much of Europe, albeit with strict (monarchical) control of their interest rates. The first Lombards arrived in The Netherlands in 1260. Clashes were recurrent as to accusations of usury (De Roover 1974). Originally the Lombard policy was a prerogative of the Count. Prince William of Orange tried, in the quest for war funds, to centralise this type of activity, but failed. In 1578 the governments of Holland and Zeeland gave the towns the right to regulate the Lombards' activity. The magistrates confined themselves to a definition of usury that brought the regulations in harmony with the local economic trend. Subsequently, they were more concerned with fixing maximum interest rates than with prohibition of Lombards (Maassen 1994, p. 94).

Several officially recognised Lombards were transformed into municipal institutions, the Banken van Leening (Banks of Loans). The first was erected in Amsterdam in 1614. The immediate cause had been a dispute over the rates of interest. Amsterdam interest rates for pawnshops had dropped from 86 per cent in the first quarter of the sixteenth century to 43.5 per cent around 1550 and to 21.7 per cent in the beginning of the seventeenth century. The magistrates thought the rates should be even lower. As the Lombards, in business there since 1467, refused to cut the rates, the municipality took over the pawnbroking establishment and prohibited its private counterpart. Amsterdam burgomasters thus gained another instrument with the Banken van Leening to stabilise conditions on the financial market.

The Bank van Leening lent money at low interest rates mainly to the meaner businessmen wishing to expand their business in return for a pledge or pawn. It raised its capital, about 1.2 million guilders by 1616, through issuing bonds and debentures bearing interest. Larger investments were financed too. But as table 3.1 shows, the Amsterdam Bank van Leening became increasingly more important for credit in small and medium securities. The Amsterdam example was followed by most of the major Dutch towns. The structure and regulations of its Bank van Leening were copied, as with the credit on securities.

Table 3.1. *Credit granting by the Amsterdam Bank van Leening, 1629 and 1678 (percentage distribution, totals, and rates of interest)*

	1629	1678
Small securities (under 100 guilders)	53.5%	69.4%
Medium securities (100–475 guilders)	19.9%	21.7%
Large securities (500 guilders and over)	26.5%	8.9%
	100.0%	100.0%
Total in million guilders	8,526	19,923
Interest rate	6.1%	3.75%

Source: GAA Archive, 5059, nr. 49.

These money changers, cashiers, pawnbrokers and Banken van Leening all performed crucial functions on the money market. Public authorities had also recourse to financial aid from tax collectors and to advances from the farmers of the taxes on consumption (see previous chapter). Receivers of taxes thus frequently acted as bankers too. Next to these semi-public institutions and officers, many private firms performed financial functions. Some merchants specialised in specie trade, others in securities. Firms often combined credit, freight and insurance (Spooner 1983, p. 16). The larger houses with commercial correspondents all over the world became brokers for international payments and loans, like Hope & Co., Clifford or A.Pels & Zn. As can be seen in figure 3.4, Hope & Co. came to the top of the commercial and financial world in the course of the eighteenth century. Their average annual distributed profits were calculated at 8.25 per cent, whereas their capital grew at 8.64 per cent on average annually (Buist 1974).

3.5 The Bank of Amsterdam

Yet most critical for this network were the functions performed by the public Wisselbanken, the Banks of Exchange, with their giro-system and their control over bullion. Above all, the Bank of Amsterdam was essential for the overall smooth running of Dutch money and the capital market. Flows of money which, in Antwerp, had passed uncontrolled through the hands of cashiers since 1609 passed through the Bank, where specie were converted into guilder deposits. The Bank of Amsterdam had emerged upon the request of several merchants, who complained about the confusion in currency. The roots of this type of public banking lay like the origins of most financial services in mediaeval northern Italy (Parker 1974, p. 544). The Bank of Amsterdam was even modelled after the Venetian one.

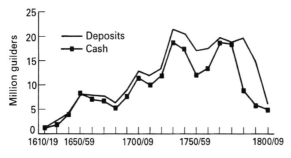

Figure 3.2 Cash and deposits at the Amsterdam Wisselbank, 1610–1810

Basically a mediaeval institution, the Bank proved to be very effective and fostered development in the Dutch financial system. Only large gold and silver coins of the correct weight were accepted at an official rate. Other coins deposited were estimated by a bank assayer according to their actual bullion value and credited accordingly.

By temporarily taking over the business of all money changers and cashiers the Bank acquired a central position on the money market. Its functions were simple: receiving money on deposit, transfer and clearing business through a giro system that was based on current accounts kept in guilders, exchanging and purchasing precious metal and uncurrent coins. All bills of exchange valued at over 600 guilders (since 1643 over 300 guilders) had to be paid through the Bank, with the result that all major merchants held an account. Not included were tasks like the discounting of bills of exchange, portfolio management, the issue of bank notes and the provision of credit. Its business was predominantly a matter of transfer between accounts with the aim to undo the confusion of the currency.

The fact that the Bank of Amsterdam did not become an issuing bank is still regarded as a shortcoming with regard to other central banks of the early modern period. The relevance of the giro system, in which monies could be transferred from one account to the other, should not be underestimated however. Merchants thought the giro transfers with other account holders in the Bank extremely convenient. In 1716 John Law expressed admiration for an Amsterdam merchant who could regulate his payments, amounting to 4,000 to 500,000 guilders, with 50 persons within 15 minutes. The giro was boosted by the increase in the number of accounts. The Bank of Amsterdam was in volume superior to any other bank in Europe: 1,350 accounts in 1625, whereas the Hamburg Bank had only 539 in 1619 and the Nuremberg Bank 663 in 1621–4 (Peters 1994). The number of account holders increased rapidly from 1609 up to 1661. Thereafter, due to warfare conditions, this growth slowed down, but a new

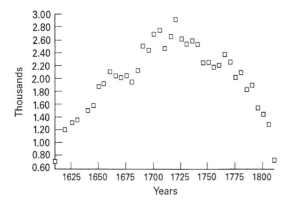

Figure 3.3 Number of accounts at Bank of Amsterdam, 1611–1811
Source: Van Dillen 1925, p. 985.

peak was reached in 1720/1 with the total number of account holders at 2,918.

The Bank radiated a solid image, due to the requirement to refrain from extending credit. As a result, it did not even run out of cash during the major crisis of 1672. The deposits bore no interest, but had the enormous advantage that they were guaranteed by the city of Amsterdam. The average deposit per account rose from about 1,300 guilders in 1610 to about 3,500 guilders in the later seventeenth century. The Bank's clearing activities reached a peak during the early eighteenth century, dropped back after the 1720 crisis but then gradually rose again to a new high in the 1760s. After the 1772–3 crisis clearing at the Bank dropped sharply and never recovered.

Overdrafts were prohibited and carried a penalty of 3 per cent. Although the provision of credit was not a function of the Bank, loans were granted to the East India Company, the city of Amsterdam, and the Banken van Leening which supplied advances to small businesses (Heckscher 1934, p. 163; Voorthuysen 1989). Figure 3.2 demonstrates that right from the start, cash levels remained under deposits, and the gap widened after 1720 and again after 1770, indicating increased clandestine lending by the Bank. It was only after the 1760s that the Bank's central role diminished, when private domestic banking by cashiers and the management of foreign state debts by major banking houses became more influential in Dutch finance. The decline after 1770 is quite clear from figure 3.3.

Whereas the Bank's functions were rather restricted, its task in the currency system was pivotal for Dutch economic development throughout the early modern period. The Bank of Amsterdam, as circumstances required, purchased or sold coined money and bullion. Bullion was converted into money or vice versa if desired. In response to market pressure, the governors of the Bank allowed this institution to swing into action by buying and selling bank money at a premium that ran mostly at about 5 per cent. Generally, the Amsterdam magistrates pretended to establish the Bank's policy efficiently by increasing or lowering this *agio* rate. The *agio* was a kind of fixed but adjustable domestic exchange rate between the official full bodied currency in which the Bank quoted its accounts and the money in circulation.

Amsterdam's position in the bullion trade was enhanced by the introduction of the *recepis* in 1683. This was an issued receipt in bank money against deposited coins as security to be taken out within six months under commission charge, which could be prolonged or negotiated (Mees 1838, p. 146). Because of the extreme low rates of interest for such deposits in hard money the Amsterdam amounts of bullion multiplied. Merchants no longer demanded their bank accounts in hard cash, as it was cheaper to buy a *recepis* on the bourse. The trade in the *recepis* papers increased speculative options on the market. From 1683 on, a wise dealer would buy and sell the paper receipts on the bourse instead of speculating on future profit opportunities of coins. The system attracted plenty of speculators with small bank accounts. In all, the receipts' leverage offered the possibility of coping with the growing demands of an expanding financial market in the second half of the seventeenth century.

Moreover, the bank was extremely important in providing a fiduciary circulation, setting the tune for regulating domestic and foreign demand and the supply of money. Around 1700 a multilateral payment system was completed with all major financial centres of the world. At least until the mid eighteenth century, the Bank network provided for a significant integration of the European markets.

Backed by the careful policy of the governors of the Bank, Amsterdam rose as the financial capital of the world. It became a major market for precious metals and a terminal station of circulating bills (Klein 1987). In foreign trade, many bills of exchange were drawn, negotiated, accepted and paid in Amsterdam. The reason for Amsterdam's success lay in the fact that direct contacts existed with virtually all other trade centres throughout the world, which made it possible to buy a bill of exchange in Amsterdam that would be honoured almost everywhere in the world. A bill on Amsterdam meant gold, silver or short-term credit. In the Baltic and in Russia, for example, only Amsterdam bills of exchange were accepted.

The States General had approved the Bank of Amsterdam in 1610 and nourished hope for Wisselbanken in other Dutch cities for some time to come. Middelburg was the first town to prohibit money changers and cashiers in 1614 and to found a Wisselbank in 1616. Upon request from

Table 3.2. *Cash and deposits of the Amsterdam and Middelburg Wisselbanken, 1616/19–1790/9 (in million guilders)*

	Amsterdam			Middelburg		
	Cash	Deposits	Avg. C-R	Cash	Deposits	Avg. C-R
1616/9	1,355	1,473	96.3	36	50	72.9
1650/9	7,129	7,815	90.9	98	168	55.9
1700/9	10,049	11,985	84.4	253	360	63.1
1750/9	13,364	17,442	75.8	177	398	43.9
1790/9	5,870	14,706	36.0	95	347	28.0
Average	9,935	12,378	81.7	158	290	53.6

Source: GAA Archive, 5077; Van Dillen (1925 II, appendix). C-R = Cash ratio: cash/deposits × 100.

cloth manufacturers, Delft established a similar Wisselbank in 1621. This foundation was in existence only until 1635, when the merchant adventurers moved to Rotterdam. This city created a Wisselbank in that very same year.

The monetary policies of the Rotterdam's Bank were in line with those of the financial capital, as to intended accumulation of specie, the bank money rate and exchange quotations. Efforts in the 1720s to gain a substantial part of the home market in bills for itself, by prohibiting the trade of bills bought elsewhere, proved of no avail. The Amsterdam influence on Rotterdam was even so direct that the Rotterdam municipality allowed in 1638 its bank governors to help merchants in drawing bills on Amsterdam at Rotterdam municipal expense in order to prevent a specie drain to Amsterdam (Sneller 1940).

Middelburg, on the other hand, had more freedom of movement. However, the Bank of Amsterdam, which held considerably more in deposits and in its balance total (see table 3.2) used various devices to forestall the Middelburg Bank on the home market. The extremely strong position of the Bank of Amsterdam was reflected in its cash ratio, which was invariably much stronger as compared with its Middelburg counterpart. In the specie trade, Middelburg fought a desperate war. In 1647–8, when Spanish silver was lured from Amsterdam to Zeeland, Middelburg initially purchased above the Bank of Amsterdam price. The latter made a tough response and launched a counter-attack, outrunning the less powerful Middelburg Bank by raising prices even more (Van Dillen 1970, p. 33). Nevertheless, Middelburg was in a position to settle the bank money rate, the reserve rate and cash ratio of its deposits, and the foreign exchange rate within a certain range.

For the local market, the Middelburg bank proved quite significant. It permitted the formation of the local Bank van Leening, and the Commercie Compagnie Middelburg which specialised in slave trade and in sawing mills. Also regional public corporations relied heavily upon capital from their home market, and a part of the Middelburg Bank assets was composed of debtor's bonds, such as from the government of Zeeland, the city of Middelburg, the isle of Walcheren and the VOC chamber, Zeeland.

The Dutch Wisselbanken met the needs of the market (Rotterdam and Middelburg, the regional parts, Amsterdam, the international part) by adapting existing structures and techniques, and through organisation and policy. They served an initially vulnerable market, that grew more sophisticated and complex, with large resources, and created a fair degree of stability. Obviously Amsterdam dominated in this period in all these aspects. There, customers required services on a scale that was beyond the local banks, as in 1672 when the invading French army caused a run on the Wisselbanken. At the height of the panic, depositors withdrew their money on a massive scale. The Rotterdam and Middelburg Banks, who had engaged to a much greater extent than Amsterdam in the provision of credit to their clients, collapsed. It took years to establish them again (Sneller 1940, pp. 85–7; Van Dillen 1925, II, pp. 1013, 1026).

Meanwhile, the central state had no control at all over these public banks. The States General had attempted to introduce prohibition in the exportation of gold and silver in 1659 according to the ruling mercantilist opinion. But the insurmountable opposition by Amsterdam rendered this attempt futile. Even the provincial governments exerted little control. Holland, for example, requested the burgomasters of Amsterdam to disentangle their complex web of debts with the Bank of Amsterdam and the Bank van Leening, but no sanctions whatsoever existed to enforce such requests when they were disobeyed (Van Dillen 1965, p. 178).

Whereas the central authorities could not impose their policies upon the public banks, the Bank of Amsterdam was of great benefit to the city. The annual profits in the seventeenth century were regularly 50,000–80,000 guilders, mainly as a result of trade in precious metals. The General Masters of the Mint proved incapable of diverting such earnings to the mint houses of the Republic. The Wisselbanken remained municipal institutions with the strong backing of the local magistrates.

However, in the later eighteenth century, the political situation changed. Assistance by the authorities for public banks had been strong in the 1670s when the Middelburg and the Rotterdam Banks were refunded. Yet such options faded. Local and central authorities were unable to raise the necessary means, as private fund holders became more sceptical about the political solidarity of the ventures. Efforts faltered to create a Stadsbeleeningskamer in the 1780s, for credits against commodity securities, with the financial support of the Bank of Amsterdam. In 1796 an attempt misfired to refloat the Bank of Amsterdam itself, after the Bank had fallen into severe distress as a result of the French invasion. The fate was sealed too of the scheme by the provincial government to erect in 1795 the Generaale Beleenbank voor het Volk van Holland. The intended transformation of the Bank of Amsterdam in 1798 into a national deposit and discount bank (Algemeene Nationaale Beleen-, Disconto- en Deposito Bank) lacked support and vanished in 1803 (Fritschy 1986). The Middelburg Bank collapsed in 1794 and the Rotterdam Wisselbanken ceased operations in 1812. Liquidation of the Bank of Amsterdam followed in 1820.

3.6 Characteristics of the Amsterdam capital market

Dutch banking had been based on the breakthrough of Antwerp's banking system. Regarding the capital market, however, the Dutch model was different. The Antwerp capital market was basically short term in character. Its organisation relied upon the creditworthiness of predominant private Italian banking houses. In Amsterdam, the specific blend of financial institutions, based upon an Italian structure of public banks, ensured a long-term basis for credit operations and allowed the development from local lending and borrowing to international finance and revenue banking. The expansion of foreign trade was financed, and funds were lent to foreign governments. Amsterdam became the cardinal clearing place and the nearly unlimited source of accumulated capital – initially for direct domestic investment and foreign private investment in trade, later mainly for the foreign public sector – consolidating government debts and expenditures.

Other important international markets were Geneva, Hamburg, Genoa, Frankfurt, Vienna and London. Yet among these cities Amsterdam was pre-eminent in having the necessary volume of capital for large-scale lending and a set of institutions that safeguarded the market liquidity and the interests of lenders and borrowers alike (Riley 1980, p. 8). Moreover, the trade in bullion was unequalled by the other centres. Table 3.3 shows the direction and volume of the bullion outflow. In comparison with other contemporary countries, the Dutch had little want of money at all. It was estimated that, by 1700, the ready money per head of population amounted to about 100 guilders on average (De Vries and Van der Woude 1995,

Table 3.3. *Bullion flow from the northern Netherlands, ca. 1600–1750 (in thousands of guilders)*

Destination	1600	1650	1700	1750	1780
Baltic and Archangel	4,375	5,625	5,000	5,000	7,500
Levant	1,500	2,000	2,500	3,750	3,750
East Indies by VOC	575	860	3,414	4,748	4,788
Total	6,450	8,485	10,914	13,498	16,038

Sources: Baltic and Levant figures: Attman 1983a, p. 103, Attman 1983b, p. 20; East Indies: Gaastra 1976, p. 253, Gaastra 1983, p. 451 and Bruijn *et al.* 1987 I, pp. 226–244.

p. 115). In addition, the network of information centred on Amsterdam. As more merchants, consular agents, and newspaper publishers congregated in Amsterdam, the amount of information available increased, and the snippets of information being exchanged rose geometrically (Neal 1990, p. 29).

However, the Dutch Republic was not always a net exporter of capital. As a result of its trade deficit, capital was imported up to the middle of the seventeenth century. In the last two decades of the sixteenth century, Amsterdam received massive resources from the southern Netherlands. Wealthy immigrant merchants joined the exodus from Antwerp and settled mainly in Middelburg and Amsterdam (Israel 1989, pp. 12–37; Den Haan 1977, pp. 61–9). These entrepreneurs did not only bring capital. Their skills in finance and banking came with them too. Investments came also from Venice (until the 1630s), Hamburg (before 1620) and Paris (1610–40) (Kors 1988; Dehing 1995). As the trade balance shifted later in the century, with the excess of exports, the Dutch Republic became a creditor nation. Thereafter, foreign investors were of only minor importance (Riley 1984, p. 552).

This shift from a debtor to a creditor nation was enacted under an inverse liquidity structure. In the Republic, short-term capital was scarce relative to long-term capital, from the early seventeenth century up to the first three decades of the eighteenth century. Compared with London and Paris, two other eminent financial centres, Amsterdam showed a short-term capital undersupply, which was reflected in high interest rates (see table 3.4). Long-term capital, on the other hand, was much more abundantly available as compared with most other financial centres. All these differences in liquidity trends added to the international mobility of capital.

Table 3.4. *Nominal interest rate structure in Amsterdam, 1540/9–1789 (ten year averages)*

Year	Sight	Short	Long	Year	Sight	Short	Long
				1660/9	11.6	4.3	4.1
1540/9			6.3	1670/9	5.9	4.1	4.2
1550/9			9.5	1680/9	11.5	4.6	5.0
1560/9			16.7	1690/9	7.6	4.3	4.0
1570/9			13.1	1700/9	9.2	4.1	4.1
1580/9			13.0	1710/19	8.3	4.9	4.2
1590/9	10.0	7.8		1720/9	8.5	4.8	3.9
1600/9	12.5	8.7		1730/9	8.4	4.0	4.1
1610/19	25.6	6.5	7.0	1740/9	7.0	3.2	5.4
1620/9	12.8	6.2	5.5	1750/9	7.1	5.0	5.3
1630/9	18.8	5.6	5.6	1760/9	8.0	5.5	7.0
1640/9	15.9	6.6	5.6	1770/9	7.0	4.0	6.0
1650/9	12.4	4.9	4.8	1780/9	6.9	3.9	4.5

Notes: Sight= 0–6 months; short= 6 months to 2 years; long= 2 years and over. Interpolated data: sight 1730/9 and 1750/9; long 1670/9 and 1730/9, 1740/9. Extrapolated: sight and short 1780/9.
Sources: 1540–1609: Tracy 1985, pp. 45, 89 and Dormans 1991, pp. 26, 64; 1590–1789: GAA (NA: obligations; RA: schepenkennissen).

3.7 The Amsterdam bourse and the trade in securities

The Amsterdam bourse, which was first mentioned at the end of the fifteenth century, was like its Antwerp example intended for both commercial and financial transactions. As early as 1639 at least 360 types of commodities were traded. By 1685 their number had risen to 550. Characteristic of many transactions was buying in advance: commodities were purchased ahead of delivery, sometimes even years ahead, which was an enormous stimulus for trade. This habit of paying in advance extended to all kinds of goods, even herrings before they were caught, or grain, cocoa and coffee before they were grown. The ability to pay in advance also meant an enormous competitive advantage for the Dutch on the international market (Spufford 1995, p. 307).

To some extent, the city authorities exerted control on the bourse through the brokers' guild. The number of official bourse-brokers mounted to 360 in 1612. In 1722 about 395 sworn brokers were working in and around the bourse. Besides, some 700–800 unsworn freelance traders performed transactions, arranging loans and insurances and the sale of real estate as well as of commodities. The regulation of insurance came early: an ordinance of 1598, which was renewed in 1744, formalised procedures. A Chamber of Assurance was set up in 1612 under the auspices of the city government (Spooner 1983, pp. 15, 22; McCusker and Gravesteijn 1991, pp. 44 ff.).

Information as to the main transactions could be had through the *beurscourant*. This paper was established by the sworn brokers, listing the main business of the bourse. The first issue appeared in 1585. After 1613 it was to appear weekly. In the eighteenth century, the Amsterdamsche Courant even appeared three times weekly with lists of prices of securities and real estate sold in public auctions.

The concentration on the bourse simplified the development of speculation. Speculation occurred first in commodities with high price fluctuations like grain, herring, whale oil and bones, and tulips. Notorious was the tulipmania of 1636–7, when speculation provoked prices of 4,600–6,000 florins per bulb. Later, after the second half of the seventeenth century, speculation ensued mainly in financial assets. Trading in securities rose steadily: around 1750 about 44 issues were quoted (Van Dillen 1964). Besides the forward business with fixed purchases, some brokers and bankers engaged in option transactions, which boosted speculation even further.

Most trading was in stock of the VOC (East India Company) and WIC (West India Company). The VOC, dating from 1602, was created out of the amalgamation of competing Dutch joint ventures, the private Voorcompagniën (Den Haan 1977, pp. 79–127; Gaastra 1982). Such companies, with a large number of investors (*partenrederij*) had been known for several centuries. A novelty of the VOC was its size and its time of operation. Initially, it was set up for a limited number of years, like most early modern trade enterprises. But the VOC continued with fresh monopolycharters for trade in the East Indies right up to the end of the eighteenth century. It was basically a federal organisation made up of six separate Chambers, that also provided the capital to a total corporate sum of nearly 6.5 million guilders: Amsterdam, Zeeland, Rotterdam, Delft, Hoorn and Enkhuizen. These Chambers were represented in the general managing committee, the Heeren Zeventien. Amsterdam furnished 57 per cent of the capital and elected eight representatives, Zeeland four, the others one each; number 17 came alternately from Zeeland and the smaller chambers (Gaastra 1989). And, although this board decided on matters of general business, it did not shut out the freedom of separate Chambers to act at their own discretion. Amsterdam of course, possessing the largest number of transferable shares, was the most powerful of all the six chambers.

Already by 1608 the method of selling and buying VOC stock was simple, but new. Sellers unofficially sold short, *in blanco*, what they expected to receive but did not have. And, although the powerless States General repeatedly prohibited this practice (such as in 1610, 1621, 1623, 1624, 1630, 1636 and in 1677), forward share selling continued. An improvement was the introduction of the three-monthly liquidations term, the *rescontre*, during which days the outstanding deals were balanced.

In the first decade of the 1600s, and in the 1680s, the volatility of VOC shares was at its highest. Their market value reached a ceiling in the early decades of the eighteenth century, with quotations generally over 600 and 700 per cent. The trade in VOC stock was accelerated by the introduction of so-called *ducaton*-shares, worth one-tenth of a normal share. This gave people with limited funds some opportunity for speculation too. After the 1740s the trend slowed down, with quotations often under 400 per cent. A decline of the company was noticeable after 1780, when quotations fell generally to under 250 per cent (Van Dillen 1931).

In the West India Company (1621), with a comparable charter for trade in the West Indies, Amsterdam was less involved. Its Chamber still furnished the largest funds, amounting to 43 per cent of the total capital sum of 6.6 million. The other WIC Chambers were Zeeland, Delft, Enkhuizen and Groningen (Den Haan 1977, pp. 106–10, 214–19).

With the development of public bonds payable to bearer (instead of the more traditional loans committed to a person) vouchers of Dutch public funds appeared on the market too. During the time of the Republic, these bonds constituted a most secure investment item. Revenues were not spectacular, but assured by the soundness of Dutch politics (see previous chapter). Later in the seventeenth century, British public funds appeared in the unofficial price lists next to the public debts of the Dutch Union, the provinces and towns. By the middle of the eighteenth century, 25 Dutch public funds were traded regularly, next to shares of three Dutch and three English companies and 13 foreign loans. Subsequently, numerous stock companies in sea, fire, and life assurance and discounting business were created. Foreign loans mounted up to 39 in 1796, next to 57 Dutch long-term loans.

Increasingly, private firms came to be involved in the transactions on the bourse. Their development in the second half of the eighteenth century was impressive. Partly, the activities of these firms were boosted by foreign governments, appealing to a certain merchant/banker. As agents, some bankers became specialists in specific foreign issues: Fizeaux and Hasselgreen for Sweden, Pels for Prussia and Hamburg, Horneca, Fizeaux and Van Staphorst for France, Deutz and Goll & Co for Austria, the Cliffords for Danzig and Denmark, and so on.

Table 3.5. *Net real capital return in London and Paris as compared with Amsterdam, 1605/9–1750/4 (percentages)*

	London	Paris		London	Paris
1605/9	13.9		1680/9	3.1	
1610/19			1690/9	7.8	
1620/9			1700/9	−11.2	
1630/9	39.4	18.9	1710/19	−18.5	
1640/9	32.2	19.7	1720/9	24.6	
1650/4	−54.7	−56.3	1730/9	−24.4	22.4
1660/9	15.1	−21.2	1740/9	4.7	−38.3
1670/9	14.4	19.6	1750/4	32.0	6.8

Sources: London: Phelps-Brown and Hopkins, 1981, Paris Hauser 1936, Amsterdam Nusteling 1985, pp. 260–1; GAA Archive/NA obligations; RA, schepenkennissen; NEHA (CCC, Commodity price, exchange rate and money lists).

3.8 Capital flows and foreign assets

Long-term Dutch capital was generally diverted to land reclamation (*polders*) and government bonds. Short-term Dutch capital was generally ploughed into trade credit but was also directed at assets with positive valuation effects, for instance in Danzig, London and Paris, predominantly at private enterprises. Naturally, those opportunities fluctuated. Table 3.5 shows the net return of capital investment in London and Paris as compared with Amsterdam.[3] In the 1630s and 1640s, Dutch merchants channelled their short-term capital overseas, to England, due to sterling appreciation, and not to Paris. Thereafter, capital apparently moved inversely. It flowed to the Republic as sterling depreciation made lending in England very unprofitable and domestic revenues for Dutch merchant houses considerably lower (Dehing 1995).

This nexus of profitability and foreign exchange marked also Dutch and foreign export of long-term capital. Dutch investment funds in the early seventeenth century were principally directed to land reclamation, extraction and manufacture of raw materials and the export sector. The examples are diverse, such as lending to the land reclamations and other hydraulic engineering of Cornelis Vermuyden in England, to the Société pour le Deséchement des Marais et Lacs de France for large-scale reclamation in France, to the possessions of the Amsterdam merchant Joachim Irgens in copper-mining in Norway, to the lending and purchases of estates by the Marselis family in Denmark, to the Dutch participation in the Danish East

India Company since 1616, to sulphur-pits in Iceland exploited by the Amsterdam Sautijn family, to the copper mines of De Geer and the Trippen in Sweden, and to loans for the Swedish government (Klein 1965).

As the demand from authorities for public loans contracted in the course of the eighteenth century (see chapter 4), other outlets were sought for Dutch capital. With public funds in The Netherlands paying between 2 and 3 per cent, transfers abroad looked attractive with returns from 4 to 6 per cent. Opportunities for foreign investment by the Dutch had been rather marginal until the 1750s (Van der Voort 1981, p. 91; Kesler 1982). From then on, however, the situation changed: Denmark, Sweden, Austria, Russia, Poland and several German princes borrowed in Amsterdam. European loans were generally issued at rates of 4–5 per cent and the West Indies loans at 5–6 per cent (Spooner 1983, p. 73). Data from Amsterdam inheritances suggest a considerable shift from investments in the Dutch Republic and England to ventures in other parts of Europe and the world in the 1780s (Carter 1975, pp. 20–65). During this decade, Amsterdam's international involvement was at its peak as foreign wars increased the demand for Dutch funds.

In some cases Dutch funds wielded enormous effects. Trade expansion in seventeenth-century Danzig was increasingly financed by Amsterdam capital. Inflation gave Polish business activity and credit demand a significant impetus. Real long-term depreciation of the Danzig *grossen* however, caused capital loss to the foreign borrowers. Dutch creditors turned into revenue bankers, managing the private debts (Bogucka 1990, p. 26; Cieslak 1983). In the eighteenth century, a shift of investments was noted into securities of the city of Danzig. The same long-term depreciation occurred in Frankfurt with similar effects until the 1670s. All in all, Amsterdam money appeared to be easily transmitted again.

Estimates of total foreign investment ranges between 200 and 270 million in the 1760s rising to between 500 and 650 million in the 1790s (Riley 1980, pp. 15–16). Initially, these loans were obtained against commodities like copper in Sweden, mercury in Slovenia, copper in Hungary and crown jewels in Bavaria. Gradually, the security for these loans shifted to sources of revenue like customs receipts in 1735 in Denmark or guarantees by governments.

The foreign states that came to the Amsterdam capital market to finance their deficit spending and wars found a welcome climate. The Dutch tax system encouraged investments in foreign loans as these bonds were generally not taxed at all. The flow of Dutch capital to England, used in financing of both private assets and British government debt, is the largest and well documented example. As early as the 1690s English shares appeared on the Amsterdam bourse. Dutch bankers also entered the London market through their local agents and acquired a large share in the English public debt. A regular communication system between the London and Amsterdam capital market remained characteristic for the eighteenth century. Dutch bankers exported long-term Dutch capital, while borrowing themselves on the short-term market in London by their agents and replacing these funds in Amsterdam to convert them into more profitable deposits and assets. The rapid reaction of foreign agents to changing market conditions was essential to exploit the Dutch market power by negotiating foreign loans. By 1739/40, even 72 per cent of all Dutch investments in English funds was in Bank of England stock. In 1720 London underwent a brisk trade in securities, offering high real returns (see table 3.5) on the South Sea Company. Dutch holdings in the English East India Company reached the 15 per cent level of the £3,200,000 company capital. Furthermore, the City of London sold annuities to Dutch investors, and a credit of 10 million guilders allowed the British government to finance plantations in the West Indies (Wilson 1942). Only after the Fourth Anglo-Dutch War did the investments in England diminish (Eagly and Smith 1976; Neal 1990; Schubert 1988).

When the activities of billbroking and exchange dealings were undermined, the number of foreign loans issued rose. American, Swedish, Silesian, Russian, and French loans were floated and the bonds easily placed. The small holdings made an enormous spread possible, as the portfolio of an investor shows. C.C. van de Meer had invested a sum totalling 141,386 guilders, of which 87,068 guilders (61.4 per cent) went abroad. One holding concerned the Bank of England (21,002) and the remainder was divided over the Danish Asiatic Company, Austrian quicksilver mines, Surinam, public loans in Russia, Denmark, the Bank of Vienna, Mecklenburg, Leipzig, Sweden and Saxony (Carter 1975, p. 47). This example points also to the typical investment habit of a single large English stock and a variety in other foreign lending.

3.9 Crises and weaknesses

While foreign financial markets expanded, the Dutch autonomy to regulate financial policy diminished. The Amsterdam authorities became increasingly dependent upon extraneous policy measures of competing capital markets, which restrained their fine tuning of rates and ratios. Gradually, the former organisational advantage of the Dutch lapsed. After the War of Spanish Succession (1702–13), lending was at the mercy of the market just at a moment of growing private off-balance activities and tougher solvability requirements of the Bank of Amsterdam. The crisis of 1720 caused a portfolio switch to foreign securities. The structure inversion in interest rates after the 1730s (table 3.4) indicates a preference for higher foreign returns, which caused high risk lending in short-term futures and the trend of borrowing long-term risk averse government loans by Dutch investors.

Typical for the Dutch capital market was that domestic investment opportunities were rather limited, in particular after 1650. The herring fisheries were damaged by competition from English and Scandinavians. Industry, closely linked to the terms of trade, was becoming less attractive and suffered from high excise rates. Land had been a traditional investment item, but these ventures were discouraged by the agrarian depression of the late seventeenth century. Furthermore, the authorities of Holland had embarked upon a policy to constrain the domestic public debt in the eighteenth century. Above all, Dutch shipping suffered from increasing international competition. Whereas seventeenth-century Amsterdam had profited as an entrepot of trade goods, eighteenth-century commercial traffic tended to sail directly from the source of supply to the point of distribution or consumption, passing Amsterdam by.

Yet the Dutch remained important within the international commercial networks. A general shift from trade to finance was noticeable. Traditional contacts furthered payments being made through Amsterdam. For example, no exchange rate was quoted between London and St Petersburg until 1763. Throughout the eighteenth century, Dutch commission agents continued to advance money, arrange insurance, discount bills of exchange, and maintained the most elaborate channels of information which furthered their role as financiers of trade.

Together with these indirect activities in trade, an altering of the repayments system overall led to an extension of acceptance credit in Amsterdam. The acceptance banker was prepared to accept bills of exchange on condition that the client ensured that there were sufficient funds on a due date. During the Seven Years' War (1756–63) such practices got out of hand. Too many bills of exchange had been issued without sufficient backing in commodities. A contemporary observer remarked that the volume of paper could have reached 15 times the currency circulating in The Netherlands. And whereas wartime needs had given Dutch bankers opportunities for large profits, peace conditions demanded payments in cash. The chains of accommodation bills, called *wisselruiterij*, were ultimately responsible for the July crisis of 1763, when the merchant banking house of De Neufville went bankrupt. Discounted bills collapsed as Frederick II of Prussia withdrew old debased money from circulation before new money was issued. To provide the latter he had bought silver on credit in Amsterdam. The crisis was redressed by the bankers Clifford & Sons and Andries Pels & Sons who met the money demand by placing a Danish loan of 2.5 million guilders (Veluwenkamp 1981; Spooner 1983, pp. 79–84).

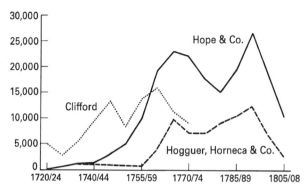

Figure 3.4 Turnover of three merchant bankers with the Amsterdam Wisselbank, 1720–1810

The numerous foreign stocks made speculation and overtrading easy play. Bad news in London concerning the results of the East India Company in 1772 tempered the speculative boom. Share prices declined, in particular after harvest failures tended to direct funds into the storage of wheat and settlements to grain dealers. A chain of bankruptcies followed in England. Loans ceased, speeding panic and the crisis spread to Amsterdam. Clifford & Sons, once the overseas correspondents of the Bank of England in Amsterdam, now had to suspend bill payments and failed in December 1772.

The monetary weakness of the Amsterdam market became evident, as no lender of last resort could restore confidence or make money available. The Bank of Amsterdam had not been designed as such. Clearing at the Wisselbanken dropped sharply, reinforcing the downward trend which the turnover of some merchant bankers already showed during the late 1760s (cf. figure 3.4). As compared with the 1763 crisis, however, recovery was rapid. The burgomasters of Amsterdam set up a fund of 3 million guilders against 3.5 per cent interest for temporary solace (Wilson 1942; Spooner 1983, p. 95).

Figure 3.4. also demonstrates the pecking order amongst Amsterdam merchant bankers. Hope & Co. surpassed the older houses Clifford and Pels during the 1760s, and recovered from the 1772–3 crisis to achieve a new peak in the 1790s. Hogguer, Horneca & Co. followed a more cautious track, thus suffered less from the crisis, and resumed growth in the mid 1700s. The great bullion traders Andries Pels & Sons appears to have gone into decline during the late 1750s after their heyday during the 1720s and again during the War of the Spanish Succession, when the firm supplied English troops in the southern Netherlands with cash. Pels suffered substantial losses in the Clifford collapse and went into liquidation in 1773.

Although some private firms continued with an upward trend (like Hope & Co. and Van Eeghen), Amsterdam's preeminence as a financial centre suffered a severe blow as a result of the crises of the 1760s and the 1770s. Several international banks lost their distinguished position after the 1780s: Stadnitski, Muilman & Sons, Hogguer, Horneca & Co., Determeijer Weslingh en Zn., Goll & Co., Fizeaux, Hasselgreen, Van Staphorst and DeSmeth (Buist 1974; Elias 1903/5). In the meantime, some smaller merchant bankers, in particular outside Amsterdam, managed to move ahead. Examples of a booming business were noticed with Ketwich & Voomberg and Van Son Brothers in Amsterdam, Osy & Sons, Chabot and Mees in Rotterdam and Van Lanschot in Den Bosch.

Overall though, in the last quarter of the eighteenth century, Dutch banking had become extremely vulnerable. When the French invaded The Netherlands in 1795, the largest private bank, Hope & Co., decided to go abroad. The combination of a weak domestic political background and strong subjection to foreign economic and political circumstances made Amsterdam less attractive. Integration into the international money and capital market had increased sensitivity to external exogenous shocks; and, at the same time, the powers of domestic policy had decreased.

3.10 Conclusion

As in the field of public finance (see chapter 2), the Dutch financial system suffered enormously from the confusion of the early decades of the Revolt. In comparison with the Habsburg era central control was significantly reduced. Gradually, however, problems were overcome by the sheer economic power of the province of Holland. In particular the city of Amsterdam managed to set the rules for control over monetary matters. The disadvantages of the federalised structure were mastered with the establishment of the Bank of Amsterdam in 1609 and the currency reform of 1694. The Bank, prospering in particular during 1683 till 1781, allowed for stable currency, flexible transfers, and the multilateral clearing of international payments. Trade coins, the *negotiepenningen*, were issued, through which international trade flows escaped the currency difficulties. Though these inducements and initiatives for improvement were basically local, its effects were nationwide.

In the meantime, in contrast to the mint and currency, the capital market seems to have thrived from the lack of central control, and relied largely on the investments of private capital. In many other states, central powers recurrently curbed the possibilities of enterprising ventures. In the Dutch case, local interests could be advanced to the full. The main impediments were dictated by local authorities, who did accommodate in general the demands of the most powerful merchant communities. In particular in the beginning of the Revolt, the uncertainties hampered many, but constituted an extremely profitable source for those who were able to operate within the available opportunities.

The system was bolstered by a growing economy, a relatively stable currency and receptive political institutions. Nowhere was there a sudden break with the past. Occasionally, the conditions were adapted to the needs of the moment. The fact that most institutions were actually quite conservative did not seem harmful (Spufford 1995). The refinement of the available instruments proved remarkably adequate. The system of small-scale local banking, without disappearing itself, gradually smoothed the way for large-scale heterogeneous international bank activities in the second half of the eighteenth century. Conducive to this global interaction of local capital markets was the Bank of Amsterdam, whose limitations did not prevent the development of the city of Amsterdam into the main financial market of the time. On the contrary, precisely through its continuity with the past, with the limits set on advances and the guarantee of the city authorities, the clearing system of the bank attained an enormous degree of reliability.

Innovations, on the other hand, were not totally lacking. The reforms, though modest and adapted to the available opportunities, did lower the general transactions costs, which allowed Dutch capital to penetrate far into European countries and their colonies. Furthermore, the fact that the Bank of Amsterdam did become an enormous storehouse for international specie meant that exchange rates became uncommonly stable. Any shipment of precious metals in any desired coinage became possible. The costs were low. Opportunities for raising capital cheaply and easily for any commercial or industrial venture were greater in The Netherlands than anywhere else at the time. Interest rates were low, perhaps not always the lowest in Europe, but the market was solid and reliable. There was great confidence in the soundness of the financial system, and, in particular, for funds destined for long-term investments Dutch rates were low by foreign standards.

In accordance with economic changes, a shift was noted from finance of trade to finance of governments and foreign investments. The climate for a thriving capital market remained profitable, not in the least because of the stability of the Dutch government. Investments were highly flexible; even the financial crises of 1763 and 1772 were short lasting. In addition, inflation was modest, at least up to the 1780s (Posthumus 1943–64 I, ci). Furthermore, Dutch authorities were willing to invest in infrastructure and communications, promoting business, and in facilities like the Bank of

Amsterdam. And, although this bank became increasingly inadequate by the later eighteenth century, the Amsterdam financial market remained of continued relevance up to the period of the Napoleonic wars.

The revolutionary transition period of the 1790s definitely altered the international balance. After 1815, Amsterdam's primacy passed on. The requirements to finance economic growth had finally passed beyond the capacity of this tiny state.

Notes

1 In the southern provinces (Zeeland for example) the Flemish pound was still used. One pound Flemish = 6 guilders. One guilder equals 20 *stuiver* of 16 pennies each, one guilder equals also 40 *groten* of eight pennies each. Posthumus (1943, p. lvi), Korthals Altes (1996).

2 A bill of exchange is an order of payment of a certain sum of money in another place, mostly in foreign currency. Endorsement allowed the transfer of this bill by a simple assignment on the back; discount means the surrender of a commercial title, mostly a bill of exchange, to a third party before the bill matured for a sum lower than the nominal value, giving the discounter a reward (the discount rate) for holding the bill.

3 Calculated: the net real return of Amsterdam investments in London (A) equals the Amsterdam real interest rates (Ra) reduced by the real London rate (Rl) minus the pound Sterling/pound Flemish appreciation (D). The real interest rate of Amsterdam (Ra) is the nominal rate of interest (Na) minus the inflation in Amsterdam (Ia). Suppose a nominal rate of 7 per cent and an inflation of 3 per cent, this makes a real interest rate of 4 per cent. A similar calculation is possible for London (Rl=Nl–Il). Then, for the appreciation (D), the increase in value of Dutch money *vis-à-vis* foreign currencies. For example, for the pound Sterling this amounted to 26 per cent between 1590 and 1609 and 60 per cent between 1630 and 1650. To conclude, A=Ra–Rl–D; Ra=Na–Ia; Rl=Nl–Il; thus A=(Na–Ia)–(Nl–Il)–D.

4   From fragmentation to unification: public finance, 1700–1914

WANTJE FRITSCHY AND RENÉ VAN DER VOORT

4.1 Introduction

The decisive event in the financial history of The Netherlands during the eighteenth and the nineteenth centuries is the transformation from fragmentation to unification. After the so-called Batavian Revolution of 1795 the provincial debts of the united provinces were amalgamated into one national debt. The first national budget was presented to an elected parliament. In 1806 a national taxation system was realised, by which the fiscal autonomy of the seven provinces was ended. Moreover, the charters of the West and East Indian Companies were not renewed after their expiration. Their tasks were handed over to a state department of colonial affairs. The local Bank of Amsterdam died a silent death in 1820 and a new national bank modelled on the example of the Bank of England was erected in 1814. In the meantime, the pound sterling had taken over the role of the depreciated Bank of Amsterdam guilder as the main international key currency at the turn of the century. London replaced Amsterdam as the main international financial centre (see chapter 3). Thus, the Dutch lead in the international financial and economic system definitely came to an end, the ancien régime federal republic became a modern unitary state, ready to embark on financial policy on a national scale.

In the seventeenth century the Dutch Republic had been remarkable for the success of its financial system. In the beginning of the eighteenth century its debts were hardly any longer compatible with its small size. Owing to their central position in the international system, however, the Dutch could not back out silently. During the eighteenth century the ever increasing financial problems still had to be solved within the worn-out institutional arrangements. Besides, competition from increasingly protectionistic neighbours, with large internal markets, caused much damage to the economic position of the core province of The Netherlands, export-oriented Holland. Its financial sector still remained strong, but industries deteriorated and employment opportunities diminished. In contrast to the developments in most other Western European countries Holland did not have an upswing in population growth or in economic development. In the maritime regions, both the population and economy stagnated. Only the agrarian, eastern provinces of The Netherlands were able to take advantage of the increasing price levels of the period and experienced population growth as well as increasing wealth in the course of the eighteenth century (Van Zanden 1984, pp. 105–31).

Whereas internal tariff barriers had never been felt as a barrier to economic development in seventeenth-century Holland, dependent as it was on foreign commerce, the better accessibility of internal markets brought about by the removal of tariff restrictions was clearly in the interest of the eastern provinces in the course of the eighteenth century. Some pressure for unification from the inland provinces became noticeable. Holland had always expressed a desire for fiscal unification in order to have the other provinces take a fair share in the unbearable load of the interest burden (Fritschy 1989, p. 670).

Initially the financial consequences of the Batavian Revolution of 1795 were even more disastrous for public finance than any of the former wars. After the temporary incorporation in France in 1810 those problems were countered by Napoleon by simply reducing the interest payments on the Dutch state debt by two-thirds, the notorious *tiërcering*, as had been done in France in 1797. After Napoleon's defeat in 1815 the prospects were promising, as the northern and the southern (or Austrian) Netherlands were joined into a United Kingdom of The Netherlands by the great powers. The Kingdom was thus a centralised Dutch state, double its former size with an interest burden reduced to a third. Its assets were, in the north, an abundant amount of capital in the hands of its wealthiest citizens and a tradition of financial and commercial know-how in the service sector, and, in the south, modern industrial developments in textiles, coal and iron.

A thorough improvement of the Dutch economic structure seemed feasible within this new political constellation. Unification, not only of the northern provinces, but also of the northern and southern Netherlands, seemed a precondition for economic mutual integration and for the integration of the colonies into a healthy national whole. It may be clear that, apart from banking and currency policy (see chapter 5), government financial policy regarding expenditure, taxation and debt creation was seen as a vital instrument to attain this goal.

Chances of success seemed to reach an utter low, however, after the Belgian secession of 1830. Financial problems of an unprecedented extent had to be solved again within the borders of the former, small country. Nevertheless, thanks to some drastic financial measures in the early 1840s and to the growing addition to public revenue from colonial exploitation of the Indies since the 1830s, rather smooth financial developments came into being in the second half of the nineteenth century. A rapidly growing population was supportive.[1] The economy expanded again, not only because of a developing industrial sector, but also because of the advancement of the German hinterland. The Dutch–Indian colonies greatly enhanced opportunities in the service sector, that had traditionally been a preponderant part of Dutch economic structure (Smits 1990, pp. 81–99; Smits 1995, p. 163). At the end of the nineteenth century, financial policy aimed at economic and social improvements without burdening the state with disastrous debts became feasible.

Most remarkable was the increasing weight of local governments in public finance, a development which was also noticeable in other Western European countries. National unification had meant primarily the curtailment of provincial autonomy. Since the middle of the nineteenth century, local financial autonomy was restricted, but only as far as the taxation side of public finance was concerned. In public expenditure and debt creation the role of local governments in public finance waxed larger than it had ever been in the heyday of autonomous cities during the old Dutch Republic.

We will start this chapter with a broad overview of the quantitative developments of public expenditure, revenue and debt in the eighteenth and nineteenth centuries. Secondly, we will analyse first expenditure and then taxation in the eighteenth and the first half of the nineteenth centuries to gain a better insight into the importance of the Batavian Revolution (1795) for Dutch financial history. In the last part of this chapter the new financial developments in the second half of the nineteenth century until the outbreak of World War I will be sketched in more detail. It is the purpose of this chapter to detect how and why the process from fragmentation to unification in public finance in the end resulted in a renewal of economic and financial strength in the twentieth century.

4.2 Quantitative developments

Figures on public finance always deserve suspicion if only because of their dependence on the nature of bookkeeping practices. Figures for early periods have to be used with even more caution because of lack of data. Reliable figures on Dutch public finance are available for the period 1850–1914 (Van der Voort 1994). Van Zanden made a reconstruction of the figures for the period 1807–50 (Van Zanden 1996, forthcoming). As for the era before 1850 the figures on public finance given in table 4.1 offer just a rough impression of quantitative developments. Besides, they are in current prices, whereas it should be remembered that the second half of the eighteenth century was a period of price rises of at least about 25 per cent

(Fritschy 1990, p. 73). Between 1815 and 1914 prices remained roughly at the same level, although significant fluctuations did occur.

To account for fluctuations in population size, fiscal revenue is also presented in guilders per head. For the nineteenth century some estimates of national income are available, permitting an indication of the development of public expenditure as a percentage of national income as well. Another measure for the tax burden is the number of days an industrial labourer had to work to pay for the amount of fiscal revenue per head per year. To account for the large wage differences in The Netherlands estimates of a maximum and a minimum of this number of working days are given in the last column of table 4.1.

Last but not least the amounts for public finance on the national level are partly dependent on the extent of local public expenditure and of fiscal revenue collected at a local level, or by public authorities other than the central government. Reliable figures in this respect, however, are even harder to come by than central government figures. We will come back to local finance below.

Notwithstanding those considerable reservations mentioned before, table 4.1 offers three major tendencies that should be pointed out. Firstly, as a result of population growth, fiscal revenue per head during the nineteenth century was lower than for most of the eighteenth century, despite higher amounts of public expenditure. The Dutch were no longer the most heavily taxed people in Western Europe. Even after the Belgian secession, when the tax burden in the north had to be increased, fiscal revenue per head collected at the central level was slightly higher than in France, where it came down to 16 guilders per head in 1841, but much lower than in Great Britain, where it came down to over 23 guilders per head in 1841.[2] If local taxes were included the picture might be somewhat different. In 1913 however, the total fiscal revenue per head, local taxes included, was in Britain about 62 guilders, in France about 54 guilders, and in The Netherlands only about 34 guilders.[3]

Secondly, despite an impressive growth in public expenditure by the central government between 1850 and 1913, the stage of growing percentages of national income per head was not yet entered upon. This figure showed even a modest decrease. The state displayed still a modest presence in social and economic life.

Thirdly, a comparison of expenditure with fiscal revenue during these centuries shows that financial means other than taxes must have continued to render significant amounts in public finance in most of our period.

To illustrate the part played by public loans in closing this gap, table 4.2 offers a survey of (estimates of) the development of the public debt between 1700 and 1914.

Table 4.1. *Public expenditure and fiscal revenue in the (northern) Netherlands, 1720–1913*

	Public expenditure (million guilders)	Fiscal revenue (million guilders)	Fiscal revenue (guilders per head)	Fiscal revenue as % of national income	Fiscal revenue per head in number of working days
1720	33	32	17.00		18–25
1750	41	37	19.50		21–29
1790	46	39	20.00		22–29
1799	57				
1806/7	50	45	22.20	9%	
1815	51				
1817	80*	33	14.70		
1820	81*	37	15.60		16–26
1830	87*	38	15.50		
1835	50				
1842	71	50	17.10	8%	
1850	68	54	17.50	9%	18–25
1860	72	55	16.70	7%	17–24
1870	100	69	19.30	7%	16–21
1880	116	94	23.40	8%	15–21
1890	123	101	22.50	8%	14–19
1900	146	120	23.50	8%	13–17
1910	195	150	25.70	7%	14–17
1913	228	165	27.10	6%	

Note:
*Southern Netherlands included.
Sources: Up to 1815 based upon: Fritschy 1983, 1988, 1990, 1996; Kappelhof 1986; Zijlstra 1983; for 1799: Schimmelpenninck 1845 vol. II, pp. 312–14; after 1815: Riemens 1935, 1937; Fritschy 1992, Van Zanden 1996; figures exclude debt redemption by Amortisatiesyndicaat during 1822–30; for 1890 including 37 million guilders for the take over of the Rhijnspoorwegmaatschappij. Estimates of national income in an unpublished research memorandum by Horlings, Smits and Van Zanden 1992. Wages are based upon Noordegraaf/and Schoenmakers 1984; Vlis 1981; De Meere 1980, p. 358 and Vermaas 1995.

Of course debt figures offer only a limited insight in real financial developments, because they do not reveal fluctuations as a result of temporary loans, redemptions and conversion measures. A special mention should be made of the rise in the debt between 1810 and 1814 which was mainly due to a conversion law at the beginning of the new kingdom. The

Table 4.2 *Development of the debt burden in the Netherlands, 1764–1914 (in million guilders and in percentage of national income)*

	Real debt	Deferred debt	In % of national income
1764	552		
1796	766		
1798	950		
1810	1,200		225
	400		
1814	617	1,205	151
1822	759	1,136	182
1829	913	837	191
1841	1,219	896	227
1845	1,226		228
1850	1,231		212
1860	1,058		135
1870	957		95
1880	927		78
1890	1,076		83
1900	1,145		74
1913	1,156		44

Sources: For 1764: Archives Nationales in Paris K 879, no. 123 Moreau de Beaumont, i. 202; for 1796: Dormans 1991, p. 156 and Bruijn 1970, pp. 87–8; 1798 and after: Houwink 1940, p. 607. As for the *deferred* debt, see below, p. 76.

whole debt, then running against interest rates varying from 1.25 to 7 per cent, was converted against one and the same interest rate of 2.5 per cent. Owners of stock against higher interest rates were compensated by higher nominal amounts of debt.

Nevertheless, table 4.2 supplies a view, firstly, of the continuing importance of the demand of the Dutch state on the capital market during the period until 1850. Secondly, the table shows the extent to which capital was set free by debt redemption between 1850 and 1880. This implies that the continuing gap between expenditure and fiscal revenue between 1850 and 1880 must have been financed in another way. In fact, between 1830 and 1850 more than 10 million guilders on average per year was diverted from the Indies to The Netherlands. This amount grew to even more than 22 million guilders per year on average in the period between 1850 and 1875 (Fasseur 1975, p. 42). Thirdly, table 4.2 shows the renewal of government capital demand after 1880. Related to the growth of national income in this same period, however, this increase was still modest, as far as the central level was concerned. The increased importance of municipal governments in public finance can be illustrated by the fact that the total of local government debts doubled between 1900 and 1913 to nearly 500 million guilders (*Zeventig Jaren* 1970, p. 133).

4.3 Public expenditure in the eighteenth century: wars and debts

Interest payments, together with war expenditure, remained by far the most important elements in public expenditure during most of our period. A striking difference with the seventeenth century, however, was the relative proportion of the two. In the 1670s, after the notorious Year of Disaster of 1672 when England and France had declared war on the Republic, interest and debt service had demanded about one-third of total tax income in Holland, war expenditure nearly two-thirds. During the War of Spanish Succession (1702–13), however, Holland's debt had been augmented with no less than 128 million guilders to about 310 million guilders. In the 1720s interest and debt service required more than two thirds of fiscal revenue, leaving for war expenditure less than one third. For the other provinces the War of Spanish Succession had disastrous consequences as well (see also figures 4.1 and 4.2). Besides the debts contracted by the provinces themselves, the Union contracted debts, which had to be serviced from the contributions of the provinces. This debt, although small as compared with that of Holland, more than tripled during the War of Spanish Succession (see figure 2.4).

For financial reasons, therefore, the Republic's role as one of the great European powers during the seventeenth century was over. The army, amounting to 45,000 men in the peace years before 1702, was reduced after the War of Spanish Succession from 119,000 to 34,000 (Zwitzer 1991, p. 176). Although after the War of Austrian Succession (1740–8) the States General voted for more than 52,000 men for its peacetime army, in fact only 32,000 men seem to have been paid (Van Deursen 1981, p. 76). For many years, the admiralties no longer received any subsidies from the federal state. Their debt-ridden position was worsened by the fact that they had to cope with a combination of stagnating sources of income and rising prices in the course of the century.

In 1715 the Union could not even meet its interest obligations, because the provinces paid less than promised. Its payments office was closed, which might have been labelled a state bankruptcy but for the fact that Holland's debt was much more important for the Republic than the Union's debt. Attempts during these years to create a stronger central executive in the Republic in order to compel the provinces to meet their financial obligations failed.

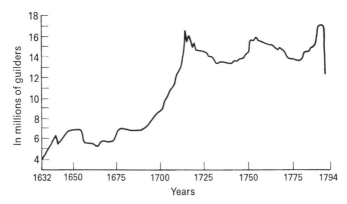

Figure 4.1 Debt service in Holland, 1632–1794
Source: Van der Ent *et al.* 1996.

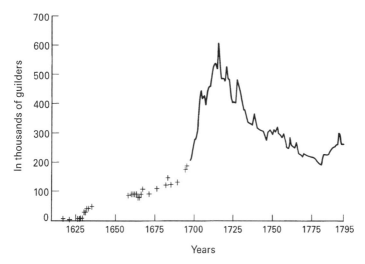

Figure 4.2 Debt service in Overijssel, 1604–1794
Source: Van der Ent *et al.* 1996.

When the Union's payments office reopened after nine months, with Holland's support, holders of its debt were forced to accept an interest reduction from 4 to 3 per cent. The admiralties had reduced the interest on their debts as well. In Holland it had already been customary to tax stock property by so-called *extraordinary* taxation, which took the form of interest reductions. During the War of Spanish Succession, freedom from such taxes had been promised in order to get the loans subscribed. The province was compelled to break these vows. All these measures were unheard of in this Republic, famous during the seventeenth century for its public credit.

The Dutch refrained in the meantime from risky solutions of their financial problems like Law's Missisippi company in France and the South Sea Company in Great Britain. The Republic simply could not afford the accompanying circulation of paper money or the risk of wild speculations on shaky grounds because of the extreme dependence of Holland's economy on international confidence in the solidarity of its guilder and on trade. Jeopardising domestic credit by interest reductions was preferred to risking its international credit by monetary experiments.

As to the provinces outside Holland we know that Overijssel also reduced the interest on its provincial debt, first from 4 to 3.5 per cent in 1732 and again from 3.5 to 3 per cent in 1744. These reductions, however, were voluntary, like Pelham's famous interest reductions in Great Britain in the 1750s from 4 to 3 per cent. Debt in the hands of stockholders who did not agree with the measure was redeemed (Fritschy 1995, p. 214).

Besides interest reductions, a policy of simple debt redemption was entered upon. The Union proved able to reduce its debt from 65 million guilders in 1717 to 17.5 million in 1795 (see figure 2.4). Holland's debt was reduced from about 310 million guilders to 295 million between 1718 and 1740, until, forced by international alliances, the Republic had to participate in the War of Austrian Succession (1740–8) (see figure 2.5). After this war the provinces failed again in their financial contributions to the Union with the result that its payments office had to close again in 1754, no longer able to meet its interest obligations. Renewed attempts to create a stronger central executive around the newly installed *Stadhouder*, William IV of Orange, after a *stadhouder*less period in most provinces from 1702 till 1748, proved abortive.

During the Seven Years' War (1756–63), the Republic succeeded in remaining neutral. Cuts in military expenditure were inaugurated. An impressive debt redemption was embarked upon in Holland. The burden was reduced from about 360 million guilders to 320 million between 1756 and 1780. Its load of interest payments decreased from 15.2 million guilders to 13 million, i.e., from about 70 per cent to – still – about 60 per cent of fiscal revenue. In order to grant the holders of government stock some degree of security, it was decided in 1747 that taxation upon stock by way of extraordinary *honderdste penningen* (see below) would no more result in a *de facto* interest below a level of 2.5 per cent.

The economic impact of this financial policy was that the Dutch investors were looking for other outlets for their capital. Although preferring domestic loans, they engaged increasingly in (risky) foreign lending. There was an increase in unemployment in the coastal provinces, which was already high due to industrial decline, because of the cuts in naval expenditure. Only in the eastern provinces, however, some signs of new forms of domestic capital investment were noted, in papermills and coppermills for example (Verstegen 1982, pp. 41–59, 48–51).

In 1780 the Republic became involved in a costly war again, the Fourth Anglo-Dutch War (1780–4). In the 1790s, before any renewed attempts for debt redemption could have been successful, the Republic got involved in a series of international wars that were even much more expensive than any of the former. The old worn *ancien regime* came subsequently to an end by the Batavian Revolution of 1795.

4.4 Public expenditure in patriot ideology and during the Batavian Revolution

From the 1770s onwards, a shift was noted in the views on expenditure priorities, which preluded the ideas on public finance after the Batavian Revolution. An increase in budgetary means for the navy was urged, not only by Amsterdam commercial interests, but also by a land province like Overijssel. Access to American cotton, vital for Overijssel's textile industry was jeopardised by British aggressive protectionist policy. After the negative outcome of the Fourth Anglo-Dutch War (1780–4), a new political movement under the appellation of Patriots blamed the *stadhouders* of the House of Orange for having favoured the army above the navy. During 1785–7, these Patriots seized power in several municipal and provincial governments and installed committees to examine the possibilities for improvement of the war finances (Schama 1977).

The suggestions to cut the size of the army, however, were not welcomed at all by the Orange oriented circles. When *Stadhouder*, William V, was restored to power, with support of a Prussian army in 1787, and Patriot leverage was curtailed; the drastic proposals were averted. The States General agreed to a peace time army of 42,000 men at the annual cost of nearly 11.5 million guilders. But they also voted for an extension of the budget for the navy of 2 million guilders on top of their ordinary customs revenue, amounting to 2 million guilders. A fundamental revision of the repartition of war expenditure, another proposal of the Patriots, was frustrated by the unwillingness of the provinces to impair their autonomy and to allow each other insight into their finances. Unification had not been on the agenda even of the Patriot movement at that time.

Despite the fact that some provinces introduced a couple of new taxes, the fiscal revenue made available by the provinces for war expenditure was still only 12 million guilders, falling short of the 13.5 million voted for by the States General. As sanctions were lacking, fragmentation allowed the provinces not to spend on the army and the navy what they had promised to do in the States General. Even Holland, forced by its interest burdens, paid less than its *quota*, at least since 1780.[4]

Holland, together with Zeeland, suffered most from the crushing burden of interest payments.[5] One of the most important accomplishments of the Batavian Revolution was the amalgamation of the provincial debts into one national debt in 1797. The amalgamation implied that from then on the inhabitants of the other provinces had to share in the debt charges of the province of Holland.

After the Batavian Revolution, in contrast to their French brethren, the Dutch patriot revolutionaries of 1795 had no intention of violating debt obligations. Maintenance of creditworthiness was their first priority. They preferred additions to government debt rather than allowing the circulation of *assignats*, which the French thrusted on Dutch shopkeepers. Despite an ideological aversion to rentiers and stockjobbers, the revolutionary government made shrewd use of stockbroking practices on the Amsterdam stock market. So-called *anticipation loans* facilitated advances on future levies. Also, a large part of the French imposition of 100 million guilders was paid by way of so-called *Batavian rescriptions*. Each year, a portion of the rescriptions were to be drawn for redemption. The French sold this paper on the stock market or used it to pay their suppliers, who then could sell it. Subsequently, the Batavian government could purchase a great part of the rescriptions at prices often far below par instead of having to redeem them at 100 per cent (Fritschy 1988, pp. 183–7, 211–18).

Revolutionary expenditure policy consisted further in attempts to realise a shift from army to navy expenditure. A conscription army was introduced, as in France. Initially the Patriots were even convinced that the Republic would have to restrict itself in the future to an army of only 25,000 men (from a total population of 2 million), to allow funds for the restoration of the glory of the national navy. Such a drastic reduction in army expenditure was not accomplished, but, on the whole, war expenditure was definitely lowered. After 1815 the army numbered about 50,000 men for the united northern and southern Netherlands from a population of approximately 5 million. Yet the navy budget was reduced also, to not much more than before the revolution. The shifts in proportion of army and navy budgets is shown in table 4.3.

The amount of the other expenses (i.e., non-war, non-debt) increased significantly. Around 1790 this expenditure had amounted to 12 per cent, two-thirds of which was spent on administrative and juridical tasks and about a quarter on infrastructure. The first budgets after the Batavian Revolution showed important shifts in this respect: other expenditure absorbed about 20 per cent of total expenditure.

Table 4.3 *Ordinary budgets for army and navy in the Netherlands between 1790 and 1844 (in percentages of the total budget)*

	Army %	Navy %
1790	33	11
1800	18	14
1815	32	11
1820	27	7
1840	16	8

Source: See table 4.1.

An important part of this was due to the fact that the Dutch East India Company was dissolved in 1799. Its administrative apparatus and debts were taken over by the state. Besides, the budget for the improvement of the waterways and other infrastructural works was raised. Likewise, the budget for salaries and pensions of government officials showed additions. As a matter of fact the state apparatus of the new centralised state was more expensive than that of the federal state of the ancien régime. The observed shift in the composition of public expenditure was reinforced in the new United Kingdom. In its first budget no less than 38 per cent was left for expenditure other than debt service and war expenditure.

4.5 National expenditure and debts from 1815 to 1850

In 1815 the debt in the north, then about 600 million guilders, still required about 30 per cent of tax revenue for interest payments. After unification with the south, a sum of 26 million guilders was added. On the whole, the proportion of the interest burden decreased to about 19 per cent of the combined state budget: now the inhabitants of the south had to share in the payment of the interest on northern debt. Also, in the southern Netherlands war expenditure had been low, whereas in the north – a small state always threatened by major states – it had been traditionally extremely high. This implied an enormous drain of money from the south to the north in the following years which added to the discontent in the south and contributed to the secession in 1830 (Horlings 1995, p. 127).

From the outset, King William I was eager to minimise the influence of parliament, which might frustrate his economic policy. In this he succeeded remarkably well. The Kingdom's constitution provided for a ten-year budget for ordinary expenditure and annual budgets for extraordinary expenditure. As a result, about 70 per cent of public finance was no longer available for parliamentary consideration between 1820 and 1830. As such, the constitution allowed the king much freedom to reallocate the funds voted for.

Even more important for his financial freedom were three new financial institutions: the Amortisatiesyndicaat, the Société Générale and the Nederlandsche Handel-Maatschappij (NHM, the Dutch Trading Company). As a result of these three institutions the Kingdom's debt and interest burden increased to a disastrous amount in the 1830s. In order to regain the goodwill of the money lenders, which were indispensable for his ambitions, King William had tried to undo Napoleon's *tiërcering* of the debt at the start of his reign. The proportion of the debt on which interest was no longer paid came to be a so-called *deferred debt*, which would gradually be converted into interest bearing *real debt*. In the years thereafter, loans had to be contracted at real interest rates of about 6 per cent. State credit improved during the 1820s, however, to the point that a major loan could be contracted in 1829 at a rate of only 3.9 per cent. In the 1830s, after the Belgian secession, interest rates on government loans increased to about 6 per cent again (Fritschy 1992, pp. 222–3).

The Amortisatiesyndicaat of 1822 obtained far-reaching powers for Bourse operations (in particular for selling and buying government bonds), the contracting of loans and the mortgaging and sale of national domains. Its statute allowed it to relieve the national budgets by taking care of the payment of pensions, the costs of improvements in the infrastructure, subsidies to industry and the renewal of coinage. In this way, the Amortisatiesyndicaat paid out 18 million guilders on infrastructure and 14 million on industrial subsidies. The institute also took care of the costs of the disastrous floods in 1825 in the Indies and for the Java War (at 21 million guilders). Besides, it covered all other budgetary deficits.

Unlike the Amortisatiesyndicaat, the Société Générale and the Nederlandsche Handel-Maatschappij (NHM) were private companies with the king as largest shareholder. Their finances, though, became heavily entangled with public finance. The Société Générale was founded in 1822 to furnish credits for the economic development of the south, but it also took over a government loan of 100 million guilders in 1824, which failed to be subscribed on the free market. It also furnished more than 6 million guilders for the construction of roads and canals (Riemens 1937, pp. 160–1).

The NHM was erected in 1824 to revive colonial trade. Its activities included, among others, the subsidising of shipping and shipbuilding, the chartering of vessels for shipment of colonial produce to The Netherlands and of Dutch industrial goods to East India, and the furnishing of credits to sugar producers to modernise their factories for the refining of Javanese sugar. The NHM also furnished the Dutch government with loans, especially after 1830 when the Société Générale was no longer available to this end due to the Belgian secession (Mansvelt 1924).

Parliament got no information on the most important financial measures, except for an incomplete survey of the activities of the Amortisatiesyndicaat in 1830. After the parliament managed to curtail the powers of this institution, the NHM took over most of the former role of the Amortisatiesyndicaat, again without any parliamentary control. As a result of the revolt of the south, public expenditure soared. This time, the NHM even furnished the necessary funds for the military campaign against the south.

Those loans by the NHM were backed up by revenues expected to accrue from the so-called *Cultuurstelsel*, a system which forced the Javanese to till certain agricultural products or to work on government plantations. But this system fell short, and failed to produce the funds needed. In 1840 the government had to ask parliament for a loan of 56 million guilders, 39 million of which was necessary to repay the NHM.

Parliament, alarmed about the condition of public finance, rejected the loan. Also, they did not accept the next ten year budget, and the king had to abdicate. The future Minister of Finance, F.A. van Hall, spoke of the 'artificial secrecy', 'confusion' and 'miserable entirety' of the financial system. He pointed out that the debts of the Amortisatiesyndicaat and of the NHM should be added to the national debt. Therefore, the actual interest burden was 42.4 million guilders, and not 15.2 million as the budget of 1839 stated. This amount came to no less than 88 per cent of government income at that moment (Van Hall 1840).

To clear the muddy financial pool which had come to the surface, the holders of the *deferred debt* were forced to accept a conversion to real debt against 6.8 per cent of its nominal value. Of course, this step raised the burden of interest, but at the same time it did put an end to this millstone round the neck of Dutch public finance. Consequently in 1844 Van Hall, by that time Minister of Finance, issued a loan of 127 million guilders against 3 per cent, which was subscribed as he threatened with a forced loan in case this voluntary loan failed. The funds were used to repay the NHM and to convert the 5 and 4.5 per cent stock into 4 per cent debt. In all, these measures reduced the debt charges by 3.7 million guilders. On this basis, rising revenues from the colonies sufficed for the restoration of public finance in The Netherlands in the next decades (see below). But first, we should return to the revenue side to obtain a complete picture of Dutch finances up to 1850.

4.6 Public revenues: the heritage of the eighteenth century

Next to expenditure, fiscal policy underwent significant changes as a result
of the process of unification. In 1806 taxes were centralised and rendered
uniform throughout The Netherlands. At the end of the eighteenth century,
drastic measures were necessary in view of the disastrous situation of public
finances. This section examines the failure to solve the financial problems of
the *ancien régime* during the eighteenth century.

Little could be expected at all from customs. The ordinary revenues
(under the heading of *convooien*) fluctuated between 1 and 2.2 million guilders. A heightening of tariffs was supposed to jeopardise international trade,
the main source of Dutch wealth. After the War of Spanish Succession the
admiralties had induced the provinces to consider a renewal of the tariff list.
The new levies of 1725 were nevertheless still extremely liberal. A proposal
for a *Limited Porto Franco* (free zone) of 1751, which might have advanced
Dutch trade in a period when it was losing terrain to other states, came to
nothing, partly for fear of the financial consequences for the navy (Hovy
1966, pp. 618–20). Obviously, customs could offer no substantial contribution to the financial problems of the eighteenth century.

As to fiscal developments inside the provinces, it is striking to see that the
distinction between *ordinary* and *extraordinary* revenues, which had been
customary in the seventeenth century, no longer made sense in the eighteenth century. *Ordinary* expenditure was no longer met by *ordinary* taxes
alone: *extraordinary* taxes had become as regularly levied as the ordinary
ones.

The most important item of the ordinary *gemene (generale) middelen* (=
common means) were still the excises on primary necessities like grain and
peat. This burden was heavy as compared with excises in other European
countries. But a shift was noticeable, conforming to the trend in the later
seventeenth century (see chapter 2). Taxes on luxury items like wine, brandy
and coaches and on signs of property like the keeping of servants were
stepped up, hitting the relatively well-to-do more than the common man. Of
the total revenue from the common means, rising from 9.3 million guilders
around 1700 to 11 million in the beginning of the 1790s, the proportion of
the duties on necessities sank from 83 per cent in 1700 to 66 per cent around
1790.

Excises remained high, however. Rising food prices during the Austrian
War of Succession caused discontent about taxes to burst out. In 1747 and
1748 tax revolts over the whole Republic were directed against the tax
farmers. A reform in the method of collection was the result: the abolition of
tax farming in several provinces in 1750. The ensuing rise in revenues was
less due to this reform than to a simultaneous rise in rates.

Of course it was the lower middle classes who were relatively hardest hit by taxes on *luxury* consumption, like meat, coffee and tea, because an element of progression was lacking in most of these taxes, though not all. We know, for instance, from the personal administration of the opulent Amsterdam merchant De Neufville that no less than 8 per cent of his income was taxed away through the luxury means tax alone (taxes on coaches and the keeping of servants, among others) (Fritschy 1988, p. 135). This is a very high percentage considering the fact that the first income tax with a progressive rate after the Batavian revolution ranged from 2 to 4 and 7 per cent. Pitt's famous income tax in Britain during the Napoleonic wars had a tariff of only 6.25 per cent. No doubt the rich in Holland were very rich and probably grew even richer in the course of the eighteenth century and they were not taxed excessively. Compared with other countries, however, Holland performed rather well in extracting resources from its wealthiest class (see also figure 2.9). Another sign of the ability of the provincial government to tax the wealthy was the increase in the yield of the stamp duty on sales registered by notaries and the tax on inheritances. Together, these funds rose from about 1 million in 1720 to about 2 million around 1790.

In the meantime, the increases in the ordinary direct taxes in Holland were rather modest. A new assessment of the land and house tax was made in 1734, to replace the former list of 1632. As a result, the yield rose slightly from about 2.6 to about 2.9 million guilders, mainly due to the fact that Amsterdam was now forced to pay more according to its expanded size.

More funds accrued from the so-called *extraordinary* means, consisting of taxes on property. Around 1720, they yielded about 6.2 million guilders; around 1790 this sum amounted to 8.5 million. From 1739 the additional *verponding* (land tax) on land and houses was restricted to houses in order to alleviate agriculture, that was plagued by low prices, rinderpest and pileworm. Additional revenue was raised through other taxes on holders of government offices: the *amptgeld*; on property of stocks and bonds: the *honderdste penningen*; and by way of cuts in military and civil salaries. The most remunerative part was the *honderdste penningen*, reducing the actual interest on Dutch bonds from the ordinary rate of 4 per cent to sometimes no more than 2 per cent. However, from 1747 onwards a real interest rate of at least 2.5 per cent was guaranteed.

In times of extreme crisis, truly extraordinary measures were added, such as a *personal quotisation* in the 1740s, a direct tax on personal wealth. Further, in the midst of the political crisis which caused the restoration of the *Stadhouder*, a national capital levy of 2 per cent upon property was imposed. This so-called Liberale Gift of 1747 proved to be an astonishing success. A forced loan of no less than 4 per cent of property was imposed in

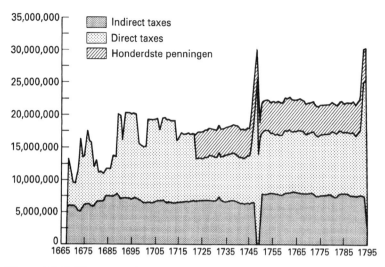

Figure 4.3 Public revenue in Holland, 1668–1794
Source: Van der Ent *et al.* 1996.

1788, followed by yet another one of 2 per cent in 1793. Even apart from these truly *extraordinary* measures, Holland's fiscal burden per capita definitely increased during the eighteenth century from about 23 to 31 guilders per head.

Figures 4.3 and 4.4 show the composition of taxation in two provinces, Holland and Groningen. They demonstrate that, although indirect taxes formed a solid base in the tax system, it was not their flexibility but the flexibility of direct taxation which was the main feature of the tax system in The Netherlands in the eighteenth century, not only in an agrarian province like Groningen, but also in urban Holland.[6] The importance of the *honderdste penningen* in Holland's tax system is obvious for the period after 1722.

Charles Wilson once argued in a famous article entitled 'Taxation and the decline of nations' that the decay of Holland was due to a fiscal policy biased towards heavy taxes on primary necessities, which raised the wage level and thereby eroded its capacity to withstand international economic competition (Wilson 1963). Despite its elegance,this explanation needs a thorough revision. Unlike in the seventeenth century, in the eighteenth century direct taxation had become much more important for the solution of financial problems than indirect taxation on primary necessities. Besides, international economic and political developments were probably more decisive for Holland's fate than domestic financial policy.

In provinces outside Holland the actual burden of taxes was often much lower and may yet have sunk in the course of the century. For Brabant levels

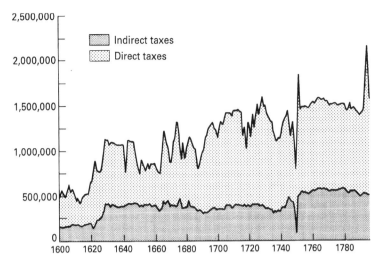

Figure 4.4 Public revenue in Groningen, 1600–1795
Source: Van der Ent *et al.* 1996.

of about 12 guilders per head are documented for the beginning of the eighteenth century and of about 5 guilders in 1790 (Kappelhof 1986, p. 381). In Overijssel per capita tax revenue was about 9.80 guilders in 1720, in 1790 – mainly owing to the population growth – only about 6.50 guilders. Besides, wealth seems to have been growing in agrarian provinces like Overijssel due to favourable developments in agricultural prices in the second half of the eighteenth century, while in Holland growth was stagnating (see table 4.4).

Naturally, this does not preclude the fact that Holland was on average still wealthier than Overijssel, which eased the levy of a high tax burden. The distribution of revenues of the first national levies on property and income after the Batavian Revolution points in that direction too. Holland contained about 40 per cent of the total population, but paid 65 per cent of the national property tax. And in 1800, while the economic circumstances were still adverse for Holland, no less than 70 per cent of the revenue of a levy on incomes originated from Holland. On the whole, taxation seemed to be much more effective in Holland as compared with the inland provinces. This was one of the main reasons to opt for fiscal unification.

4.7 Taxation during the Batavian Revolution

Holland, therefore, was the great advocate of fiscal unification after the Batavian Revolution. In other provinces, much more hesitancy as to the desirability thereof existed. Complete fiscal unification of The Netherlands

Table 4.4. *Percentage of per capita income appropriated by taxes, 1720 and 1790*

	Circa 1720	Circa 1790
Holland	9 to 12%	10 to 14%
Overijssel	7 to 10%	4 to 5%

Source: Fritschy 1990, p. 64.

was nevertheless decided on in 1798. It was brought into effect in 1806 by the first national Minister of Finance, the famous Isaac Gogel. Barriers to internal trade were removed, which must have been welcomed especially by tradesmen in the eastern part of the country who now gained better access to the populous markets in the maritime west. A new personal tax based on house rents was introduced in an attempt to tax people according to their ability to pay.

But the revolutionary endeavours to replace all taxes by an income and property tax, soon proved to be idle. Therefore, the new fiscal system had to maintain excises on primary necessities at sometimes higher rates than the former Dutch ones. This policy was necessary in view of the priority given by the revolutionaries to maintain public credit, as credit allowed them to raise the loans needed for the pay of the French armies. In their attempts to gain the support of the rentier class, property of newly created stock was no longer taxed by way of the *honderdste penningen*. The margins for a progressive fiscal policy proved to be utterly small in the new unified state (Fritschy 1988).

Anyhow, Gogel succeeded in his *tour-de-force* to raise revenues from about 39 million guilders to about 46 million in 1807; i.e., from about 20 to about 22.20 guilders per head. At an average wage level of about 0.90 guilders a day, this would require 25 working days. In fact, Gogel's measures were an extraordinary achievement, considering that this level in guilders per head was only reached again after the 1870s. By then, the average wage level had risen to 1.20 guilders. Consequently, the tax burden had declined to about 8 per cent, requiring only about 19 working days to earn the same amount in fiscal revenue per head.

After the incorporation of The Netherlands into France in 1810, Napoleon lowered the tax burden. It is evident that he could only afford to do so because of his decision to reduce the interest payments on the national debt. He was able to act without having to fear the loss of support of the domestic investors, a support that had been indispensable for all previous Dutch governments.

4.8 Taxation in The Netherlands up to 1850

The financial integration of the northern and southern Netherlands implied a severe augmentation of the fiscal burden in the south, despite specific efforts to keep the increase for the southerners within limits. The basic rate for the land and house tax in the north was fixed at 8.9 million guilders, the basic rate for the south – with an area not much smaller and a population 1.5 times as large – was settled at only 7.2 million. The onerous tax on milling grain was not introduced in 1816, but, as it had been the most remunerative of the Dutch excises, the tax had to be imposed in 1821, along with additions and reforms in some other taxes in an attempt to cover the continuing budgetary deficits. Thereafter, the fiscal revenue per head in the south turned out to be on average about 11 guilders against 16 guilders in the north. These figures signified that fiscal pressure in the north was lower than in the previous two centuries, but much higher than the south had ever experienced before (Coppens 1992, p. 217).

In the interest of the south, import tariffs were raised to rates varying from 10 to 20 per cent. Though moderate in themselves, they were much higher than had ever been customary in the north. Nevertheless most industrialists in the south thought them still too low, as industry in the south had flourished during the French occupation thanks to the protection of the Continental Blockade and thanks to uninhibited access to the French market. Such frictions added to the discontent about the strenuous efforts of the king to impose unification and productive boom for his country. The tragedy of this period was that contrary to other nineteenth-century European states the functioning of the parliamentary system up to 1850 was not eased by increasing fiscal revenue, as economic growth in the north languished and proclivity to tax evasion was high in the south.

As the south had been much more populated than the north – about 3.8 million against about 2.7 million inhabitants in 1830 – especially the revenue from excises was drastically curtailed by the Belgian secession, as can be seen in table 4.5.

The same table shows the drastic increase realised in the years after the Belgian secession by means of putting surcharges on all taxes, but mainly on excises. The dramatic character of this last increase stands out even more clearly in a comparison with Great Britain, where government was able to reduce the number and the rates of excises in this period. Thereby, between 1831 and 1850 the fiscal burden per head decreased from about 10 to about 6.20 guilders per head, whereas in The Netherlands it increased from 3.40 to 6.80 guilders per head in the same period.

In addition, national income in Great Britain increased, thereby lowering the fiscal burden as a percentage of national income per capita. For The

Table 4.5. *Distribution of fiscal revenue, 1824–1850 (selected years in million guilders)*

	1824	1829	1831	1835	1840	1850
Direct taxes	28.1	28.2	15.0	16.4	15.5	19.0
Excises	24.6	25.7	8.8	15.9	15.7	20.4
Customs	6.4	6.6	3.0	3.5	4.1	5.0
Stamps, etc.	11.7	13.8	5.4	8.4	7.5	9.3
Other*	3.7	2.6	5.6**	6.1**	6.2**	3.2
Total	74.5	76.9	38.0	50.3	49.0	56.9

Notes:
*mainly postal service, domains, lotteries.
**including 3.0 million, 3.1 million and 3.5 million guilders respectively in surcharges on all taxes on behalf of the Amortisatiesyndicaat.
Source: *Rekeningen.*

Netherlands, the modest economic growth between 1830 and 1850 (Griffiths 1979) could not have been sufficient to offset the rise in fiscal revenue per head. The total burden of fiscal revenue of the central government as a percentage of national income per capita definitely increased between 1830 and 1850. In contrast to fiscal policy in the eighteenth century, this time heavier excises were mainly to blame.

In fact, the weight of local taxation should be added. In 1849 the total yield of all local taxes in The Netherlands was 11.5 million guilders, 72 per cent of which consisted of indirect taxes and levies. This burden of local taxation varied over the country. In the inland provinces it averaged 2.60 guilders per capita, but in the coastal provinces the load amounted to no less than 5.40 guilders. Of the latter, 4.10 guilders was paid in indirect taxation (Griffiths 1979, pp. 58–60).

In some cases the incidence of local taxation was even much higher. In Amsterdam, for example, the levy per capita for local taxes in 1849 amounted to 10.50 guilders. This implied that an Amsterdam wage labourer had to work about 29 days to earn the amount of central and local taxation combined. The burden was much heavier as compared with the end of the eighteenth century, when the Amsterdam local fiscal revenue had been on average about 6.80 guilders per capita.[7]

If the adverse effect of heavy excises on primary necessities on wage levels has ever been a factor in Dutch economic development (cf. Wilson 1963), it must have been in these two decennia after the Belgian secession in the province of Holland. In fact, the possibility to levy surcharges on excises for the financing of local expenditure in the first half of the nineteenth century was a serious impairment of the fiscal unification realised by the Batavian Revolution. As a result, wages rose in the coastal provinces. Mechanisation in industry was handicapped by the way the tax on milling grain was collected. A guild-like cartelisation of related local industries was necessary to secure the collection of all local surcharges. These cartels subsequently proved obstructive to the initiatives of daring individuals in the mechanisation of grain mills (Van Zanden 1991).

After 1850 excises on primary necessities were gradually abolished. Furthermore, the right of cities to augment their fiscal revenue by way of excises or surcharges was curtailed. From then on municipal governments were partly subsidised by central government. Their local funds relied more on direct capitation taxes according to wealth assessments. Still, inequalities in fiscal pressure due to the extent of local taxation was to remain a feature of the Dutch fiscal system until the Second World War.

4.9 Public expenditure during the heyday of liberalism

In the years between 1844 and 1914 the unification of public finance was lifted on to a more social plane through the unfolding of parliamentary democracy. Since the liberal constitution of 1848, accepted by King William II under pressure from European revolutionary threats, the ministers were responsible for the financial deeds of the government. In order to prevent the emerging of a new Amortisatiesyndicaat the new constitution stated explicitly that all public expenditures were subject to approval by parliament, together with all means by which the budget had to be covered. Besides, budgets and accounts had to be presented annually to parliament, including a detailed report about colonial finances.[8]

A period of balanced budgets, and even of budgetary surpluses and debt redemption could start (see table 4.2). This did not result, however, in a decline in the amounts of public expenditure (see table 4.1). On the contrary, expenses rose, not only due to the impressive debt redemption, but also to a rise in army expenditure to consolidate Dutch colonial power in the Indies and the renewal of the Dutch system of fortifications. In 1860, during the heyday of doctrinal liberalism, parliament agreed to an extensive scheme for railway construction. In 1863 it was decided to realise the ambitious plans for giving both Amsterdam and Rotterdam a direct connection to the North Sea by digging the Noordzeekanaal and the Nieuwe Waterweg. All expenditures for infrastructure combined, including the municipal ones, accounted for a sum of 3 guilders per head in 1850, but of 7 guilders per head in 1913. In particular, the increase in local public finance for expenditure in public works was remarkable, which is shown in table 4.6.

Table 4.6. *Investment in and maintenance of*
public works on the national, provincial and local
level in million guilders, 1850–1910

	1850	1880	1910
Central government	3	20	13
Provinces	1	2	2
Municipalities	4	11	24

Sources: De Jonge 1978, p. 282; Van der Voort 1994.

Local finance became more important for other expenditure items too. The most important after public works was education. In the 1870s a new generation of liberals had come to the fore which confessed a belief in using the state to reform and improve society. The Education Bill of 1878 was an important step in the direction of a universal school system, paid for and carefully inspected by the state. Teachers' salaries were raised and school buildings improved. Primary education became the responsibility of the municipal administrations. Local expenditure on education rose from 1.70 guilders per head in 1870 to 2.90 guilders per head in 1880. This amount was to increase to 5.75 guilders per head in 1910 after the new Education Bill of 1889, introduced by a new government including both Catholics and Protestants, had allowed all schools – including those founded by the various religious denominations – to pass on one-third of their costs to the state.

The central state subsidised the municipalities for these and other tasks, like poor relief and public health. Such subsidies became an important slice of public expenditure, rising from 8 per cent of total national expenditure in 1870 to 14 per cent in 1910. Total municipal public expenditure per head rose from 8.35 guilders in 1860 to 24.50 in 1910, of which about 20 per cent was covered by the subsidies from the national government. In all, about 35 per cent of total public finance was now paid for out of local revenue, against 22 per cent in 1860. This growing importance of the local level could be looked upon as a remarkable counterpoint to the overall process of unification and centralisation of public finance in our period. On the other hand, unlike local taxation in the first half of the century, the objects of their expenditure policy – education, infrastructure, building, public utilities – furthered economic unification and development.

Local governments remained restricted in their opportunities to impose taxes, but they commanded other sources of income, like loans. The interest burden on the total of municipal debts was in 1910 nearly as high as that on

Table 4.7. *Revenues of the central government, 1850–1910 (in million guilders)*

	1850	1860	1870	1880	1890	1900	1910
Taxation	55	57	71	96	105	120	153
(direct taxes)	(19)	(20)	(21)	(25)	(28)	(35)	(47)
(customs)	(5)	(5)	(5)	(5)	(6)	(10)	(13)
(excises)	(20)	(18)	(28)	(39)	(44)	(49)	(62)
(stamps, registration, mortgages, legacies)	(9)	(13)	(15)	(25)	(24)	(26)	(28)
Revenues from public enterprises	2	3	5	9	15	22	31
Revenues from the Dutch East Indies	19	27	13	–	2	4	14
Loans and other	2	6	6	13	19	6	2
Total	78	93	95	118	140	152	200

Source: Overhagen and Wolff 1969, pp. 226–7; *Statistiek Koningrijk* 1911.

the national debt, which means that interest payments at the central plus the local level required about 20 per cent of total expenditure. Actually, the total public debt, which had been kept outside parliamentary control by King William I, continued to grow outside the supervision of the States General, in this period, but now because of the importance of local public finance. Yet this local autonomy as to debt creation can be seen as a blessed device. While parliament was still hesitant to increase the national public debt, local expenses funded by local loans surely contributed to the economic development of The Netherlands in the second half of the nineteenth century.

The renewed government demand on the capital market did not have any negative consequences on the supply of capital for private investment. The rate of interest could decline, allowing even for a conversion of a major part of government bonds at a rate of 3.5 per cent to stock against 3 per cent in 1897 (Riemens 1949, p. 68).

4.10 Public revenue between 1844 and 1914

Table 4.1 showed that fiscal revenue kept rising in the later nineteenth century, although not enough to offset the rise in public expenditure. Until 1875 this deficit was solved by revenues from the Indies. Thereafter, parliament hesitantly issued loans again. Table 4.7 offers a breakdown of public revenue in its main categories with ten-year intervals. Next to loans, revenues from public enterprises constituted an increasing part of state revenue after the 1880s, of which the most important were postal services with a total revenue of almost 20 million guilders in 1910.

Revenues from the *Cultuurstelsel* in the Indies diminished as a liberal colonial policy allowed more room for private initiatives. A start was made with the abolition of the state plantations in the 1860s. More important for the decline in revenues was the costly war in Achin on Sumatra, as a consequence of Dutch attempts to establish their authority in the outer provinces of their colonial empire. Annual costs amounted to 15–20 million guilders from 1873 to 1885, and – after a reduction in Dutch ambitions – about 7 million per year between 1885 and 1903. In 1877 profits from the Indies had turned into losses. Private capital, on the other hand, was increasingly invested in the Indies (Kossmann 1978, pp. 271, 400–1). In fact, economic growth in The Netherlands since the last quarter of the nineteenth century owed a lot to the intensification of the relations with its colonies outside the realm of public finance.

In 1876, when colonial revenue had already shrunk to 2.3 million guilders, the first state loan since 1850 was issued to be followed by many more, until 1913 on average 6 million guilders per year. Parliament became gradually convinced that loans were justified for productive investments. However, a separation between current and capital expenditure, which would have been the logical counterpart of this principle of revenue policy, was not made in government accounts before 1928.

Regarding ordinary revenue our attention is drawn to the effects of liberal trade policy on customs revenue. After the abolition of the Navigation Laws in Great Britain in 1849, The Netherlands lowered several import duties. In 1862 all export duties were abolished. The immediate effect was a decrease in the part played by customs in total revenues, from about 10 per cent of total revenue in 1844 to 6.5 per cent in 1864. The international crisis of 1878 led to a nadir of 5 per cent in 1879. Absolute amounts however had risen in between, thanks to the resulting expansion of trade, from 4.2 million guilders in 1864 to 13.3 million in 1910. By then, customs revenue accounted for 9 per cent of total revenue.

Not only customs duties were lowered in the age of liberalism, but also excises on primary necessities. From 1852 onwards the excise on meat was restricted to beef. The tax on the milling of bread grain – after the duty on brandy the most remunerative of excises, yielding about 22 per cent of all excise revenue – was abolished in 1855. In 1863 the excises on peat and coal were abolished as well. The reductions and cessations resulted in a loss of 8.3 million guilders.

Even more important was the abolition of local excises in 1865. Already in 1851 municipalities had started to levy surcharges on direct taxes instead.

Table 4.8. *Tax burden in the Netherlands, 1850–1910 (in guilders per head of the population)*

		1850	1870	1880	1890	1900	1910
Municipalities	indirect taxes	2.11	0.09	0.03	0.03	0.01	0.01
	direct taxes etc.	1.08	2.69	3.70	4.38	4.78	6.90
Provinces	indirect taxes	0.20	0.20	0.30	0.40	0.40	0.50
	direct taxes etc.	0.20	0.20	0.30	0.30	0.30	0.50
Central level	indirect taxes	13.60	15.00	17.40	17.00	16.00	17.50
	direct taxes etc.	4.40	4.90	6.50	6.80	7.40	8.40
Total public	indirect taxes	15.91	15.29	17.73	17.43	16.33	18.01
revenue	direct taxes etc.	5.68	7.79	10.50	11.48	12.58	15.80
Grand total		21.59	23.08	28.23	28.91	28.91	33.81
Average industrial daily wage		0.91	1.07	1.33	1.43	1.54	1.63
Number of working days required to earn the amount of *indirect* taxes per head		17	14	13	12	11	11
Number of working days required to earn the amount of total public revenue per head		24	22	21	20	19	21

Source: De Jonge 1978, p. 281; Vermaas 1995.

The loss of excises was compensated for by allowing local governments a maximum of 80 per cent of the so-called personal tax levied by the central government, which yielded about 7.8 million guilders. Instead, the central state raised the tariffs on sugar, wine and brandy, which produced an increase of approximately 7 million guilders. On the whole, the increase in excise revenue from the low of 1860, 17.7 million guilders, to 62.2 million in 1910 was mainly due to the duties on sugar and brandy. Together they accounted for 84 per cent, leaving only 16 per cent for levies on wine, beer, salt and beef.

Table 4.8 offers a summary of the development of the tax burden between 1850 and 1910.

The proportion of indirect taxes in total public revenue decreased from 74 per cent in 1850 to 54 per cent in 1910. As a result, the tax burden on the poor diminished after the 1850s as a result of the declining role of primary necessities in excise taxation. The wealthy noticed a relative increase because of the expansion of direct taxation. A first step in this direction, decided upon as colonial revenues were declining, was the addition of the direct lineage to succession duties in 1878, which proved to yield nearly 3 million guilders annually.

Since the 1840s the desire was expressed to introduce an income tax for a better distribution of the tax burden. Four bills of income taxes were presented to parliament between 1860 and 1885. Four times the proposals failed. But chances improved as the political climate changed, mainly as a result of the extension of the vote from about 100,000 to about 350,000 males in 1886 and the passing of the Education Bill of 1889. The proposals for an income and a property tax by the Minister of Finance, Nicolaas Pierson, were accepted in 1892 and 1893, fifty years after the introduction of an income tax in Great Britain. The tariffs were still low. Higher rates were only introduced by the Germans in 1941 during the Second World War. Pierson's income tax contained a progressive scale starting at 0.15 per cent. The top tariff was 3.2 per cent. The tax yielded 5 million guilders in 1895. Licence fees, which had produced also about 5 million guilders, were abolished. The property tax, its corollary, ranged from 0.8 per cent to 3 per cent of property income. Its revenue in 1895 amounted to 7 million guilders. To compensate property owners, registration and mortgage duties were reduced, which was a loss of 4 million guilders. In fact, the introduction of the new income and property tax did not alter the distribution of the tax burden significantly. Capital wealth in the later nineteenth century must have been furthered by the lenient way in which property was treated in the tax system, even after Pierson's tax. Nevertheless, the road was open to an improvement of the tax system as a whole.

4.11 Public finance, institutional change, economic development and capital export

The development from fragmentation to unification in public finance was not a smooth process. Obviously, the transformation was related to the vicissitudes of political and institutional change and economic development. These interrelations will be highlighted in this last section.

In the course of the eighteenth century attempts to improve administrative and financial efficiency – induced by state bankruptcies at the central level – proved abortive. At the same time capital abundance still allowed continuous growth of public debt at the provincial level. The vulnerability resulting from being rich *and* small compelled the provinces to keep military expenditure high *and* to maintain their public credit.

Holland refrained from monetary experiments to solve its financial problems, as its economy was highly dependent upon the international reliability of the guilder. More than in the seventeenth century, however, the wealthy holders of Holland's bonds had to shoulder a part of the tax burden. Nevertheless, taxes on primary necessities were still burdensome and some excises even increased. The Batavian Revolution put an end to the paradox, resulting from the institutional structure of the Dutch state, that the tax burden per head rose in the province where population and economy stagnated, and declined in the provinces where population and economy expanded. But as long as the state was forced into a policy of maintaining public credit, the financial unification resulting from the Batavian Revolution could offer no solace for the huge debt burden. Not even the successful heightening of the tax ceiling realised by Finance Minister Gogel solved the deficit. Taxation simply could not keep pace with the staggering amount of debt servicing required since the demanding alliance with France.

Prospects seemed more promising after Napoleon had reduced the debt burden during the incorporation of The Netherlands in the French empire. Favourable also was the doubling in territory and population through the addition of the southern Netherlands in 1815, where modern industry, indispensable for a more healthy economic structure in the future, had already gained a foothold. An expenditure policy directed at economic development and further unification of the new kingdom could, however, be a success only temporarily in a situation where a heightening of the tax burden was thought to have serious political and economic repercussions in the south. After the United Kingdom of North and South had proved to be a failure, public debt rose, hidden from parliament, to such heights that The Netherlands were on the verge of state bankruptcy once more.

In the meantime an effective and unified fiscal policy was still hardly possible as long as municipal governments remained autonomous in the levying of taxes. Recent research has shown how this had adverse effects not only on wage levels but also on mechanisation. Local tax autonomy was curtailed after 1850. Public finance was rescued by the shrewd financial policies of Van Hall and a new liberal constitution in 1848, followed by rapidly increasing revenue from the Indies after 1850 and the process of modern economic growth somewhat later. During the 1860s public expenditure per head was still, thanks to population growth, lower than the amount that had been reached at the end of the eighteenth century. After the 1870s however state expenditure per head grew faster. Local public finance grew considerably in importance. If local expenses are included, total public expenditure as a percentage of national income per head rose from about 11 per cent in 1870 to about 13.5 per cent in 1913. Local autonomy as to expenditure policy and debt creation seems to have offered a positive contribution to economic development in a period when the national parliament was still hesitant as to the acceptability of renewed debt creation.

Regarding debt creation, one last point should be made. Characteristic of Dutch public finance, contrary to many other European states, was that the state could rely as a rule on the domestic capital market for the financing of deficits and public investments. It was striking that Amsterdam, in the very same century when Dutch government debt more than doubled, became the capital market for international government finance (Riley 1980). Partly, this paradox can be solved by pointing to Dutch capital abundance resulting from Holland's commercial wealth combined with a high propensity to save among the rich and a lack of feasible private investment opportunities at home. Recent research has shown, however, that the specific rise in foreign investments by Dutch capitalists which has been documented for the later eighteenth century (Riley 1980, p. 84; Van Stipriaan 1993, pp. 209–11) and the later nineteenth century (De Vries 1986), was induced also by the remarkable redemption of state debt in both these periods (table 4.2).

Furthermore, the integration of the international capital markets in the nineteenth century gave rise to a new phenomenon. In 1844 Finance Minister Van Hall informed parliament that no less than 300 million guilders, about a quarter of the Dutch debt at that moment, was in foreign hands. It was observed that this situation forbade taxing the holding of government stock in the same way as had been done in the eighteenth century, as long as government was dependent on the capital market to finance its deficits.[9] It is not even sure whether the domestic capital market could have absorbed all the debt creation during the reign of King William I, if not for the remarketing of part of it on the international market.

Debt redemption, thus, had generally induced capital export, and debt creation in the first half of the nineteenth century seems to have been accompanied by capital import. But the increase of investment possibilities at home, at the end of the nineteenth century, seems not to have gone with a smaller share of foreign investments in Dutch portfolios (De Vries 1986, p. 207). Whereas Dutch foreign investment was about 600 million guilders in the 1790s and in the 1810s (Riley 1980, p. 84) and about 650 million in the 1850s (Bos 1990, pp. 566–7), it rose to no less than 3,000 million guilders in 1913 (excluding 1,000 million in investments in the colonies; Brugmans 1961, p. 401). In 1850 about 10 per cent of Dutch capital was tied in foreign investments and about 20 per cent in domestic government debt. In 1913 these percentages were reversed (De Jonge 1968, p. 306). Renewed demand on the domestic capital market since the 1870s, mainly by local governments, did not prevent Amsterdam from regaining some of its lost position as an international financial centre (Riemens 1949, p. 71).

Notes

1 In 1800 The Netherlands had 2.1 million inhabitants, in 1850 3.0 million, in 1900 5.1 million (Hofstee 1981, pp. 124–5).
2 Calculations Great Britain: fiscal revenue 51.6 million pounds, population 26.7 million, 1 pound = fl. 12; in France: fiscal revenue 1,198 million francs, population 34.2 million, 1 franc = fl. 0.48 (Mitchell 1992).
3 Schremmer 1989, pp. 400–6. If the wage levels are accounted for (Zamagni 1989, p. 118; Vermaas 1995) the tax per year required in Great Britain 25 working days, in France 30, in The Netherlands 19–24 workings days.
4 Between 1780 and 1792 Holland paid 55 million guilders of the promised 61 million (Fritschy 1986, p. 19).
5 In 1796 Holland spent 69 per cent of their budget on debt charges (after deduction of the taxes on property), Zeeland 75 per cent, the other provinces ranging between 5 and 48 per cent (Fritschy 1988, p. 156).
6 De Vries and Van der Woude 1995, pp. 130 and 140, stress the flexibility of the common means in the seventeenth century and the immobility of the tax system in the eighteenth century.
7 ARA, Gogel, inv.nr. 168 'Rapport van het Committe der Finantie van de municipaliteit der stad Amsterdam, 19-2-1795': the Amsterdam revenue amounted to 1,471,621 per year with a population of 220,000.
8 Constitution of 1848 art. 119, 120 and 60. Complete accountability of the colonial finances was realised only after the bill of 1864.
9 Verstegen, 1995. The author kindly informed us that already in 1832 a Dutch Minister of Finance reported that 'foreigners recently became the owners of a considerable part of the recent 6 per cent loan of 39 million'.

5 The alternative road to modernity: banking and currency, 1814–1914

JOOST JONKER

5.1 Introduction

From about 1780, The Netherlands dropped back from a leading position in trade and banking to a rank more befitting its size, content to follow international developments rather than steering them. For long, this downgrading was hidden and softened by the riches accumulated during the Golden Age, which ensured Amsterdam a continuing position in international finance. The character and importance of that position changed irrevocably as well, however. In 1834 the government of the United States moved their European account from W. & J. Willink of Amsterdam to Rothschild in London (Chapman 1984, p. 21). From the end of the 1840s Hope & Co.'s unique hold over Russian government issues slipped (Platt 1984, pp. 70–2). Around 1850 several big German–Jewish bankers shut their Amsterdam branches, sealing the city's slide to second rank.

The adaptation to changed economic circumstances proved long and painful. Industrialisation and corporate joint-stock banking both came late in the nineteenth century, inspiring many observers to suggest a negative link between the two, blaming conservative bankers and wary investors for the prolonged economic decline. If that suggestion fails to stand up to scrutiny, it still leaves to be explained what actually happened in Dutch banking during the nineteenth century.

The themes dominating this period may be summed up as the evolution towards a national economy in tandem with a financial system centred on Amsterdam, and the slow emancipation of banking from trade and other activities. Only the convergence of these developments in the decade after 1860 created the opportunities for the first joint-stock banks. As an important proxy to the first two factors the currency vicissitudes will be treated first.

94

5.2 Cleaning up the circulation, 1814–1850

The new Kingdom of The Netherlands started off with money circulation in a state of confusion (Korthals Altes 1996). Provincial minting was abolished for a single national mint established at Utrecht, but old and clipped silver guilders continued as the mainstay, around which a wide variety of coins circulated. The 1816 Currency Act, intended to remedy the defects by establishing a *de facto* bimetallic system based on silver coins of one and three guilders plus ten guilder gold pieces, only made matters worse. The Act overvalued both gold in relation to silver, and, to accommodate the union with Belgium, the franc in relation to the guilder. As a result only the new gold pieces circulated alongside a trickle of very worn silver coins, the rest disappearing to be melted down for francs. Around 1820 small coin became so scarce that merchants in Utrecht and Den Bosch introduced their own substitutes (Van den Eerenbeemt 1959, pp. 41–2). King William I's government, always hard-up, could not afford the necessary complete overhaul of the system and half heartedly patched it up to little avail.

From the late 1780s confidence in the Wisselbanksystem declined, causing the virtual disappearance of *bankguldens*. Since there was no widely accepted fiduciary issue to compensate the sorry state of coinage, local *kassiers* (cashiers) in Amsterdam, Rotterdam and probably elsewhere too, stepped in to fill the gap by issuing various types of *kassierspapier*, tender paper quite like the London goldsmiths' notes. Since most *kassiers* firms were small, the notes would not as a rule stray very far from their origin, but according to people at the time they circulated on a large scale, despite frequent bankruptcies amongst the cashiers during the French occupation (Jonker 1992).

Given time, *kassierspapier* could conceivably have evolved into a national system. It was not to be. In 1814 King William I, keen to weld his diverse regions together, set up the Nederlandsche Bank, intended as a circulation bank for his Kingdom. The bank's notes gained only slow acceptance. Until the late 1830s, average advances regularly outstripped the amount of notes issued. The standard explanation for this phenomenon blames the public's supposed old-fashioned preference for specie, reinforced by unhappy experiences with the French *assignats* (De Jong 1967a I, pp. 82–3, 110). Yet the public accepted *kassierspapier* quite willingly, and the *assignats* did comparatively little damage in The Netherlands. The true reason lies in the limited scope of the bank's activities and the stiff competition offered by the *kassierspapier*. In Amsterdam, *kassiers* had been pivotal in the payments system of the mercantile community for centuries, so the banknotes at first made little headway and only gained the upper hand after the bank provoked, and won, a sharp conflict over control of the circulation in 1839/40

(Jonker 1992). Until the local system of *kassierspapier* collapsed after a bankruptcy in 1836, Rotterdam cashiers treated the bank's notes as bills on Amsterdam and would handle them only against a discount (De Jong 1967a I, p. 285). Elsewhere, the government's declared readiness to accept paper money for all payments underpinned its credit, but the lack of integration between the various regional economies, and the bank's wariness to expand beyond its grasp, as yet prevented the notes from building up a national circulation. The internal border with Belgium presented the most formidable barrier. Until at least 1824, exchange rates between Brussels and Amsterdam fluctuated so much that the cost of specie settlements outweighed the risk of drawing bills (De Jong 1967a I, p. 146). The relations with other provinces within the Kingdom probably did not come under such extreme stress, yet complaints about bank notes suffering a discount outside Amsterdam were still aired ten years later (quoted in Boissevain 1902, p. 17).

Yet the bank's average note issue grew by just over 9 per cent a year during the late 1820s and early 1830s, with circulation per head of population also increasing by leaps and bounds, so the extent of the problem should not be exaggerated. By 1846 circulation of and confidence in the banknotes had grown enough for the Minister of Finance to start worrying about safe issuing limits, a matter not raised until then (De Jong 1967a I, pp. 298–9, 576–7, 589).

Without a well-established circulation bank such as the Nederlandsche Bank now was, the solution to two long-standing and pressing problems would have been much more difficult, perhaps impossible. In 1843–5 Minister of Finance, F.A. van Hall, finally succeeded in reorganising the huge public debt (see chapter 4), thus paving the way for the badly needed currency overhaul, which took place during 1846–8. Acting as the government's cashier, the bank played a pivotal role in both operations, with circulating capital, bullion stock, note issue and deposits reaching unprecedented levels during these years (De Jong 1967a I, pp. 576–7). At the same time the government built on the bank's established note circulation to issue paper money in small denominations, the so-called *muntbiljetten*, as temporary replacement for withdrawn specie. Within three years 30 million guilders of these notes were issued and withdrawn again to cover the 80 million guilders of specie taken out of circulation, melted down, re-coined and reissued, a remarkable operation directed smoothly over the counters of the Nederlandsche Bank (De Jong 1967a I, pp. 308–23).

The currency overhaul was completed by dropping bimetallism. From the late 1830s expert opinion, supported by the conclusions of the 1836 Currency Commission, moved towards a single standard to eradicate the effects of fluctuations in the ratio between gold and silver. The

Nederlandsche Bank saw no practical reasons for a change, but urged strongly to take silver if the government wanted a single standard, mainly since the board expected more volatile and higher interest rates from a gold currency as being cheaper to send abroad and forever draining to the UK. Minister Van Hall, himself in favour of gold, took the advice. From May 1845 the guilder was in practice tied to silver, with the legal groundwork following two years later (Korthals Altes 1996, pp. 173–6). This switch and the subsequent demonetisation of gold further strengthened the Nederlandsche Bank's position as national circulation bank. Note issue rose to 74.5 million guilders in 1852–3, almost double the previous high of 1848. At the same time average advances dropped below 20 million guilders, a level unrecorded since 1835, the difference being made up by a doubling of the bullion reserves. The reorganisation of the public debt thus created the scope for a currency clean-up which moved the Nederlandsche Bank firmly into central position, an achievement of three vital and interdependent steps which turned the 1840s into the crucial decade in Dutch financial development during the nineteenth century. From then on, both bank and currency enjoyed the confidence necessary for building up a sound financial system.

5.3 Managing the currency, 1850–1914

The silver standard did not last. The sudden and rapid international depreciation of the early 1870s forced governments across Europe to adopt gold whether they wanted it or not. The Dutch government suspended the free minting of silver in 1873, followed by the adoption of the so-called limping standard in 1875, a gold currency helped out by the old silver coins remaining in circulation. Both the currency and the position of the Nederlandsche Bank had gained considerably in strength since the 1840s. For, while the suspension of free minting left the guilder without formal backing for two years, the guilder exchange rates against foreign currencies rose at the same time. Though that may have been the result of capital repatriation following the international financial panic (Schimmel 1882, pp. 233–4), it also points to undiminished confidence abroad. The Nederlandsche Bank was a reluctant convert to the gold standard. However, from the first signs of trouble in the autumn of 1872 until the new Currency Act became law in 1875, the bank's judicious policies significantly contributed to maintaining stability during the prolonged political debate, by sensibly anticipating events while keeping all options open (De Jong 1967a II, pp. 224–311). From the early 1850s onwards, the board deliberately built up a position as keeper of the nation's silver reserves. Starting in October 1871 it moved cautiously to attract gold as well, buying bullion on the market, and offering cheap lombard facilities to bullion traders, at the same time keeping the mint occupied with orders to check the free minting of silver.

The compromise of 1875 introduced the gold standard in a curiously hybrid form. Superimposing gold coins on the existing silver circulation may have been an expedient and cheap way of switching to the gold standard, but at the price of upward pressure on the exchange rates. A reduction in the amount of silver coin in 1884 eased the strain somewhat, but the increased need for fine tuning led the Nederlandsche Bank to bolster its quietly assumed position as manager of the guilder. In 1888 the board obtained permission to start dealing in foreign bills, a practical and profitable way of controlling exchange rates. The bank prided itself on always sticking to the rules of the game and never resorting to gold points manipulation (De Jong 1967a III, pp. 319, 517–21). Yet, not being obliged to redeem its notes in gold coin, the bank starved customers at home. The famed *gouden tientjes* quickly became a rarity, leaving the field to the bank's notes and joining the nation's bullion reserves in the vaults of the head office at the Turfmarkt. As a result the gold standard practically turned into a gold bullion standard, as advocated by the Dutch economist G.M. Boissevain in 1889, and subsequently given wider berth during the 1920s by the British Cunliffe Report (Kindleberger 1984, pp. 332–3). In 1903 this informal policy gained official confirmation by the banknotes being made legal tender, against the bank's formal undertaking to the government of exchanging gold for guilders at the rate pitched in 1881.

5.4 The early pattern of banking, 1814–1860

5.4.1 Regional banking

Very little is known about provincial banking during the seventeenth and eighteenth centuries. No firms seem to have survived apart from the Middelburg Wisselbank, which operated until the 1830s. During the first half of the nineteenth century, most major provincial towns had a cashier or perhaps two, changing money, retailing securities, and offering short-term advances and sometimes long-term loans. These firms remained quite small, however. Few seem to have taken deposits; most developed from other business which continued alongside. The Schiedam firm Jos. Loopuyt dealt in money, grain and Dutch gin. Fransen van de Putte & Zn. in Goes started as a brewery. Until the middle 1850s, Doijer & Kalff in Zwolle made more money from the tea trade than from their cashier's business (Van der Werf 1988, pp. 20–1). The Kingma family in Makkum provided some financial services to customers of their widespread and varied shipping and industrial business, which originated in the eighteenth century. From about

1840 these services grew in importance, but a formal separation between them took place only in 1869, and the manufacturing side of the family empire outweighed the cashiers' firm Gebr. Kingma until the turn of the century (D.P. de Vries 1989, pp. xxiv–xxv). Lissa & Kann could afford to concentrate on banking and retailing securities from the 1830s, patronised as they were by the rich citizenry of The Hague. The firm's capital more than tripled in under thirty years to reach 300,000 guilders in 1866 (Stevens 1970, pp. 80, 83). The Utrecht firm of Vlaer & Kol traded on a similar capital in the 1830s, having established itself in much the same way as Lissa & Kann by virtue of its links with the provincial gentry (Louwerens 1993, pp. 59–68). F. van Lanschot in Den Bosch wound up his commodity business only in the early 1880s, when the firm had a capital of about 170,000 guilders (Govers 1972, pp. 292, 295).

Overall, provincial banking thus remained small scale and closely interwoven with other activities. This comes as no surprise. The sluggish economic development kept trade and manufacturing on an equally modest footing, tied to the region or tenuously linked to the outside world by a chain of middlemen all giving credit hidden in late payments at higher prices, as evidenced by the widespread discount-for-cash custom. Only the gradual breakdown of barriers between regions by the building of roads and railways and canals after the 1850s, coinciding with the lifting of restrictive taxation, created enough economic scope for a separation between financial and other services.

5.4.2 At the old centre: Amsterdam

In the two main mercantile centres Amsterdam and Rotterdam, commercial banking stood on the brink of that separation towards the end of the eighteenth century. This trend slowed, however, and may even have reversed during the slump which followed.

Until the 1860s, financial services in Amsterdam were spread over four quite different types of intermediaries: the *kassiers*, whom we have already met above, the merchant houses and commission traders, the Jewish banks and the Nederlandsche Bank. Each played a distinct role on the money market, and thus contributed to the curious fragmentation which remained a feature until the early twentieth century.

Merchant firms like Hope & Co., Van Eeghen & Co., Crommelin & Sn. and Stadnitski & Van Heukelom, to name but a few, all retained links with the commodity trade throughout the nineteenth century, sometimes close, sometimes less so. However, as a rule they made most of their money by providing financial services. A fifth of gross earnings coming from interest charges on advances in current account or on *prolongatie* was normal, a quarter common, and a third not exceptional. During the 1830s and 1840s, Crommelin & Sn. regularly topped 50 and even 60 per cent. Commissions accounted for a further 20–30 per cent of gross earnings, and, even though partly springing from commodity dealing, most of it represented financial services like guaranteeing payment, covering costs, brokering, providing insurance, etc. Investments and stock broking made up most of the remainder, for, next to functioning as market makers in any available securities, these houses kept a large portfolio for own account (Jonker 1996b).

The commission traders or *commissionairs*, one rung below the merchant houses in the hierarchy, sometimes specialised in finance altogether. Foremost amongst them was the formidable Wed. W. Borski, ostensibly no more than the chief agent and underwriter for Hope & Co., but in reality a powerful banking firm in its own right.

The Nederlandsche Handel-Maatschappij, set up by King William I in 1824 to revive foreign trade, worked the same field between trade and finance as the merchant houses. The company is usually described as having crossed over to banking in 1882, when the board formally sanctioned the backing of rights issues (Wijtvliet 1993, pp. 107–50; cf. however Renooij 1947). Now merchanting undoubtedly formed the NHM's main concern, more so than with the merchant houses. Even so it acted like a bank all the time, though not always voluntarily. The importance of the company's commodity interests is reflected in commissions providing 50 per cent of net profits from 1824–79, but even so interest charges came to 23 per cent (Mansvelt 1924, appendix 7). During the 1830s the government bullied the company into providing advances totalling 39 million guilders. Generous credit terms were used to manipulate the markets in tin and coffee, and to prop up calico manufacturers and sugar refineries, in one case leading to a conversion of frozen advances into a direct shareholding of half a million guilders. During the 1850s the NHM embarked on self-confessed *crédit foncier* or mortgage banking activities in the Dutch East Indies, supplying planters and manufacturers with long-term loans in return for their produce (Mansvelt 1924 II, pp. 359–61). At the end of the 1870s these advances exceeded 10 million guilders, about 20 per cent of total assets, well over half of it locked up in mortgages or shareholdings (Wijtvliet 1993, pp. 111, 135).

During the last quarter of the eighteenth century, the cashiers started to move from cash-keeping towards commercial banking, building up a wide circulation of notes or *kassierspapier*, and converting deposits into advances. A combination of inexperience, generally a small amount of capital, and economic upheaval during the Napoleonic Wars decimated the cashiers' ranks; just 16 out of 54 mentioned in 1780 survived the French occupation (Jonker 1992, p. 115). One such firm, Bosch & De Clercq, had a capital of only 200,000 guilders on a balance sheet of 2.2 million in 1810, with a liquidity ratio of about 65 per cent. It suspended payments in the general panic of November 1813.[1]

These mishaps reduced the appetite for further experiments. In 1806 a group of prominent merchants set up the Associatie Cassa, a limited company with a capital of 500,000 guilders, and put it under strict instructions to keep deposits in cash and limit advances to the available capital. When Bosch & De Clercq reorganised into the Ontvang- en Betaalkas seven years later, the firm publicly embraced the same principles, and installed a supervisory board to inspire confidence. Clients paid for the cashkeeping instead of earning interest on their deposits, and the firms' income depended on the commissions charged on transactions, less so on the difference between interest paid out and received. The Associatie Cassa derived as a rule two-thirds of gross earnings from commissions, and the rest from interest. In the long run this basis proved too narrow. During the 1840s a combination of circumstances severely undermined the cashiers' position. The compromise ending the conflict with the Nederlandsche Bank cut down the issue of *kassierspapier*. After hectic trading following Minister Van Hall's conversion of the public debt and the subsequent currency clean-up, activities on the money market turned down sharply, while the introduction of new coinage ended the need for an intermediary to help order the confusion of specie. From a vital link in the city's economic life, the cashiers withered to a small group running the settlement system on the exchange, paying dividends and delivering securities, too small a pool to sustain many fish. By 1860 the Associatie Cassa and the Ontvang- en Betaalkas stood out in a depleted field, monuments from a long-gone era, their backs firmly and proudly set against change. After 54 years in business, the Associatie Cassa's capital and reserves had reached 1.7 million guilders on a balance total of 15.5 million. Its capital–assets ratio of 11 and capital–public liabilities ratio of 12.5 compared favourably with the commercial banks entering the field from the 1860s, the difference of course being the staggering 90 per cent of balance total lying unused in the vaults. This policy paid rather handsome regular dividends of 8 per cent, culminating in 50 per cent for the year 1851–2, justified by directors lamely pointing to the difficulty of employing the money profitably.[2]

If their overall business went downhill, why didn't the cashiers adapt, for instance by moving back into banking? Part of the answer lies in the pickings left for surviving *kassiers* like the Associatie Cassa, but the question boils down to asking why commercial banks made such a belated entry, and to explain that we need to look deeper into the structure of the Amsterdam money market.

A striking feature of Dutch banking history is the slow development of deposit taking. The cashiers' refusal to pay for deposits has always been taken as a mark of sclerotic conservatism, and no doubt part of it was. However, when during the 1860s some firms did start offering interest, they met with little success, and the commercial banks entering the fray somewhat later showed a distinct lack of deposits until the World War I. The usual explanation points to the thriving *prolongatie* or on-call money market at the Amsterdam stock exchange, which attracted available cash from all over the country until its collapse in August 1914 (Eisfeld 1916, pp. 269–73). First described by Joseph de Vega in 1688 as a technique to facilitate forward securities trading, *prolongatie* served speculators, merchants, and manufacturers alike as a flexible means of short-term credit against securities (Smith 1919). This secured investors against the loss of their deposits, and turned the *prolongatie* into the safe and stable lynch pin missing in most other nineteenth-century financial systems, which may well explain the scarcity of runs in Amsterdam. The *prolongatie* deals consisted of simple sale–repurchase agreements or repos in today's parlance. Being cheap and easy to obtain, they created wide opportunities for what is known as margin trading, speculating on price differences over time with securities bought on credit to be paid off with the expected gains. Boosted by the vicissitudes of the Dutch government bonds or *NWS* (Nederlandsche Werkelijke Schuld) and Amsterdam's role as an arbitrage centre, the system already operated on a fairly large scale during the first half of the nineteenth century (*pace* De Jong 1967b, p. 90). On-call intermediation formed the bread and butter of Amsterdam stock brokers and cashiers. This large pool of liquid savings regularly attracted customers from abroad. British bankers apparently lombarded large quantities of American stocks in the late 1830s on this market. French and German bankers were regular customers during the 1850s (Riemens 1949, p. 59; Van Winter 1933, II, p. 425; De Jong 1967b, pp. 94–5).

If the *prolongatie* market explains the scarce supply of deposits in The Netherlands, its long domination of course also suggests that demand for credit exerted not enough pressure on cashiers and bankers to switch from passive to active intermediation. The very high yield on government debt until after Van Hall's reorganisation will have reinforced this slant from excess pull and lack of push on the money market during the first half of the nineteenth century. It rarely fell below 4.5 per cent and regularly touched 5 per cent, whereas in surrounding countries with the exception of Belgium 4 per cent or below became the norm from the 1820s.

The second important feature concerns the top-heavy structure of the money market. The establishment of the Nederlandsche Bank in 1814 put a lid on market-induced developments like the evolution of the *kassiers* at the end of the eighteenth century. At 5 million guilders, the bank's initial capital

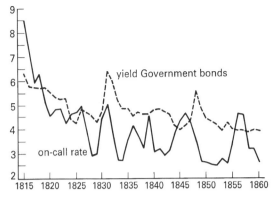

Figure 5.1 Interest rates in the Netherlands, 1815–1860
Sources: On-call rate: GAA PA 599 Stadnitski and Van Heukelom, unnumbered
ledgers (1815–28); *Algemeen Handelsblad,* 1828–64; and De Jong 1967a II:
pp. 624–6 (1864–1914). The yield on Government debt is taken from the
Prijscourant der effecten (1815–28); the *Algemeen Handelsblad* (1828–46) and De
Jong 1967a II: 621–3 (1846–1914).

together with a privileged note issue ensured domination of the discount
and lombard market. Though others could and did undercut its rates, no
one matched it for power, even more so after the capital was doubled in
1820, and raised again to 17.2 million guilders including reserves 20 years
later. For that reason, and because of its close connection to King William I
and his centralising efforts which antagonised local pride, the new institution started off on a bad note. By 1830 the bank had become firmly established, however; the turmoil surrounding the Belgian revolt and subsequent
well-founded rumours about clandestine advances to the government failed
to shake its position. Until the appointment of four Rotterdam agents in
1852, operations remained largely confined to Amsterdam. Yet the influence of the bank's interest rate probably made itself felt somewhat earlier,
either directly or as a business barometer. In 1846 the Rotterdam banker
R.A. Mees complained about its high level (Mees 1920, p. 43).

Figure 5.2 demonstrates that after the early 1820s the *prolongatie* rate and
bank rate on average more or less coincided, the longer term of the three-
month bank loans cancelling out the quicker and more extreme reactions of
day-to-day business at the exchange. However, bank rate became an
effective instrument only during the 1860s; the crises of 1864–6 still largely
bypassed the Turfmarkt (De Jong 1967a II, p. 157).

The Nederlandsche Bank's advances were limited to orthodox three
months' discounts and lombards on collateral of Dutch securities,

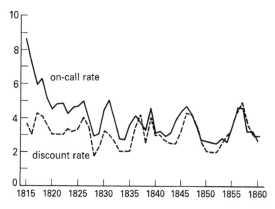

Figure 5.2 Average on-call rate at the Amsterdam exchange and the
Nederlandsche Bank's discount rate, 1815–1860
Sources: As Figure 5.1.

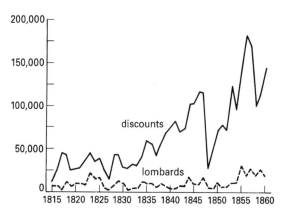

Figure 5.3 Annual turnover on discounts and lombards of the Nederlandsche
Bank, 1815–1860, ×1,000 guilders
Source: De Jong 1967a I.

commodities and later bullion. Figure 5.3 shows the development of operations. Average discounts outstanding rose from 2.4 million guilders in
1814–15 to around 6 million ten years later. Soaring to 10 million and
beyond in the later 1830s, the amount topped 21 million guilders in 1847–8
before dropping back to about 14 million in the early 1850s. In 1854 the
figure passed the 23 million mark, to end at 42 million guilders in the early

1860s. Discount turnover rose from an initial 20 million guilders a year to a steady 30–40 million until the middle 1830s, and just over 100 million ten years later. The downturn on the money market following Van Hall's reorganisation, the currency overhaul and the crisis of 1848, brought about a sharp setback, but by 1853 the amount recovered to about 70–80 million guilders a year, and from there climbed to 180 million in the late 1850s and over 200 million in the early 1860s.

Lombards seemingly lagged far behind, once in a while rising above 10 million guilders but mostly staying well under that amount until the mid 1850s, when the rules were changed to allow foreign securities as collateral and the practice of charging interest at 0.5–1 per cent higher than discounts ceased. As a result the amount doubled to around 20 million guilders. However, average lombards outstanding topped average discounts until the early 1840s. Both transactions carried a mandatory three-month term, so lombards were often rolled over without being registered as new. Consequently lombard turnover must have been at least equal and probably higher than discounts until the 1840s.

The services of the Nederlandsche Bank are universally regarded as very beneficial to the Amsterdam economy, and the figures certainly do impress. No other institution extant in 1814 could have grown into providing advances on anything like a similar scale. Nor could a new private initiative have done that. Still, some qualifications may be made as to the impact of these benefits, since the support they afforded to the much-lauded commodity trade seems to have been rather less than that given to the often maligned stock exchange. Until the 1860s, the commodity trade struggled in vain to turn the once favourable terms of trade, and consequently few bills came on the market from that sector. Merchants preferred to keep them in portfolio, as discounting cut into profits. Most firms possessed ample means, on which the prolonged economic slump put little pressure. When in 1856 a new steam shipping line was set up, the board specifically earmarked some of the company's capital for the bills expected (De Boer 1921, p. 96). Not discounting at the Nederlandsche Bank was supposedly seen as a mark of high standing, since the big and even the middle-ranking firms simply did not need to. De Jong's data for the 1850s show remarkably few commodity traders using the bank's facilities (De Jong 1967a II, pp. 503–6).

As a result, bills from the booming stock trading provided the main fare on the discount market. Until about 1850, the high yield on government stock must have attracted foreign investors. Combined with modest short interest rates it also created a lively arbitrage market. No fewer than seven German Jewish banks specialising in this work established a branch linking Amsterdam with other offices around Europe, amongst them well-known names such as Königswärter, Bisschoffsheim, Raphael, Stern, Oppenheim and Sichel. These branches liquidated one after the other roughly between 1850 and 1860, when the interest gap disappeared, the telegraph cut margins and the blocking of initiatives for a Dutch Crédit Mobilier dashed hopes of finding a lucrative replacement (Jonker 1994). After the lifting of restrictive legislation Dutch capital repatriated during the French occupation found its way back abroad from the 1820s, generating a steady flow of bills from foreign interest earnings. The latest estimates put the amount of foreign stock held in The Netherlands at about 500 million guilders in 1807, or 19 per cent of total national assets, rising to 600 million or 21 per cent by 1832 (Verstegen 1995). Conservatively taking interest at 4 per cent, that means annual payments of around 24 million guilders flowing to the Amsterdam money market.

This stock exchange business depended rather more on discounting. Big houses like Hope & Co. probably followed fellow merchants in preferring to keep paper in portfolio, but specialist firms like the German branches and stock brokers building themselves up to emerge as bankers in the 1860s, ran a much tighter ship and thus discounted more. Contemporary criticism of the Nederlandsche Bank's advances supporting the stock exchange are borne out in several ways. Firstly, turnover on securities lombards exceeded discounts until at least the 1840s. Secondly, in its annual reports the bank's board attributed its business fluctuations more often than not to the pulse of stock broking rather than that of the commodity trade. Thirdly, owing to a very large number of small customers, advances to commodity firms outstripped those to others during the 1850s. Even so securities traders easily topped the individual table, two discounting on average just under 9 million guilders a year, two around 4 million and five were in the 2.5 million bracket, next to the two biggest commodity firms (De Jong 1967a III, pp. 504–6). With the arbitrage market in decline, and commodity trading on the rise following the abolition of restrictive legislation and the colonial commodities monopoly of the Nederlandsche Handel-Maatschappij, the preponderance of stock trading bills was probably even more pronounced before the 1850s.

The acknowledgement that the Nederlandsche Bank provided advances on a scale which otherwise would not have been available, must therefore be qualified by pointing out that, to a very large degree, these served the needs of finance rather than trade or industry. This was definitely not the board's intention. The bank stifled further initiatives, however, and by freezing the market structure helped to strengthen the hold of finance over other sectors. Developments in Rotterdam offer a tempting example of what might have happened without it.

5.4.3 The need for mobility: Rotterdam

During the first half of the nineteenth century, two Rotterdam firms, M. Ezechiëls & Zn. and J. Osy & Zn., are known to have operated as bankers in contemporary parlance, dealing in money, securities and foreign bills. The full scope of their activities remains unknown. Osy disappeared around 1840; Ezechiëls liquidated in 1888 (Mees 1920, pp. 63–4).

Except for these firms, banking remained closely tied to insurance, following the example of the Maatschappij van Assurantie, Disconto en Beleening der Stad Rotterdam, set up in 1720 with a nominal capital of 12 million guilders. The four cashiers, Gebroeders Chabot, R. Mees & Zn., Ian Havelaar and later Schaay & Madry, all ran banking services in tandem with insurance broking. Until World War I, Mees and Chabot derived a large part of their profits, 25–30 per cent, from insurance (Krans 1977, p. 165; Kämper-Attema Vleesenbeek 1986, p. 47; Van de Laar and Vleesenbeek 1990, pp. 57–9). The available data suggest the firms mainly operated as true cashiers to their clients during this period, keeping cash, settling accounts and discounting bills. Just as in Amsterdam, profits in banking derived less from the difference between interest paid and received, than from the commission charged on transactions. Until 1863 only family members' deposits carried interest. As a rule advances were given on a small scale only, and often not provided by the firm, but by the partners in private account, a common practice during the eighteenth and nineteenth centuries. Even so it could be hard to maintain a grip on clients. Chabot ran aground in 1836 on a credit of about 300,000 guilders, roughly a third of its balance total, to a single company (Krans 1977, pp. 156, 162). Overall, the Rotterdam cashiers moved into banking slowly and cautiously. In 1860 Mees still had only about 1.8 million guilders of deposits and 1.4 million of advances on a capital of 2.2 million and a balance total of 4.3 million. From 1815 the firm's capital growth consistently outpaced its balance sheet.[3]

Despite this slow progress, the Rotterdam cashiers clearly moved in the opposite direction to their Amsterdam colleagues. Three factors explain why they did: the economic climate, the character of the local money market and the position of the Nederlandsche Bank. Firstly, buoyed up by its great harbour and rising transit traffic to Germany, Rotterdam experienced healthy activity during the 1850s, while Amsterdam remained caught in a slump (Nusteling 1974; Van Tijn 1965). Secondly, Rotterdam resources seem to have been rather smaller. Top Amsterdam firms like Hope & Co., Van Eeghen & Co. and D. Crommelin & Sn., stayed in position, trading on capitals of about 1.5–2 million guilders or more carried over from the late eighteenth century. The Rotterdam firms making the running, such as A. van Hoboken, W. Ruys and A. van Rijckevorsel, all started more or less from scratch during the first decades of the nineteenth century, to edge alongside their northern rivals for 20–30 years (Muller 1977; Oosterwijk 1983, 1989). As a result these merchants and shippers had to rely more on discounting and other credit, thus creating a regular demand which by the 1850s started to outstrip local resources (De Jong 1967a I, pp. 1069–70, pp. 1102–4). Moreover, they and their cashiers grew side-by-side to reach a similar size by 1850, whereas the Amsterdam cashiers started from, and remained in, a subordinate position to the big houses. Thirdly, in 1852 the Rotterdam cashiers successfully thwarted the establishment of a branch of the Nederlandsche Bank by agreeing to work as the bank's agents instead, thus securing a slice of the credit business which otherwise would have bypassed them. From the late 1840s the four cashiers discounted a sharply growing amount at the Nederlandsche Bank, on average about 20 million guilders a year jointly (De Jong 1967a III, pp. 504–5). Most of this business was new, for the bank's discount turnover rose, and while Mees sent on average just over 6 million guilders a year to Amsterdam, the firm's own portfolio grew rapidly to 1.3 million in 1860. In striking contrast, none of the Amsterdam cashiers discounted at the bank, while at least the Associatie Cassa never held bills to any significant amount.

These factors mark out the difference between Rotterdam enterprise and Amsterdam financial conservatism. As became clear during the 1850s, however, the former could not do without the capital power of the latter, thus reconfirming the ascendancy of the old financial centre, now in the shape of the Nederlandsche Bank. From the 1860s this phenomenon would be repeated as the bank branched out into the country.

5.5 Structural changes, 1860–1890

The founding of the Amsterdam Credietvereeniging in 1853 heralded two decades full of initiatives aimed at breaking the mould of Dutch banking. With economic development lagging behind expectations, that push met only with partial success. By 1873 the big undertakings had all failed, and the modest and prudent ones were being scaled down. Even so, the money market acquired a framework for renewed growth from the 1890s. The institutional changes have always attracted a good deal of attention. However, two underlying developments were at least as important in determining the shape of things to come. Though unconnected, both aimed to draw the Dutch money market tighter together on Amsterdam, sealing the capital's financial ascendancy over the rest of the country and thus setting a ceiling to regional banking initiatives.

5.5.1 Towards a national system, I: the Nederlandsche Bank

During the lean years of the early 1850s, the contrast between declining Amsterdam business and the swelling discounts coming in from Rotterdam slowly persuaded the Nederlandsche Bank of the need for branching out to restore profits. This coincided with public opinion pressing for a nationwide service to match the bank's national monopoly. Consequently, the Bank Act of 1863 committed the Nederlandsche Bank to set up a national grid of agencies and correspondents. By January 1865 the bank operated a full-blown branch in Rotterdam, agents in 12 towns and correspondents in a further 56.

This momentous step turned the advance side of the Amsterdam market into a national system and thus sealed the capital's financial ascendancy over the rest of the country. It remains unclear whether or not provincial discount rates dropped by 1 per cent as expected. Otherwise the immediate effects were quite dramatic. In 1863 nearly 75 per cent of the bank's business came from Amsterdam; within five years this fell to 50 per cent, with the Rotterdam branch taking nearly 24 per cent and the provincial agents just over 25 per cent. By 1880 the rankings were roughly, 40 per cent for Amsterdam, 10 per cent for Rotterdam and the rest going elsewhere. The Nederlandsche Bank's advances (see figure 5.4) soared from an annual average of 63 million guilders in 1863–4 to 106 million ten years later, before reaching a peak of 120 million in 1878–9. The ensuing depression then brought a setback, but from 1890 advances rose by two-thirds to reach an annual average of 147 million guilders in 1910–11 and 159 million in 1913–14. Note circulation increased by leaps and bounds, levelled at about 200 million guilders during the 1870s and 1880s, then took off again during the late 1890s, rising to 250 million in 1905 and 313 million guilders in 1913–14 (De Jong 1967a III, pp. 164–5, 546–9).

However, it must remain a moot point whether the Nederlandsche Bank's expansion into the regions was indeed beneficial overall. To begin with, the agency network may have pushed down provincial interest rates, but provincial business certainly eroded the effectiveness of the bank rate as a policy instrument. A lot of provincial business came as lombards; most discounts consisted of discounted *promessen*, finance bills habitually rolled over, and not redeemed, on expiry. Both forms were quite impervious to interest rate changes. Time and again the Nederlandsche Bank's board warned agents not to accept the *promessen*, only to relent in the face of opposition and on realising their importance for its provincial business and profit. By 1900 these IOUs formed 60 per cent of the bank's bill portfolio, while as a rule lombards represented just over half of total advances. Thus the bank rate remained an efficient policy instrument for only about 30

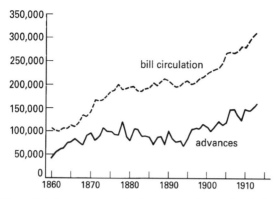

Figure 5.4 Average annual advances and note circulation of the Nederlandsche Bank, 1860–1913, ×1,000 guilders
Source: De Jong 1967a III.

years, from the late 1860s to about 1900. Nor did the bank possess other instruments of persuasion, for banks and bankers did not deposit funds at the Turfmarkt. At the same time the Amsterdam on-call rate replaced the bank rate as the leading indicator. For parallel to the Nederlandsche Bank's expansion the *prolongatie* became a nationwide system.

5.5.2 Towards a national system, II: the on-call market

No firm data for the spread of the *prolongatie* system exist, but there are enough indications pointing in the same direction to sketch a tentative picture.

Until the late 1840s postal services were so slow and haphazard that it paid for a group of Amsterdam stockbrokers to run private courier services supplying the quotations from European exchanges. The speeding up of public communications following the 1851 Post Act and the joint spread of railway and telegraph did away with the need for such private arrangements, and helped to turn the deposit side of the Amsterdam money market into a national system. Coinciding as it did with the codification in 1856 of local trading rules and customs into a new set of regulations upheld by a society of stockbrokers, the improved communications opened up the stock exchange for outside investors, thus helping to draw money towards the old centre via the finely woven network of provincial cashiers and stockbrokers. In Rotterdam a thriving on-call market operated during the 1830s. The local Chamber of Commerce complained about its capacity being too small in 1851. By 1860 the stock market there had accepted a subsidiary position to

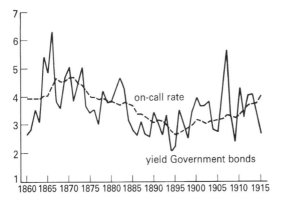

Figure 5.5 Dutch interest rates, 1860–1915
Sources: As figure 5.1.

its great rival in the north, and funds seem to have started flowing thither (De Jong 1967a I, pp. 821, 1069–70; Camijn 1987, pp. 20–7). During the 1840s and 1850s, R. Mees & Zn. had an average of no more than 150,000 guilders put on-call at end of year. Part of the money may have stayed in Rotterdam, but the total more than trebled during the early 1860s and continued rising. A lively public debate raged in 1866 about the wisdom of town councils putting their spare cash on *prolongatie* (Doorman 1866). The Rotterdamsche Bank started out in 1863 with high hopes of building up a strong base of deposits, only to give up the struggle against the more attractive on-call market in 1871 (Wijtvliet 1993, p. 201). Presumably this new supply from all over the country met a keen demand for short-term funds, as speculative American railroad securities started flooding the market at more or less the same time (Veenendaal 1996). The result may be seen in figure 5.5; from the early 1860s long and short rates drew much closer together, suggesting that the newly nationwide *prolongatie* system succeeded in paring down differentials to a minimum. Summing up then, improved communications probably transformed the Amsterdam short money market into a national deposit system. The volume of the system must remain a mystery but for tentative estimates for the early twentieth century when it was put at about 400 million guilders. At that time deposits at the five biggest commercial banks totalled only 270 million guilders (Jonker 1995). So clearly the on-call system prevented the Dutch banking system from building up a strong base of deposits until the 1920s as banks did in the UK, Germany and elsewhere.

Now it can be argued that just as the Nederlandsche Bank's expansion took the advance business, the *prolongatie* system siphoned off deposits, together robbing local and regional initiatives of a viable basis. This pincer movement stifled the Amsterdam market before, as we have seen, and indeed Dutch provincial banking remained curiously weak overall. The prima facie evidence for this case looks strong, but of course it would not do to press charges against the Nederlandsche Bank alone. Firstly, local funds would have flowed to the *prolongatie* market anyway. Secondly, the bank helped to offset the deposit drain by channelling its own resources to the regions. No other institution could or would have provided the same service, and that must have consoled the bank's board, once hopeful of nursing local cashiers and brokers to full banking status but seeing its provincial assets more and more turning into liabilities during the 1920s and 1930s.

Thus, judging by the volume and geographical spread of its business and the increases in note circulation, following the Bank Act of 1863, the Nederlandsche Bank became a truly national institution. It also moved in the direction of a central bank by trading bills and bullion and using the bank rate for broader monetary purposes, operating as lender of last resort, and monitoring other institutions. However, in retrospect it would seem this lasted for no longer than about 30 years. By 1900 the bank rate was no longer an effective weapon; the commercial banks' expansion rapidly outpaced the Nederlandsche Bank's resources, and the open market liberated the fledgling *kredietverenigingen* from the Turfmarkt's embrace. On the eve of World War I the bank had become an anachronism, out of touch with the money market, 'rather an old men's bank', as the incoming president G. Vissering complained in 1912 (Joh. de Vries 1989, p. 31).

5.5.3 Commercial banking: the false dawn of the Crédit Mobilier

The failure of all Crédit Mobilier-type initiatives provides the first indication that around 1860 the time was ripe for change, but not yet for growth, not on the vast scale this group of initiators had in mind anyway. In 1856–7 the Ministry for Justice received five schemes for Crédit Mobilier-type investment companies for approval. Three of them aimed to set up with a capital of 30–50 million guilders, way beyond the existing scale of business. The two biggest companies, the Nederlandsche Bank and the Nederlandsche Handel-Maatschappij, had capital and reserves of just over 17 million and 34 million guilders respectively. The average capital of limited companies was only 600,000 guilders. It was no surprise that the plans were rejected for fear of their projected size and function fanning speculation. Two similar projects submitted in 1863 did gain approval, if only because of their much more modest scale of 10–20 million guilders. Yet despite support from prominent businessmen neither succeeded in realising their objectives. Within three years one of them was heading for liquidation, and the other started transferring its activities to Belgium and France (Hirschfeld 1922; Kymmell 1992). Envy and a lack of entrepreneurial spirit in financial circles and official animosity no doubt helped to frustrate these initiatives. Yet they failed mainly because they were ill-conceived and ill-timed. With the economy caught in a slow transition, the Dutch market suffered from a mismatch between abundant and very mobile capital, and few productive openings at home, so there was no need for imported schemes devised to mobilise scarce capital towards promising opportunities. Moreover, the intermediation provided by the Amsterdam stock exchange was strong enough to render it quite unnecessary for corporate institutions to mobilise capital for large projects. By the mid 1850s Dutch railway companies had successfully raised about 53 million guilders of equity and bond issues through syndicates of bankers, underwriters and brokers.

Bankers and investors have often been criticised for their supposed preference for government issues and especially for exotic foreign stock, to the detriment of Dutch manufacturing investment and thus the development of home industry. This case can no longer be upheld. True, foreign securities always attracted a keen interest in The Netherlands, both respectable government issues such as Russian loans and the more speculative paper floated by American railways, etc. According to the latest estimates, however, the amount of foreign securities held in The Netherlands rose from about 600 million guilders in the 1830s to only 740 million around 1865, and, since total national assets rose, the share declined from around 20 per cent to 14 per cent, against 16 per cent for home and colonial securities, and 42 per cent for property. From the 1860s the amount of foreign securities rose, however, to 2 billion guilders or 22 per cent around 1880, and 2.4 billion or 28 per cent 15 years later. Even then the declining trend in interest rates does not suggest any shortage of capital. When economic growth started to pick up around 1895, capital exports continued to climb, reaching a peak of 2.8 billion guilders in 1910, but their share in total national assets declined again to 21 per cent, so it is hard to see where the supposed preference for foreign securities could have hit home investment (Verstegen 1996).

Moreover, any collusion against profitable opportunities would have foundered on the competition, keeping the money and capital markets keen, flexible and open. Perhaps the formal institutions extant or coming on stream during the 1860s and 1870s provided too little support for budding industrialists. However, there were plenty of private financiers eager to bridge any gaps. Amsterdam firms like the engineers Koninklijke Fabriek voor Stoom- en andere Werktuigen, the sugar refineries of C. de Bruyn &

Zn. and the Hollandsche Stoom-Suikerraffinaderij, all grew from modest beginnings into concerns worth one to three million guilders on the strength of private finance. Nor did the stock exchange offer an insurmountable hurdle. The formalities governing rights issues and listings were very light: a minimum capital of half a million guilders, the backing of two brokers and the prospect of regular trading, sufficed. Company promoters and investors could also call on a large and active parallel market ranging from regular securities auctions to the direct placing of issues. Prime unlisted companies like Heineken's brewery used this until the early twentieth century. The first insurance companies only bothered to obtain a listing in the 1950s. Other companies went abroad to obtain the conditions they wanted. The margarine magnate H. van den Bergh, co-founder of Unilever, floated a rights issue in London in 1895, and the Rotterdam trading company R.S. Stokvis and several others followed him. The Philips brothers seriously considered it when they wanted to make their budding electrical company public in 1911, but opted for a flotation in Amsterdam. Considering the Amsterdamsche Bank's stiff conditions for a rights issue to Van den Bergh's rival margarine producer Jurgens in 1906, one can understand why those who could voted with their feet (Wilson 1970, II, pp. 52–4, 80–2; Heerding 1986, pp. 362–7; Brandes de Roos 1928, pp. 111–12). The Amsterdam stock exchange thus formed only one of several doors to the capital market, and the appearance of the first industrial listings during the 1880s signified the start of trading in old listings, not a supposedly long-delayed entry into the capital market. Due to the weakness of provincial banking, manufacturers there often had to be more inventive to find the right supply, but here as well consistent signs of finance failing enterprise are lacking. Moreover, the ups and downs of home-grown joint-stock banking initiatives underline the inability of finance to force the pace of change.

5.5.4 Joint-stock banking: changing colours while keeping the pattern

The 1860s are usually described as heralding Dutch banking coming of age with the belated entry of modern joint-stock commercial banks (Brugmans 1963; Kymmell 1992). However, closer analysis shows continuities with the preceding period running deeper than supposed, for the new joint-stock banks covered much the same ground as the private banking firms and merchant bankers before.

The first initiatives for banking renewal aimed at the smaller end of the market. In 1853 a group of Amsterdam merchants, doctors and lawyers supported by three private banks founded the Credietvereeniging, a mutual credit society inspired by the French *crédit mutuel* or the German

Kreditvereine (De Jong 1967a II, p. 131; Louwerens 1993, pp. 23–9). The Credietvereeniging, intended for shopkeepers, merchants and manufacturers with businesses too small to obtain credit on the existing market, proved an immediate success. Starting with 400 members and a guaranteed capital of around 2.2 million guilders, the bank had doubled in size by 1856, and counted 1,136 members and just under 7 million guilders of guaranteed capital after ten years. Further expansion and a string of imitations followed until the middle 1870s, when along with the big joint-stock banks these institutions lost steam.

Some points must be brought out to put the *kredietverenigingen* into proper perspective. Firstly, small businesses paid a price for entering the system, for as a rule they were charged interest at 1.5 per cent over bank rate plus 0.125 per cent commission for advances. Secondly, the *kredietverenigingen* remained chronically underfunded. Members had to pay up just 10 per cent of their share in the guarantee capital, and the interest rate of 0.5 per cent over bank rate made deposits uncompetitive against the *prolongatie*. As a result the credit associations leant heavily on the Nederlandsche Bank or on their parent bank for rediscounting members' bills and *promessen* and thus came to resemble the London discount houses.[4] The Nederlandsche Bank accepted its part with a commendable mixture of business sense and an understanding of its wider responsibilities, using its power wherever possible to exercise a close monitoring of the *kredietverenigingen*. As for relations with commercial banking, the fact that two of the new joint-stock banks set up a subsidiary credit association provides an interesting clue to the nature of changes in the 1860s and 1870s.

Joint-stock banking began in 1861, when B.W. Blijdenstein moved the seat of his firm from Enschede to Amsterdam and incorporated it as the Twentsche Bankvereeniging B.W. Blijdenstein & Co. Two years later the four Rotterdam cashiers set up the Rotterdamsche Bank, and in 1872 the Amsterdamsche Bank opened for business. Together with initiatives like the Internationale Crediet- en Handelsvereeniging Rotterdam or Internatio (1863), the Nederlandsch-Indische Handelsbank (1863) and the Kas-Vereeniging (1865) in Amsterdam, this clutch of new banks supposedly broke the existing mould of Dutch banking. Some of them indeed specifically aimed to do so, notably the Rotterdamsche Bank and the Kas-Vereeniging. However, by the mid 1870s their innovative drive was largely spent, and analysis of the banks' balance sheets and performance shows them to have been far less revolutionary than generally understood.

In many ways the Twentsche Bank was the most innovative and successful of the three new commercial banks. Set up as a private limited company, it enjoyed the support and custom of the textile and allied manufacturers

concentrated around Enschede and thus escaped the confines of other provincial firms. Blijdenstein's move to Amsterdam formed part of an
expansionary drive which established a *kredietvereniging* and several
branches, including one in London. As a result, the Twentsche Bank
became the biggest of the newcomers. Balance total rose tenfold in 30 years
from 3.5 million guilders in 1867 to 31.3 million in 1890, while capital and
reserves grew from 750,000 guilders to 11.7 million.[5]

The two other banks, setting sail in a competitive environment and
without their own customer base, followed a much more erratic course of
development. After early disappointments in financing colonial enterprises,
the Rotterdamsche Bank soon concentrated on general commercial
banking. The board established a separate *kredietvereniging* and ventured
into company promotions from the early 1870s, only to be caught out by
heavy losses in 1879–80. As a result the bank's accounts show a peculiar
zigzag pattern, with peaks in 1866 and 1874, a dip in 1875–6 and troughs in
1867 and 1879–80. The balance total doubled between 1863 and 1878 to
reach 30 million guilders, only to fall back again until well into the 1890s to
the 15 million achieved in 1865. Capital and reserves show a similar pattern,
trebling to 10.1 million guilders in 1875, and then dropping to around 5.5
million.

The Amsterdamsche Bank forms a rare instance of imported initiative
succeeding on the Dutch money market. German and Austrian banks supplied three-quarters of the 10 million guilders capital, yet the executive
remained in Dutch hands and the bank was soon regarded as Amsterdam
born and bred. As with the Rotterdamsche Bank, the economic climate of
the 1870s frustrated the original intentions of building up a business in
company finance and promotion in the German mould. Adjusting to the
prevailing circumstances, the board switched to general mercantile business, reduced capital accordingly to 6 million guilders and started to build
from below. This cautious policy was rewarded by a steady growth of capital
and reserves to 7 million guilders in 1890, the balance total rising from 17.8
million in 1875 to 21 million in 1890.

Combined with the failure of the crédit mobilier, the vicissitudes of the
three new banks show that during the second half of the nineteenth century
the Dutch money market simply was not ready for radical change and could
only support an expansion of the existing mercantile credit system. A closer
look at the banks' combined accounts underlines this point. Figure 5.6
shows the capital–assets and capital–public liabilities ratios. As a rule the
former would be 35–40 per cent, and the latter 60 per cent or more, and
notably before 1875 both would be higher still by taking into account
capital pledged but not paid up by the shareholders of the *kredietverenigingen* of the Rotterdamsche Bank and the Twentsche Bank, and the share-

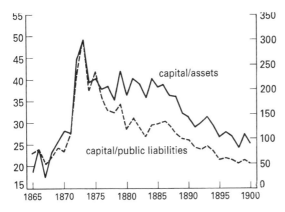

Figure 5.6 Capital–assets ratio (left scale) and capital–public liabilities ratio (right scale) in three commercial banks, 1865–1900
Source: Annual reports.

holders in the latter bank itself. Compared with joint-stock banks abroad these figures were very high. English banks for instance, often taken as a model by Dutch bankers, had capital–assets ratios of 14 per cent and capital–public liabilities ratios of 20 per cent in the 1870s (Collins 1984, p. 47). The banks' earnings structure further reveals their dependence on mercantile credit operations. Exact figures are impossible to give due to different accounting practices, but on a cautious estimate commission, bills and interest each supplied a third of gross earnings.

The earnings structure of the old Amsterdam merchant houses and of the Associatie Cassa provides an interesting comparison here. For their ratio of commissions to interest as a percentage of gross earnings was often roughly the same, the only difference being the commercial banks' higher earnings on bill transactions. We must therefore conclude that the three joint-stock banks were rather less revolutionary than generally thought. They conformed to the long-established mercantile credit pattern, even to the extent of listing commission trading amongst their functions, as the company statutes of the Twentsche Bank and the Amsterdamsche Bank did.

In one respect the new banks even turned the clock backwards. The old merchant houses held large amounts of securities as investment and as a trading portfolio, but the commercial banks would not touch them after early disappointments. On the other hand, the new banks increased the scale of available credit and probably extended the market downward. Up to 40 per cent of the Twentsche Bank's advances came under its *krediet-vereniging*, while at the Rotterdamsche Bank this figure declined from 36 per cent to 20 per cent as the parent bank absorbed more and more customers from its subsidiary.

The rest of the money market mirrors the partial modernisation in commercial banking. The Amsterdam cashiers responded to the impetus of the 1860s by starting to offer interest-bearing deposits and using these for advances, but stopped short of a complete transformation. The Associatie-Cassa exemplifies the lack of change. Its board set up a subsidiary, the Rente-Cassa, to experiment with the new-fangled ideas, so allowing the parent company to continue in the time-honoured ways. However, even the new Kas-Vereeniging, which specifically aimed to break the mould by emulating the London joint-stock banks, failed to do so. Time and again the board voiced disappointment at the failure of its original expectations, though from 1866 to 1890 its capital and reserves grew from 1 million guilders to 5 million, and balance total from 2.8 million to 15.6 million guilders. The capital ratios remained on a similar level to those of the three commercial banks, but at 2:1 the ratio of interest earnings to commissions was significantly higher. The Ontvang- en Betaalkas shows the same pattern.

The 1860s also saw the creation of mortgage banks. The first two were set up in 1861, and during the next 30 years 17 more followed. By that time the amount in mortgages supplied by them stood at just over 100 million guilders, only 10 per cent of the total outstanding, though the banks slowly edged towards capturing a fifth of new mortgages (Van der Woud 1947, p. 56; Jaarcijfers 1900, pp. 206–8).

Finally, the network of savings banks grew from 135 in 1860 to 255 in 1890, with total deposits climbing from 7.8 million guilders to 58.3 million (Van der Voort and Van Heijningen 1988, p. 45). Deposits per customer rose much slower, however, and the sector as a whole remained in the paternalistic mold of nursing the lower classes towards respectability by teaching them to save. More modern notions reached the market only with the Rijkspostspaarbank (RPS, or post office savings bank) in 1883.

5.6 New horizons, 1890–1914

During the 20 years or so leading up to World War I, Dutch banking entered an era of unprecedented growth, hesitant at first, but accelerating after the turn of the century, and again after about 1906, to culminate during World War I. This growth manifested itself on all fronts. The number of banks, their balance total, deposits, capital and reserves, and staff numbers all rose rapidly, and a whole new sector of Raiffeisen-type agricultural cooperative banks sprang up out of nothing to cover the countryside. Around 1910 a process of concentration set in which created five big banks which would dominate the scene by 1925.

Underneath however important structural weaknesses persisted. With the exception of the Raiffeisen-type cooperatives provincial banking never really got off the ground. The majority of the new firms disappeared before 1914, and the rest fell into the lap of the Big Five during the crisis of the 1920s. More importantly, growth failed to break the mould of commercial banking. Rights issues closely followed expansion, so the capital–assets ratio of the Big Five, while declining, still stood at a conservative 27 per cent in 1913. Assisted by the inverted interest rate structure the dominance of the *prolongatie* market over bank deposits continued unabated. Estimated at about 400 million guilders around 1914, this system drew twice the amount of the commercial banks' fixed deposits, thus keeping their capital–public liabilities ratio at an anaemic 62 per cent (Jonker 1995; *Financiële instellingen* 1987, pp. 32–3).

Still, the developments are interesting enough to merit attention. The data of the Twentsche Bank, Rotterdamsche Bank and Amsterdamsche Bank summarised in figure 5.7 show commercial banking's quickening pulse to good effect. From 1890 to 1913 their combined balance total increased sharply to 380 million guilders, capital and reserves to 84 million and deposits to 193 million guilders, mainly through the growth in current account business. The slightly arbitrary convention of including the Incassobank and the NHM from 1900 to make the Big Five brings out these developments more markedly still. Between 1900 and 1913 this group's balance total increased to 525.5 million guilders, capital and reserves doubled to 147 million and deposits trebled to 273 million guilders. Despite this spurt demand deposits as a percentage of money supply M_1 stood at a paltry 34 per cent in 1913, compared with, for instance, 66 per cent in Belgium (Kuné and Van Nieuwkerk 1974, p. 14; Van der Wee and Tavernier 1975, pp. 532–3).

Combined with the banking concentration, usually dated to start from 1911, this rapid development inspired contemporaries to herald a new, heroic spirit, with banking finally waking up to take the lead in matters economic and embrace closer ties with trade and industry (Van Tienhoven 1917; Westerman 1919). Most later observers have followed this interpretation, pointing to the Rotterdamsche Bank's surge from tail-end Charlie into the biggest of the Five in 1915 as the hallmark of the period. The underlying figures do not suggest a radical break with the past in the long run, however. We have already noticed the continuing high capital–assets and capital–public liabilities ratios. The commercial banks' heyday lasted only about ten years, for after a sharp rise from 1910 to 1920 bank assets as a percentage of national income at market prices (NNImp) declined again. Increasing business meant more of the same, passive intermediation in current accounts.

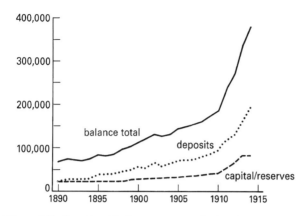

Figure 5.7 Combined balance total, capital and reserves, and deposits of three big commercial banks, 1890–1914, ×1,000 guilders
Source: Annual reports.

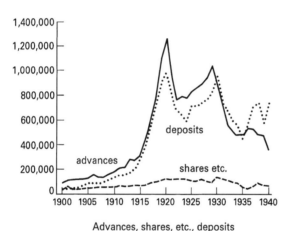

Advances, shares, etc., deposits

Figure 5.8 Advances, deposits and the amount of securities, participations and consortia at the Big Five, 1900–1940, ×1,000 guilders
Source: Financiële instellingen 1987, pp. 42–3.

After a rare peak in the early 1900s the amount of securities, participations and consortia in total assets, while never high, continued to decline, as figure 5.8 shows. Finally, tentative data on company finance and bankers' directorships suggest that banking concentration followed rather than led business development, and continued to do so (Jonker 1991b, 1995).

One truly important innovation of this period happened in the countryside. From 1896 farmers set up a fast-growing chain of small credit cooperatives in the German Raiffeisen mould, often with the help of local landowners, lawyers, mayors, teachers and priests. In 1900 there were 67 such banks; by 1910 the number had increased tenfold and continued rising. The banks organised themselves into two separate national chains, roughly along the denominational divide between Catholic and Dutch Reformed churches, with head offices in Eindhoven, for the Catholic-oriented Centrale Coöperatieve Boerenleenbank, and Utrecht, for the Centrale Coöperatieve Raiffeisenbank. The importance of these banks during this period did not lie in their capital power. By 1913 the balance total of the whole cooperative banking sector amounted to 53.5 million guilders, with capital and reserves of 2.1 million and deposits of 48.5 million (*Financiële instellingen* 1987, pp. 44–5). Nor did their success rest on the much-vaunted liberation from the manifold extortionate short credit practices in the countryside. The fast-growing farmers' trade and production cooperatives, of which the banks were a somewhat belated off-shoot, put a stop to those. The importance of the Raiffeisen banks lay in their building on the mutual trust of small communities rather than capital, and the pooling of local savings into a national grid.This gave them the flexibility to supply medium- and long-term advances to farmers at low cost. The extent of this innovation can be read from their low main ratios, capital–assets standing at 3.9 and capital–public liabilities at 4.3 in 1913. The trade-oriented banking establishment of course frowned on such practices, and indeed during the crisis of 1907 the Eindhoven chain came close to foundering. By 1913 these teething troubles were largely over, however (Jonker 1988).

Based as it was on a national network of low-threshold post offices, the Rijkspostspaarbank (RPS) mirrored the success of the Raiffeisen-type cooperatives in drawing from a pool of hitherto untapped savings. From 1890 deposits rose quickly to 183.8 million guilders in 1913, and two-thirds of it was invested in safe government paper. The general savings banks enjoyed a healthy growth without coming anywhere near the RPS's success. Between 1890 and 1913 their deposits doubled to reach 129.8 million guilders. Finally, the mortgage banks had rather mixed fortunes. From 1890 the number of banks, their balance total, capital and reserves, amount of mortgages supplied and mortgage bond circulation, all rose steadily, and the banks managed to increase their market share to a third of new inscriptions around 1905. Then came a sharp turning point. The expansion slowed down on all fronts, the mortgage banks' assets as a percentage of NNImp fell, and their market share plummeted to 17.6 per cent in 1914, while they were overtaken by other banks venturing into mortgages (Jaarcijfers 1915, p. 295; Jonker 1995; *Financiële instellingen* 1987, pp. 56–7). Large-scale frauds discovered in two mortgage banks during 1905–6 dented investor confidence, while far-reaching changes to the housing market following new legislation in 1901 presumably explain why the banks lost ground (Van der Woud 1974, p. 56–7; Klein and Vleesenbeek 1981, p. 14).

5.7 Conclusion

During the first half of the nineteenth century, Dutch banking and currency were tied down with the new Kingdom's interlinked political and economic problems. This Gordian knot unravelled only when the political deadlock broke during the 1840s, paving the way for the desperately needed public debt reorganisation, currency clean up and tax reforms. The removal of these key obstacles laid a firm basis for a national economy, and, helped by improved communications via new canals, railways, post and telegraph, the provinces now drew closer together. During the 1860s a national money market came into existence, resting on the Nederlandsche Bank and the stock exchange *prolongatie* system.

This grid extended the idiosyncrasies of Amsterdam's mercantile-oriented financial system to the whole country. Provincial enterprise undoubtedly profited from the wider availability of uniform and reasonably priced bill credit and a very flexible deposit system, but at the hidden cost of losing a sound basis for regional banking. For the same reasons commercial joint-stock banking appeared late on the scene, and made only modest headway until the 1890s.

As a result the nineteenth-century Dutch money and capital markets appear remarkably invertebrate through modern eyes, conditioned as they are to look for the firm structures and big institutions associated with the Gerschenkron–Cameron model for late industrialisers. As a rule European countries usually developed corporate banking and the crédit-mobilier to facilitate large manufacturing companies and/or the railways, but there was no such need in The Netherlands. Three factors combined to create a very flexible, stable and capacious money market without the familiar landmarks: firstly, the capital accumulated during the Golden Age; secondly, the high degree of securitisation to which the public was accustomed; and, finally, the dense network of intermediation by brokers, commissionaires, and bankers through which securities found their way to the public, and savings went to the open market.

The ease with which the enormous public debt of the 1830s and 1840s was absorbed, the generally low interest rates after the mid 1840s, the range of alternatives available to budding firms and companies, and the constant high level of capital exports, all testify to the remarkable ability of the market to allocate the available resources. Thus, rather than weak or backward, the nineteenth-century Dutch financial system was admirably suited to its purpose.

Notes

1 Gemeentearchief Amsterdam, (GAA) PA 583 Ontvang- en Betaalkas, no. 729. I
   am indebted to the NV Kas-Associatie for permission to consult these records.
2 GAA PA 748 Associatie Cassa no. 1, minute book, 7 September 1852.
3 Data for Mees from GA Rotterdam, Records R. Mees & Zn. No. 138A. I am
   indebted to the Board of Mees Pierson for permission to consult these records.
4 The comparison in Kymmell 1992, p. 97 with London bill brokers seems less
   apposite, for there existed a separate group of true brokers intermediating
   between buyers and sellers of inland and foreign bills.
5 Data taken from the surviving balance sheets, the earliest available of which are
   for 1867. Synopses for the early years of the three commercial banks in Kymmell
   1992, Wijtvliet 1993, Verrijn Stuart 1935, Harthoorn 1928, De Vries 1921, and
   Eisfeld 1916.

6 Old rules, new conditions, 1914–1940

JAN LUITEN VAN ZANDEN

6.1 The development of the banking system: from 'revolution' to stagnation

As a result of the relatively slow development of the banking system in the nineteenth century, its size and structure in 1913 differed from that of banking systems in other industrialised countries. The data presented in table 6.1 illustrate these differences clearly. The system of monetary transfer was much less developed in The Netherlands than in neighbouring countries; the proportion of total money supply (M1) accounted for by notes and coins in circulation was 64 per cent, about twice the corresponding figure for Belgium and Germany. The importance of the composition of the money supply was reflected in the structure of commercial banks' liabilities: in The Netherlands the relationship between equity and deposits was much more favourable than in other countries. The background to this situation, a situation Johan de Vries has labelled archaic (Joh. de Vries 1989, p. 44) is discussed in chapter 5. The foremost factor behind this delayed development of commercial banking in The Netherlands was the large and very efficient *prolongatie* system, which brought together the supply of and the demand for short-term credit. As a result, banks played a relatively modest role in the money market and, because of the small or absent differences between short-term and long-term interest rates, had difficulties in attracting deposits to enlarge their activities. Only after about 1906 did the large commercial banks, which had hitherto almost exclusively provided short-term credit to commerce, begin to expand rapidly (figure 6.1 and table 6.2).

The outbreak of World War I and the temporary closure of the Amsterdam Exchange in 1914, led to sharp acceleration of this revolution in banking. The freezing of the *prolongatie* system as a result of the closure of the Exchange, led to a sudden loss of confidence in this market. Attempts during and after World War I to revive the system failed and it finally disappeared in the 1920s. The revolution in the banking system that occurred during the 1910s meant that the large commercial banks filled this gap.

Table 6.1. *The composition of the money supply and the solvency of the banking system (the large commercial banks) in the Netherlands and other countries, 1913–1920*

	Banknotes as a percentage of money supply	Solvency: ratio of banks' own resources to public liabilities	
	1913	1913	1920
Netherlands	64	53	29
Belgium	29	24	15
Germany	37	39	4
UK	4	10	7
France	43	20	12
Denmark	14	31	15
United States	16	20	12

Source: Solvency ratios: League of Nations 1929; Money supply: Friedman and Schwartz 1982 (UK and US); Van der Wee and Tavernier 1975, pp. 432–3 (Belgium, Germany and France); Mitchell 1975; Boeschoten 1992 (Netherlands).

Without the competition of the *prolongatie* system, and with the help of the high liquidity of the war years, they were increasingly able to attract deposits. In search of profitable outlets for their booming funds, the banks experimented with the model of the universal or mixed banks, combining traditional short-term business with the long-term business of investment banking. This experiment ended with the financial crisis of the early 1920s.

Data on the level and composition of the money supply clearly illustrate the chronology of these changes (figure 6.1). Between around 1906 and 1920 bank deposits as a proportion of total money supply increased from 23 per cent to almost 56 per cent, after which this figure stabilised at around 50 per cent. Other figures show a comparable development: the combined assets of Dutch banks and giro organisations increased from 61 per cent of net national income in 1900 to 134 per cent in 1918 (see table 6.2).

There were several aspects to the banking revolution of 1906–20. Firstly, there was a significant growth in the *breadth* of the system. The number of independent banks increased spectacularly, especially during and immediately after World War I. Despite a considerable number of takeovers, the number of commercial banks increased from 242 in 1900 to 375 in 1925, after which growth slackened (*Financiële instellingen* 1987). The growth of the agricultural banks in this period was remarkable: the assets of these banks as a proportion of the total assets of all Dutch banks increased from 0.1 per cent in 1900 to 4.2 per cent in 1918 and 6.9 per cent in 1928 (table

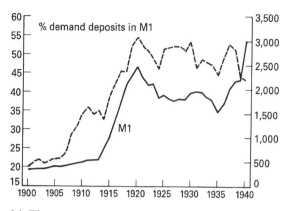

Figure 6.1 The money supply (M1; right-hand axis) and the composition of the money supply (share of bank deposits; left-hand axis), 1900–1940
Sources: Boeschoten 1992, p. 100.

6.2). In rural areas a dense network of more than 1,000 agricultural cooperative banks emerged; in the 1920s the number of account holders (around 220,000) was almost identical to the number of farms (around 230,000) (*landbouwverslag 1930*). Less spectacular was the growth of those banks specialised in providing credit to small- and medium-sized firms, but the number of Middenstandsbanken or banks for small and medium-sized enterprises nonetheless increased considerably up to 1920 (Stoffer 1986).

In addition to a broadening of the banking system, there was also a process of *concentration* and *increase in scale* among the large commercial banks (Westerman 1919; Joh. de Vries 1989, pp. 203–8) The assets of the big five (the Amsterdamsche Bank, the Incassobank, the Nederlandsche Handel-Maatschappij, the Rotterdamsche Bank, and the Twentsche Bank) as a proportion of total bank assets increased from 17.4 per cent in 1900 to 26.6 per cent in 1918 (table 6.2). The process of concentration occurred particularly after 1911. It began with the then startling merger between two large banks, the Rotterdamsche Bank and the Deposito- en Administratiebank, which together became the Rotterdamsche Bank-vereeniging (Robaver). From then on the number of takeovers of smaller banks quickly increased; between 1901 and 1910 only three banks disappeared on account of takeovers, for the period 1916 to 1925 the corresponding figure was 106 (*Financiële instellingen* 1987). A further important aspect of the expansion of the banking system was the extension of the activities of the large commercial banks outside the traditional centres of Amsterdam and, to a lesser degree, Rotterdam, as a result of the banks opening branches in other areas, or alternatively, taking over local banks. A

Table 6.2. *Assets of banks and giro organisations as a percentage of total assets of the banking sector, 1900–1940*

	1900	1913	1918	1923	1928	1933	1940
The Nederlandsche Bank	25.4	15.7	22.3	17.9	13.0	17.8	24.6
Commercial banks	36.2	44.9	52.4	48.5	53.8	36.6	32.0
5 largest	17.4	22.7	26.6	23.3	22.2	18.0	17.6
colonial banks	2.6	4.6	4.7	6.2	6.0	3.3	4.2
Savings banks	8.2	6.4	3.4	4.7[d]	5.4	7.7	7.5
Rijkspostspaarbank	7.8	8.8	5.0	5.4	5.8	9.6	8.7
Agricultural banks	0.1	2.3	4.2	5.6	6.9	7.7	8.1
Mortgage banks[a]	22.3	21.9	10.9	10.7	12.5	16.2	11.1
Giro services	–	–	1.8	7.3	2.7	4.4	8.1
Total assets[b]	1,091	2,315	5,472	6,441	7,384	6,651	7,217
Idem, as a percentage of national income[c]	61	83	134	122	113	138	125

Notes:
[a] three largest mortage banks only
[b] in millions of guilders
[c] Net National Income at market prices
[d] estimate
Sources: Nederlandsche Bank 1987; CBS 1987b.

large number of independent local and regional banks were taken over by the Big Five. This probably had negative effects on the relations between these local banks, which became branch offices of one of the Big Five, and small-scale industry in the region.

The expansion of the commercial banks and the agricultural banks was achieved partly at the expense of the specialised savings banks. The Nutsspaarbanks, which had been established in the nineteenth century by sections of the Maatschappij tot Nut van 't Algemeen to help pursue their humanitarian objectives, and the Rijkspostspaarbank (RPS), established in 1880, were unable to respond to the fiercer competition, and they saw their market share halve between 1900 and 1918 (table 6.2). Unlike the commercial banks, their function as savings institutions left them unable to respond to the growing demand for new banking services, such as arranging payments for or providing credit to clients. After 1920 these traditional savings institutions succeeded in recapturing part of the market they had lost, probably helped in this by their reputation for solidarity during a period in which several commercial banks were experiencing difficulties (Buning 1957).

The tendency to concentration among the commercial banks was paralleled by greater cooperation and centralisation among the various smaller banks. As a result of pressure from the most important customer for mortgage bonds, the Rijkspostspaarbank, as early as 1907 mortgage banks were forced to cooperate more and to accept common management guidelines (De Knocke van der Meulen 1981). The many hundreds of savings banks, the number of which fluctuated at around 260 during the interwar period, began to work together to a growing extent under the auspices of the Nederlandsche Spaarbankbond, partly because of the banking crisis at the beginning of the 1920s. After establishing their central bureau in 1924, there was a greater degree of supervision of individual savings banks (Buning 1957, pp. 26–32). Cooperation between the agricultural banks dated from as early as the establishment in 1898 of the two most important banking *centrales*, which acted as a type of banker's bank for the agricultural banks, in Eindhoven and Utrecht, but it continued to develop during the interwar period. The Centrale increasingly became the policy-making centre of the agricultural credit system and its individual-member-cooperative banks were reduced to branch offices (*Landbouw en landbouwcrediet* 1948). Finally, the system of small business credit, which had grown between 1905 and 1920, was centralised in response to the major problems that emerged after 1920. A large number of *middenstandsbanken* went bankrupt in the first half of the 1920s. With the assistance of the government the Nederlandsche Middenstandsbank (NMB) was formed in the 1920s from the then rudimentary Algemene Centrale for small business financing and it subsumed the largest surviving *middenstandsbanken* (Stoffer 1986).

These developments meant that the degree to which the banking system was intertwined with the rest of the economy increased considerably between 1900 and 1920. In this period countless entrepreneurs – industrial, small business, almost all farmers – started to make regular use of banking services, and in time they became dependent on the (short-term) financing provided by the banks. The increasingly close relationship between the large commercial banks and industry can clearly be seen in the growth of the number of *commissariaten* or non-executive directorships held by the directors of the banks (table 6.3). Between 1910 and 1923 the banks' involvement in industry increased significantly. The most expansive was the Rotterdamsche Bank: the number of seats it held on company boards increased from 30 in 1910 to 127 in 1923 (Jonker 1991b, p. 121).

The background to this development was of course the need for certainty on the part of the banks. In this respect the financing of industry had requirements quite different from those related to the financing of commerce, which was normally secured on the goods involved and took the form of loans for periods of three or six months. After the transaction had been concluded the loan could be repaid. Because of the nature of industrial companies, financing industry was mostly conducted on a longer-term basis. Credit facilities on current accounts were usually automatically renewed, while the value of the form of security offered and the probability that the company could repay the loan in the future depended on the company's solvency and its degree of profitability. To be able to assess this realistically, and to be able to exercise a degree of supervision, the banks asked for the right to appoint a representative to the board. The considerable growth in the number of non-executive directorships therefore paralleled the provision of credit to industry (Jonker 1991b). Moreover, in a number of cases the large commercial banks played an active role in the establishment and expansion of major industrial companies. For instance, C.J.K. van Aalst, the president of the Nederlandsche Handel-Maatschappij, was actively involved in setting up Hoogovens, the first iron-and-steel plant in the Netherlands in 1918 (De Vries 1968).

As a result of the considerable growth in the number of banks and the number of people regularly using their services, the need for better regulation of the system of giro transfers also increased. Even before World War I plans had been drawn up to establish a Giro system or *Girodienst*. These plans led to legislative proposals for this purpose at the beginning of 1915; the Postcheque- en Girodienst subsequently began operating at the beginning of 1918 (Van den Berge 1939). The growth in the number of giro transactions was so spectacular – the proportion of the banking system's total assets accounted for by giro services increased extremely rapidly after 1918 to 7.3 per cent in 1923 (table 6.2) – that, partly on account of the strong decentralised nature of the organisation, the system's administration collapsed into chaos and in 1923 the Giro had to suspend operations for a year (Joh. de Vries 1989, pp. 263–4). After this debâcle, the Giro was slow to win back the trust of its clients.

In trying to analyse the causes of the revolution in the banking system, one first has to look to the more rapid pace of economic development in The Netherlands after about 1890. According to J.A. de Jonge, these years saw the emergence of large-scale industrial enterprises (De Jonge 1968). Westerman accounted for the process of concentration and increase in scale in the banking system after 1910 mainly in terms of the same tendency in industry (Westerman 1919; Verrijn Stuart 1935, p. 192). More rapid economic development led to an extremely swift growth in the demand for credit and business capital. The banking system was involved in industrial bond issues, offering credit in anticipation of the sale of the bonds, and was, in general, no longer averse to providing short-term credit to industry. As a result of the rise of the large-scale enterprise, industrial firms could increasingly be regarded as reliable partners. In a certain sense the banking system was the last sector of the economy to be rapidly modernised, particularly given the fact that the expansion of the large commercial banks only dates from around 1906. The tendency to concentration after 1911 has to be seen against the background of the strong growth in lending to industry. In order to minimise the considerable risks attached to this the commercial banks had to be large enough or, as in the case of the establishment of Hoogovens, prepared to cooperate in order to raise the necessary finance. On the other hand, concentration after 1911 can also be seen as a defensive reaction to the fact that the growth in the number of banks led to a decline in the market share of the large commercial banks. In order to retain their position as market leaders, they were forced either to take over other banks or develop new activities, or both.

The rise of the agricultural cooperative banks must also be seen against the background of the modernising of agriculture in the years after around 1890. Those traditionally offering financial services in rural areas, the notaries and the RPS, were in general unable to meet the demand for the financial services that emerged in these areas (Jonker 1988).

The growth in the development of the banking system after 1914 can be attributed to a number of factors. With the closing of the Amsterdam stock exchange in August 1914 the flourishing call money market came to an end. Prior to 1914 companies, organisations and private investors had invested temporary surplus liquidity in this market and financed temporary shortages of liquidity by using shares as collateral. A substantial proportion of the market for short-term credit thereby circumvented the banking system because lenders and borrowers could deal with each other directly through the call money market, which had an estimated size of about 325 million guilders (Joh. de Vries 1989, pp. 61–3). As a result of closing the stock exchange on the outbreak of war, a measure taken to avoid prices falling so heavily that the money market would collapse, this short cut was no longer available. The explosive growth in the level of deposits with the commercial banks after 1914 has therefore partly to be explained in terms of the suspension of this market; in a certain sense it marked the elimination of one of the banks' competition, and henceforth creditors and debtors increasingly drew on the services of commercial banks.

Another competitor to the Dutch banks, namely the London banking system, was also temporarily eliminated by the events of 1914. Assisted by the Nederlandsche Bank, after 1914 the largest Dutch banks were increasingly involved in financing international trade, and in particular Dutch imports (Joh. de Vries 1989, pp. 86–7). The growth of this acceptance business also continued after 1918, though in the course of the 1920s London succeeded in winning back much of the ground it had previously lost.

Acceptance business remained an important source of income for the large commercial banks (Joh. de Vries 1989, pp. 213–21).

Besides, high war-time inflation led to large profits for certain groups of producers, for farmers, for example, who then deposited these profits with the agricultural cooperative banks. But it also increased the demand for credit from other groups of entrepreneurs. In 1918–20 above all, when the Dutch economy experienced a post-war boom, the demand for credit took extreme forms: credit was necessary not only to replenish stocks, which had been exhausted during the war, but also for large-scale investment projects. Moreover, the shortage in the capital market was exacerbated by the government's substantial budget deficits (see 6.2).

The 1920 crisis and the depression of 1921–3 put an end to this phase of rapid development. The background and particularly the conclusion to the financial crisis is considered in more detail in section 6.3.2. It should be noted here, however, that it was particularly those banks that had considerably expanded their activities during the boom years prior to 1920 and which had become important in the modernisation of the banking system that were affected most by the financial crisis. The Robaver is the best known example here. A number of new banks, in particular the *middenstandsbanken*, also faced considerable difficulties. The agricultural banks weathered the problems with signal success though.

Despite the serious problems experienced by a number of banks, public trust in the banking system was not fundamentally damaged by the 1921–3 financial crisis. There was no massive run on the banks. There was, however, a change in the relationship between the components of the money supply, which can sometimes give a rough indication of the degree of public trust in the banking system (Friedman and Schwartz 1963). After a considerable rise up to 1920 in the proportion of the money supply accounted for by bank deposits, this proportion declined significantly until 1924 (figure 6.1).

This decline could have been related to the deflation of these years though. The financial strength of the large commercial banks also showed that in general there was little reason for panic (table 6.1), certainly if one compares what happened with the experience of other neutral countries which had boomed during the World War I (Norway, Sweden and Denmark) (Jonker and Van Zanden 1996). Further, the financial crisis remained largely restricted to the financial sector; the productive economy experienced continuous growth between 1920 and 1923 (Van Zanden and Griffiths 1989, p. 111).

After the considerable shock of the 1921–3 crisis, banks wanted a return to the situation that prevailed prior to 1914, and to stop providing credit to industry. This position could be seen most clearly in the considerable decline in the number of seats the banks held on the boards of industrial and

Table 6.3. *Numbers of bankers' non-executive directorships, 1910–1940*

	1910	1923	1931	1940
By bank				
Amsterdamsche Bank	23	36	34	34
Rotterdamsche Bank	30	127	27	74
Twentsche Bank	31	46	22	34
Nederlandsche Handel-Maatschappij	31	55	27	52
Incassobank	5	18	7	12
Hope & Co.	25	32	15	27
Van Eeghen & Co.	28	61	17	38
R. Mees & Zn.	27	56	18	46
By sector				
Finance	67	132	55	141
Insurance	9	14	7	13
Trading	11	62	12	29
Transport	37	44	25	29
Manufacturing industry	34	107	42	63
Colonial plantations & trading	30	31	20	23
Various	12	41	6	19
Total	200	431	142	317

Source: Jonker 1991b.

commercial companies (table 6.3). This undoubtedly reflected a decline in the willingness of the banks to offer credit to business (Jonker 1991b, pp. 125–6). At the same time, after the boom of 1918–20 had given way to more gradual growth in the period 1921–9, industry's credit requirements were similarly less in the 1920s, all the more so because businesses remained extremely profitable. This is evident from, among other things, the fact that up to 1929 the level of industrial bond issues remained far below the corresponding level of 1919–20 (De Roos and Wieringa 1953, pp. 121, 149).

The other elements of the pre-1920 banking revolution survived intact. Indeed, the tendency to concentration, in which a large number of smaller banks were taken over by the large commercial banks, continued during the 1920s. In total, the relationship between the banks' assets and national income hardly changed at all during this period (table 6.2).

After a considerable increase in employment in the banking sector between 1909 and 1920, which saw the proportion of the total labour force occupied in banking increase from 0.4 per cent to 1.1 per cent, employment declined between 1920 and 1930 from almost 30,000 to 28,000, or 0.9 per cent of the total labour force (Joh de Vries 1989, pp. 204–5). A study conducted by the League of Nations into the development of the banking system in the period 1913–29 concluded that this sector had grown most in The Netherlands, where the activities of the banking system had increased threefold in real terms in this period. The report attributed this rapid development to The Netherlands' catching up the ground it had lost before 1913 following the late rise of universal banking there (League of Nations 1929).

However, the banks lost ground in one major field, the export of capital. In the nineteenth century capital exports consisted mainly of the buying of foreign bonds and shares, in which the big banks played a large role as intermediators. After World War I this kind of capital export stagnated and foreign direct investments by the large Dutch industrial firms such as Royal Dutch Shell, Philips, Unilever, AKU came to replace it. According to the latest estimates the share of direct investments in the accumulated foreign investment rose from about 20 per cent in 1900 to 56 per cent in 1938 (Gales and Sluyterman 1993, p. 65).

Partly on account of the cautious policy followed by the banks during the 1920s, the banking system survived the depression of the 1930s intact. Only the Nederlandsche Handel-Maatschappij had to be reorganised in 1934, as a result of which its working capital, which had been significantly diminished after considerable losses in Netherlands East Indies, was reduced by 75 per cent. The continued high level of liquidity enabled the rest to weather the storms. The consequences of the events of 1931, which first led to the freezing of substantial German assets and consequently to the decline in the value of the equally substantial sterling assets, were averted by the decision to close the market for a day, 21 September, soon after sterling went off gold. As a result of liquidating foreign assets and of the inflow of flight capital to the stable Netherlands, the gold reserve of the Nederlandsche Bank and the liquidity of the banking system increased considerably in this period, and the banking system was thus able to cope with the ups and downs in public confidence. Moreover, within The Netherlands the demand for credit declined significantly, except for government borrowing. The most important problem facing the banks was therefore how to invest their swollen reserves (Keesing 1947, pp. 202–4). The size of the budget deficit, which was partly financed by treasury bills, offered some solace here.

At first glance the stability of the Dutch banking system in the 1930s seems curious. In most industrial countries the economic depression was paralleled by a serious financial crisis, which, as Friedman and Schwartz have argued in the case of the United States, exacerbated the depression in the real economy (Friedman and Schwartz 1963). The financial sectors in Austria, Germany, Italy and a number of East European countries had already been severely hit by a banking crisis in 1931. Of those countries that remained on the gold standard, France, Belgium and Switzerland all faced some kind of banking crisis. The Netherlands did not. Belgium came through the financial crisis of 1931 undamaged, but public confidence in the banking system declined gradually after 1931, as a result of a number of lingering bank scandals and the considerable investments by Belgian banks in large loss-making heavy industries. The crisis in the Belgian banking system was exacerbated in 1933 and 1934 and became an important factor in the devaluation of the Belgian franc in April 1935 (Van der Wee and Tavernier 1975). But even this crisis did not lead to instability in the Dutch banking system. It was evident from this though that the great stability of the Dutch banking system, the result among other things of the conservative policy followed in the 1920s, was partly responsible for the Nederlandsche Bank's ability to stay on gold until the end of 1936.

When one examines the long-term development of the banking system, the period between 1920 and 1940 can be said to have been one of relative stagnation after the tumultuous growth prior to 1920 and the renewed expansion that was to follow World War II. The structure of the banking system changed relatively little, only the agricultural cooperative banks continued to expand, and the degree to which the banking system was interwoven with the rest of the economy declined rather than increased. The conservatism of the banking system prior to 1900 seemed to have returned, and the complaints common in the nineteenth century concerning the inaccessibility of the capital market for most businesses reemerged, particularly in the 1930s. Partly as a result of their institutional ties with the major commercial banks, ties which did not disappear completely of course, large companies had achieved almost unlimited access to the capital market. It is characteristic that in the 1920s and 1930s industrial bond issues were dominated by just four companies: AKU (Algemene Kunstzijde Unie), Unilever, Philips and Royal Dutch Shell. Between 1925 and 1929 these four companies accounted for 74 per cent of all industrial bond issues (De Roos and Wieringa 1953, p. 149). Medium and small companies had no access to this market, however, and after 1920 they realised that the willingness of the commercial banks to provide credit to industry had disappeared almost completely. Moreover, the process of concentration within the banking system led to many local banks, which had hitherto provided credit to local industry, being absorbed by the large commercial banks and having to adopt the conservative policy of these banks. As a result, complaints about the gap between medium and small companies and the banking system became much louder in the 1920s and 1930s than they had ever been in the nineteenth century. Discussion about the problem of obtaining finance for small- and medium-sized companies resulted in various plans to establish a special bank for industry designed to bridge this gap. Because these large commercial banks and the Nederlandsche Bank failed to commit themselves to this idea and because until well into the 1930s central government saw no role for itself in providing a solution to this problem, nothing resulted apart from the plans (De Hen 1980). The continuation of the depression led to a modest change in government policy and saw the establishment of the Mavif (Maatschappij voor Industriefinanciering) in 1935 on the initiative of the Minister for Economic Affairs, Gelissen. However, as the result of a combination of factors, such as a limited budget, an extremely cautious policy, and, in order to avoid unfair competition, the imposition of stringent criteria to be met before credit could be provided, the Mavif played almost no role in financing the modest revival of the economy after 1936 (De Hen 1980). The lacunae in the structure of the banking system remained.

6.2 Government finances: the golden rule of accumulation in practice

The development of public finance in the period 1914–40 shows a paradox. All political parties accepted as the point of departure of budgetary policy the so called *gulden financieringsregel* or golden rule of accumulation, the principle that the government may only borrow to finance productive investment and that the current budget should be balanced. But in practice the rule was continuously evaded and undermined, and in fact all attempts to monitor actual public expenditure in the 1930s became impossible. Given the renewed attention this principle of budgetary policy has attracted in the past few years, we shall discuss the background to this paradox in more detail.

In introducing the 1907 budget the Minister for Finance, De Meester, made a clear distinction between the current budget, which was required to balance, and the capital budget, to which only expenditure could be charged that resulted in a direct increase in public revenue and that could therefore be financed by loans (Stevers 1976, pp. 119–22). Other extraordinary expenditure items, for defence construction or large-scale road, dike, and canal construction projects, were not considered capital budget items. This rigid principle, established in 1907 and adopted by successive finance ministers, could not be reconciled with the political necessity to increase certain expenditures in times of war (1914–18) or depression (1929–35). Because it was considered undesirable to jettison the *gulden financieringsregel*, since balancing the current budget was considered particularly sacrosanct, it was systematically undermined instead. Current expenditure was transferred to the capital budget and direct profitability as a criterion for capital expenditure was abandoned. In addition, special funds were created to reduce current budget expenditure. Because parliamentary debates concentrated almost exclusively on the current budget and on whether the current budget was in balance, it was possible for the government to maintain the fiction of a balanced budget and to claim that it remained committed to the *gulden financieringsregel* (Stevers 1976, pp. 119–47). The process of undermining this principle began almost immediately after 1907: as early as 1908, scarcely a year after De Meester had formulated the *gulden financieringsregel*, a separate fund was established for the rapid construction of fortifications around Amsterdam.

In general, two cycles can be distinguished: during World War I public expenditure increased significantly as a result of mobilisation and food provision. Social and political pressures in 1917–20 led to considerable expenditure on housing, social security, etc. too (Van Zanden and Griffiths 1989, p. 4). Most of this expenditure was charged to a separate crisis fund, which showed a substantial deficit. This crisis fund was financed by special wartime taxes on profits, but these were insufficient to balance the budget. The considerable size of the public budget deficits in 1918–22 led to serious financial problems. In 1923 and 1924 public finances were reorganised by De Geer and Colijn. In 1926 the cycle was completed, when Colijn returned to the principle adopted by De Meester (Stevers 1976, p. 124).

Between 1926 and 1929 the principle was adhered to reasonably consistently in practice but after 1929 the tide turned again. On the one hand, public income declined as a result of the depression, while on the other hand at the same time political pressure from various sides led to new expenditure to limit the consequences of the depression. The agricultural crisis policy is the best known, and was the most expensive example (Van Zanden and Griffiths 1989, p. 64). Various measures were taken to avoid a deficit on the current budget. In 1930 and 1931, for instance, recourse could still be made to the accounting surplus on the Leningfonds 1914. Subsequently, other funds were created alongside the current budget in order to accommodate certain crisis expenditures, for example the employment fund and the agricultural crisis fund, partly financed by increases in consumer prices. Finally, many items were transferred from the current budget to the capital budget, and in due course the other way, too. Since the 1927 Comptabiliteitswet had introduced the distinction between capital budget and current budget, transfers between these two items had not been consistently reported in the published budgets since 1929. Consequently, these transfers largely escaped the scrutiny of parliament, which only debated the current budget (Van Zanden and Griffiths 1989, pp. 145–8; Stevers 1976, pp. 132–9). As a result of these developments, the budget became extremely obscure. Even after the depths of the recession had been reached and public revenues began to recover, attempts after 1936 to construct an overview of the budget in order to estimate the actual size of the deficit were well nigh impossible. Even the experts, including the most senior civil servants at the Ministry of Finance, were more or less unable to distinguish between the reality and the appearance of public finance (Stevers 1976, p. 132).

In practice the budget discipline imposed by the *gulden financieringsregel* was thus abandoned in the 1930s, but, in order to keep the myth of a balanced current budget alive, an enormously complex public accounting system was created, one that could be reorganised only with considerable difficulty. After 1936 a few attempts were made to restore order, but this aim had to be abandoned soon after because of renewed political pressure to increase expenditure considerably, this time for defence and war preparations. Even then, when the De Geer administration came to power in 1939 with expenditure plans that were simply impossible to finance with the resources then available, balancing the current budget remained the unquestioned point of departure in budgetary policy.

It is apparent then that the *gulden financieringsregel* was soon continuously evaded and undermined. The reason is that in the budget negotiations such a principle proved weaker than the hard political necessity to make certain expenditures, or not to cut existing expenditures, or at least only modestly. This necessity was sometimes the result of circumstances beyond their control, for example the cost of mobilising troops during World War I, but mostly these expenditures were important in preserving the power and legitimacy of the state. The resulting conflict between theory and practice continued to be solved by camouflaging what happened in practice, and the myth of the balanced budget was thereby preserved. Because the measures taken to camouflage what happened in practice were particularly ingenious, it was in fact possible to avoid all forms of budgetary discipline, especially after 1929 when the budget reports presented to parliament left much to be desired. Paradoxically, the general acceptance of the need for stringent budgetary control thus led to a lack of real supervision and a lack of insight into the real development of public expenditure and revenue.

The extensive government deficits in the period 1914–22 were partly financed by issuing government bonds and partly by an extremely rapid growth in the level of short-term, i.e., unfunded, debt, especially in the form of treasury bills (table 6.4). Until 1919 treasury bills, a new phenomenon, could easily be placed because, on account of the increased supply of deposits and the low demand for credit by industry, the banking system had extensive reserves. The post-war boom of 1918–20 put an end to this situation and led to increasing problems in financing the budget deficit, as a result of which interest rates rose to a record high of almost 7 per cent (Keesing 1947, pp. 54–64). The public debate about the Nederlandsche

Table 6.4. *Budget deficit and the change in the level of short-term and long-term debt, 1914–24 (millions of guilders)*

	Deficit	Short-term debt	Treasury bills with private banks	Long-term debt
1914	114	174	68	1140
1915	241	168	97	1406
1916	223	251	185	1508
1917	145	335	257	1609
1918	490	614	350	1851
1919	116	643	474	2183
1920	110	514	382	2557
1921	281	859	688	2490
1922	422	838	635	2728
1923	112	666	472	2780
1924	58	360	357	2916

Source: Keesing 1947.

Bank's base-rate policy and the depreciation of the guilder against the dollar in 1920 has to be seen against this background: because the capital market was under pressure, the government could not consolidate its short-term debt. Each increase in the level of the base rate would have led to a further increase in the level of interest payments borne by the government and to an intensification of the problems it faced (Joh. de Vries 1989, pp. 231–3).

The economic crisis of 1920 reduced pressure on the capital market considerably as domestic demand for credit suddenly ceased, but at the same time the government's budget deficits increased again after 1920 because of a decline in revenues (table 6.4), leading to a further rise in the level of short-term debt. Several banks began to experience severe problems too at that time, in short, a serious financial crisis was brewing.

In 1922 De Geer began to reorganise public finances. The government took out a series of loans at the extremely high rate of 6 per cent. Typically, these loans were partly raised in New York. Under normal conditions The Netherlands was a capital exporting country with a traditional preference for investing in the United States (Keesing 1947, p. 60). In the course of 1922 and 1923 confidence in the finances of the Dutch government was restored, partly as a result of the relatively severe expenditure cuts made by De Geer and Colijn. The budget deficit was sharply reduced and after 1924 there was even a surplus. From 1923 onwards the level of short-term debt was gradually consolidated (table 6.4), and the surpluses recorded after 1924 were used to repay the public debt more rapidly and to reduce several taxes (Van Zanden and Griffiths 1989, p. 124).

Financing the budget deficits was less problematic in the 1930s than in 1914–22, partly perhaps because the deficits were in general lower. On average the size of the budget deficit in 1914–22 was 4.8 per cent of GDP, reaching a peak in 1918 of 11.3 per cent, compared with 2.8 per cent in 1931–5, with the peak being 5.4 per cent in 1933 (CBS 1987a, p. 88). The fact that the government could profit from the continuing savings surplus of the private sector in the 1930s was of decisive importance though; the period 1918–20 had been characterised by significant savings shortages. After 1930 domestic investment was very low, while the collapse of the international monetary system made investment abroad, the traditional outlet for Dutch savings surpluses, unattractive. Investing in government bonds was really the only remaining option available. Raising government loans in a period of deflation and falling interest rates therefore presented almost no problem. Only in 1931, when the government was quickly faced with a significant fall in revenues, did the level of short-term debt increase, but by 1932 this short-term debt had been converted into long-term borrowing. As a result of accumulated deficits the national debt increased from 2.4 billion guilders at the end of 1930 to 3.7 billion at the end of 1937. By converting debts incurred in the 1920s, the cost of interest payments increased significantly less rapidly though (Keesing 1947, pp. 194–202).

Changes in the structure of public finances were not restricted to the erosion of the *gulden financieringsregel*, however. At least as radical were the changes in the composition of public expenditure. In general, until 1914 public expenditure still reflected the characteristics of the classical laissez-faire state. The primary functions of government, such as administration, justice, defence, managing the national debt, accounted for almost three-quarters of the budget, and expenditure for economic and social purposes was modest (Van Zanden and Griffiths 1989, p. 63). As a result government expenditure as a share of Net National Income was at a historical low point; between 1900 and 1913 this figure fluctuated at about 10 per cent (figure 6.2).

During World War I this changed. In 1918 government expenditure amounted to almost 30 per cent of National Income, and, because income increased much more slowly, the deficit was more than 14 per cent of National Income. With the decline of defence spending after 1918, political pressures led to considerable increases in expenditure on social functions, including housing and education. The proportion of total public expenditure for social purposes increased from 3 per cent in 1913 to 21 per cent in 1921 (Van Zanden and Griffiths 1989, p. 64). Although the cuts made in 1922–5 hit these new expenditure items most of all, compared with the

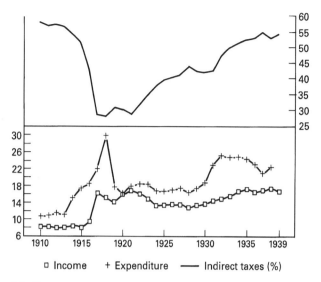

Figure 6.2 Government expenditure as a share of Net National Income and the share of indirect taxes in total taxation, 1910–1939 (in per cent)
Sources: Boeschoten 1992, p. 98 and CBS 1969.

period before 1914 they continued to be of considerable importance. As a result, in accordance with the theoretical expectations formulated by Peacock and Wiseman, public expenditure did not return to its pre-World War I level but fluctuated at about 17 per cent of National Income in the 1920s (Peacock and Wiseman 1967).

The structure of taxation shows the same changes: the share of indirect taxes declined radically as a result of the introduction of direct war taxes and the increases in the direct taxes on income and wealth (figure 6.2). But the financial reforms of De Geer and Colijn after 1921 shifted the tax burden again to the lower income classes by increasing the share of indirect taxes (Fritschy 1994b).

Consequently, during the 1930s depression government expenditure on agriculture increased enormously, rising to about 20 per cent of total public expenditure in the period 1934–7. As a result public expenditure as a share of National Income again went up to about 25 per cent in the depth of the depression, declining to about 22 per cent between 1937 and 1939 (figure 6.2). Because these expenditures were financed by indirect taxes, the share of these in total taxation continued to rise in the 1930s. Further, measures aimed at protecting and stimulating industry and the more rapid build up of a modern infrastructure were adopted in this period. In effect, the 1930s marked the end of the old tradition of free trade and a minimal role for the government in the (inter)national economy. As a result of these developments, the proportion of total public expenditure devoted to the primary functions of government was halved; the nineteenth-century laissez-faire state was now definitively a thing of the past.

6.3 Monetary policy and the development of the Central Bank

6.3.1 The period 1914–1920

The ten years after the outbreak of World War I were perhaps the most hectic in the history of the Nederlandsche Bank. Until the middle of 1914 the bank was a relatively lethargic institution and played only a very modest role in the Dutch banking system. It involved itself little with public finance. This changed radically after July 1914. As a result of several related developments, the Nederlandsche Bank soon took up a pivotal position in the evolution of the banking system, the provision of credit to international commerce, and in public finance, a development culminating in the measures taken by the Nederlandsche Bank during the banking crisis of 1921–4. From 1925 onwards there was a return to normality, the influence of the Nederlandsche Bank declined visibly, and once again its role was largely restricted to monitoring the gold standard (Joh. de Vries 1989).

With the outbreak of war on 28 July 1914 it was decided to close the Dutch stock exchange; share prices had fallen considerably during the previous few days and it was feared the stock market would crash. This did little to quell unease, however. There was a run on a few offices of the Nederlandsche Bank as the public tried to exchange banknotes for specie. In order to guarantee the liquidity of the banking system and to avert the problems caused by the freezing of the *prolongatie* system after the stock exchange was closed, the Nederlandsche Bank agreed to permit the commercial banks to set up a syndicate to provide support. The high demand for silver coins compelled the Nederlandsche Bank to create a new, temporary, means of payment, the *zilverbon* or silver certificate, in theory a promissory note backed by silver yet to be issued, in practice a type of banknote. Finally, because of the rapid growth in the amount of banknotes in circulation the percentage of the money supply that the law required to be backed by gold was reduced from 40 per cent to 20 per cent and gold exports were prohibited; in effect, The Netherlands left the gold standard (Joh. de Vries 1989, pp. 61–70).

As a result of intensive cooperation with the large commercial banks and the cabinet, the Nederlandsche Bank was able to contain the financial crisis of July–August 1914. The problem of an extremely tight money market at the end of 1914 disappeared during 1915. Large balance-of-payments surpluses led to a significant increase in the level of the Nederlandsche Bank's gold reserve in the period 1915–17. The expansion of the money market following the influx of gold was further stimulated by the gradual increase in the budget deficit, which was financed largely by issuing treasury bills. During the financial crisis the Nederlandsche Bank's base rate was raised to 6 per cent from 1 August 1914. As early as 14 August 1914 the Nederlandsche Bank was able to reduce the rate to 5 per cent, and in July 1915 to 4.5 per cent. In February 1915 the stock exchange was reopened. As a result of the increasing expansion of the money market, the interest rate charged to individual customers fell, even to a level below the rate charged to banks by the Nederlandsche Bank (De Roos and Wieringa 1953, pp. 131–3).

This left the Nederlandsche Bank free to return to its ordinary routine. The bank was deeply involved in attempts to direct the war economy, and particularly to organise Dutch imports and exports. The Nederlandsche Bank was thereby very much involved in the provision of credit abroad. Partly because of the collapse of the London money market, which had dominated the financing of international commerce, the acceptance business of the large commercial banks grew extremely rapidly during and shortly after the war, a development encouraged by the Nederlandsche Bank. The expansion of Amsterdam as the centre for credit for international trade also continued in the 1920s, when German companies in particular set up offices there in order to take advantage of the low interest rates on the Dutch money market (Joh. de Vries 1989, pp. 213–20).

During the post-war boom, from the middle of 1918 to the end of 1920, the pressure on the money and capital markets increased considerably as a result of balance-of-payments deficits in The Netherlands, the budget deficits of central government and the high demand for credit from companies. Whereas the Nederlandsche Bank had played an active role during the financial crisis of 1914, the bank now took a relatively passive role, despite the fact that the boom was accompanied by an extremely sharp rise in the level of prices and that, in 1920, the value of the guilder decreased against the dollar, and the pre-war parity, by around 30 per cent. The bank rate remained unchanged throughout the whole period July 1915–July 1922. In 1920, amid fierce criticism, the bank was pressed to increase the lombard rate to slow down the rate of economic expansion, but this only led to a rise in the rate of interest charged on secured loans. It is doubtful anyway whether a rise in the bank rate would have been effective in slowing down economic growth, given the considerable expansion of the money market, which above all was the result of the considerable level of short-term public debt (Joh. de Vries 1989, pp. 320–8). The Nederlandsche Bank was more or less powerless in the face of the problems posed by the considerable size of the budget deficits, and in any case prior to 1922 it was unable to put sufficient pressure on the cabinet to limit the deficits. Furthermore, the Nederlandsche Bank did nothing to limit the expansion of the banking system either. The president of the Nederlandsche Bank, Vissering, seemed more preoccupied with international negotiations concerning the post-war monetary system, but this can hardly have been the reason for his remarkably passive policy during these years.

6.3.2 The banking crisis of 1921–1924

In the first half of the 1920s a large number of banks, including a few large commercial banks, experienced serious problems. Scores of mostly local banks went bankrupt or were taken over by larger banks, and the collapse of the extremely large Rotterdamsche Bankvereeniging (Robaver) could only be avoided by the intervention of the Nederlandsche Bank. As such, this period was unique in Dutch banking history. It is perhaps the only classic banking crisis experienced in The Netherlands in the entire period 1600–1990. For this reason alone the crisis of 1921–4 deserves special consideration, but the events of 1921–4 were also a turning point in the development of the Dutch banking system as a whole.

The origins of the banking crisis undoubtedly have to be sought in the inflationary boom of the period 1914–20. As outlined above, the banking system provided large-scale credit to industry in these years, resulting in ever closer relationships between industry and the banking system. The Robaver set a pattern in these developments. Not only did the establishment of the Robaver in 1911 mark the beginning of a period of concentration in the banking system, from then on the Robaver followed an extreme expansionary policy aimed at increasing its interests in trade and industry. By 1923 the directors of the Robaver had by far the most positions on the boards of industrial and commercial companies (Jonker 1991b, p. 121).

Despite having achieved a strong position in the Dutch money market since the outbreak of World War I, the Nederlandsche Bank made no attempts to regulate the rapid expansion of the banking system in this period. Rumours concerning, among other things, incompetent management and concealed losses at the Rotterdam bank Marx & Co. were ignored, and no move was taken to restrict the provision of credit to this bank, since the Nederlandsche Bank still did not consider it one of its functions to supervise the banking system (Jonker 1996a). After the economy peaked in 1920, the Nederlandsche Bank was quickly confronted with the consequences of its failure to do so. In 1921 problems were restricted to runs on a few small banks, but in 1922, fearing a major run on the banking system, the Nederlandsche Bank was forced to offer help to two medium-sized banks: the Bank-Associatie, which was reorganised, and the Rotterdam bank Marx & Co., which was wound up. The Nederlandsche Bank had insufficient reserves to meet the huge losses associated particularly with winding up Marx & Co. It thereby paid for the fact that it had not increased its capital reserves in the favourable years prior to 1921 and had distributed almost all the profits earned in that period. The losses resulting from the liquidation of Marx & Co. amounted to almost 27 million guilders, at a time when the Nederlandsche Bank's total equity was 28 million (Joh. de Vries 1989, pp. 227–66; Jonker 1996a). When a few local banks went bankrupt, the involvement of the Nederlandsche Bank also mounted to several million guilders.

It is clear that when, in 1924, the even larger Robaver began to experience difficulties and immediately asked for a loan of 41 million guilders, the Nederlandsche Bank would have to appeal to the government for assistance. As soon as the Nederlandsche Bank had guaranteed the liquidity of the Robaver, the Minister for Finance, Colijn, was prepared to offer a government guarantee of 50 million guilders, an amount that was increased to 60 million guilders the same day to help form a syndicate to support the share price of the Robaver. The Robaver was subsequently reorganised, without resulting in losses for the Nederlandsche Bank and the state. This procedure was so successful that when the Centrale of *middenstandsbanken* had to be reorganised in 1925 the Nederlandsche Bank again asked for, and got, a similarly secret credit guarantee of 10 million guilders from the government (Joh. de Vries 1989, pp. 259–62; Stoffer 1986).

Although in several aspects the performance of the Nederlandsche Bank was decidedly lacklustre, its policy during the banking crisis was generally successful. Because assistance was usually offered in time, though there were sometimes long delays before assistance was approved, and because the fact that the Nederlandsche Bank was prepared to offer assistance was made public, the Nederlandsche Bank avoided a situation in which the problems faced by a few banks caused a general run on the banking system, leading to a large-scale withdrawal of deposits. The proportion of bank deposits in the total money supply (M1) clearly decreased during the crisis (figure 6.1); but it later stabilised at around 50 per cent. Studies show that where a banking crisis leads to a sudden decrease in the money supply, it can have severe consequences for the real economy (Friedman and Schwartz 1963; Bernanke and James 1991). Because the banking crisis in The Netherlands was relatively mild, the real economy successfully recovered from the post-war depression, and in 1922 and 1923 it even grew significantly. Of the Big Five only one, the Robaver, experienced significant problems. The other banks had operated a more conservative policy and were well able to withstand the deflationary shock of 1920–3.

One can be more critical about the policy of the Nederlandsche Bank prior to the banking crisis. The bank preferred to avoid the consequences of the rapid growth of certain banks during and shortly after the war, and insufficient reserves were built up in favourable years to cope with the problems of 1921–5. Political discussions concerning the role of the Nederlandsche Bank in regulating the banking system flared up only during and shortly after the crisis, but even then it did not lead to a clear formulation of the tasks of the Nederlandsche Bank in relation to the banking system. In an internal memorandum it was even denied that the Nederlandsche Bank should have such a regulatory function (Joh. de Vries 1989, pp. 256–8). The role of the bankers' bank should, the memorandum argued, be restricted to assisting large banks that were experiencing liquidity problems. And after 1925 the Nederlandsche Bank returned to this policy of limited intervention.

6.3.3 Bank-rate policy and the rules of the game, 1925–1936

In the extensive literature on monetary developments during the interwar period, the discussion on the return to and the eventual decline of the gold standard is of considerable importance. The failure of the gold standard to function adequately is partly attributed to the fact that the monetary authorities followed internal political considerations rather than the rules of the game when it suited them. In particular, criticism was voiced against the sterilisation of gold inflows – for example, the large growth of the French gold reserves between 1928 and 1932 was largely sterilised – and against the inconsistent use of the bank rate to defend the gold standard. An example of the latter is that in September 1931 the Bank of England raised the bank rate by too little to prevent speculation against sterling, as a result of which Great Britain was forced to leave the gold standard. Domestic political considerations, i.e., an increase in interest rates would have exacerbated the depression, played an important role in this (Eichengreen 1990).

Another focus of criticism by economists and historians concerns the introduction of the gold exchange standard in the 1920s. In order to counteract the supposed shortage of international liquidity and to shore up the position of sterling, the international financial conference held in Genoa in 1922 recommended that central banks hold part of their reserves in foreign currencies, in particular in sterling. An additional money multiplier was thus introduced, and over time this increased monetary instability. When sterling came under intense pressure in 1931 and fell off gold in September of that year, the central banks converted their sterling reserves into gold, precipitating a sharp reduction in the level of international liquidity. The introduction of the gold exchange standard was seen as an important departure from the rules of the classic gold standard as it operated prior to 1914 (cf. the discussion in Eichengreen 1990).

In what follows, we discuss to what degree the Nederlandsche Bank stuck to the rules of the game above between April 1925, when The Netherlands rejoined the gold standard, and September 1936, when The Netherlands left the gold standard. To begin with the issue of the gold exchange standard, the Nederlandsche Bank was in a somewhat ambivalent position *vis-à-vis* this system. Under the terms of the 1888 Bankwet the Nederlandsche Bank was permitted to use part of its assets to hold and trade foreign currencies, a power it immediately began to use on a large scale (De Jong 1967a III, pp. 321 ff.). One motive for this was profitability. Strictly speaking, the Nederlandsche Bank was a private enterprise which aimed to make a profit. To a not insignificant extent the earnings of its directors and board members were also dependent on the level of profits made. By investing part of the reserves in sterling, for example bills on London, profits could be made from this part of the reserves. The profit motive was also of considerable bearing in the 1920s. In the second half of the 1920s the international activities of the Nederlandsche Bank were by far the most important source of income for the Bank (Joh. de Vries 1989, pp. 361–3, 392).The Nederlandsche Bank's normal activities on the domestic money market declined after 1923 when, once again, the Bank began to play only a marginal role in the money market. In a certain sense then the fact that the Nederlandsche Bank accepted the gold exchange standard and held a proportion of its reserves in foreign currencies was motivated by its desire to make handsome profits and can be seen as a continuation of the policy operated prior to 1914.

In cooperation with Great Britain, in 1924 and the beginning of 1925 steps were taken to return to the gold standard. A large portfolio of foreign currencies was built up, and the gold reserve was reduced for the purpose, from 582 million guilders at the start of 1924 to 504 million by March 1925. Nurkse claimed that the Nederlandsche Bank was virtually the only central bank to actually convert part of its gold reserve to a foreign exchange reserve by exporting gold to the United States and Great Britain (Nurkse 1944). The Nederlandsche Bank regarded the foreign exchange reserve as a buffer which could be used to limit fluctuations in the reserves, while the gold reserve was held at a virtually stable level of around 50 per cent of the amount of banknotes in circulation (see figure 6.3).

The law was not modified to take account of the introduction of the gold exchange standard though. Legally, until the beginning of 1929, the gold reserve had to be sufficient to back at least 20 per cent of the money supply, after which this figure was increased to 40 per cent, the percentage required

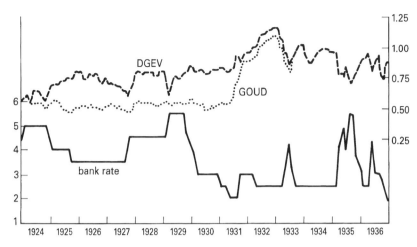

Figure 6.3 The Nederlandsche Bank's bank rate (left-hand axis), and the gold reserve (GOUD) and the gold and foreign exchange reserves (GDEV) as a share of banknotes in circulation (right-hand axis): monthly averages, January 1924 to December 1936
Sources: CBS 1924–36.

before 1914. De facto the Nederlandsche Bank employed a figure of at least 40 per cent in the 1920s too. Until the end of 1931 the reserves had three components:

the gold backing required by law: 20 per cent up to 1928, 40 per cent from 1929;
the additional gold backing that the Nederlandsche Bank wanted to provide: around 30 per cent (up to 1928) and around 10 per cent from 1929, as a result of which the de facto gold backing remained at around 50 per cent (see figure 6.3);
the foreign exchange reserve, used to compensate for shifts in the reserves (De Roos and Wieringa 1953, p. 155).

On account of this interpretation of the gold exchange standard, in practice until the second half of 1931 there was a more or less constant link between the gold reserve and the amount of banknotes in circulation, the ideal of the classic gold standard. Bank rate policy was used to neutralise fluctuations in the foreign exchange reserve and to prevent a reduction in gold cover to below 50 per cent. Moreover, in 1924 and 1925 the bank rate was reduced to help support the ailing pound in order to accelerate and promote a return to the gold standard (Joh. de Vries 1989, p. 361–3). Increases in the bank rate in October 1927 and March 1929 were principally aimed at stemming the fall in the foreign exchange reserve, the result of a rise in interest rates elsewhere, i.e., in Germany (1927) and the United States (1929) (Keesing 1947, pp. 88–9). Figure 6.3 demonstrates that these measures had an immediate success.

After the Wall Street Crash of 1929, the monetary relaxation that followed led to a series of falls in the bank rate; partly as a result of this, the size of the gold reserve did not increase until the middle of 1931. In The Netherlands, significant growth in the size of the gold reserve began only in July 1931, when the crisis of that year was already under way, much later than in France and Belgium, where the gold reserve had begun to increase substantially as early as 1928 and continued to increase until 1932 (Eichengreen 1990). During the first few years of the depression, between the Wall Street Crash and the collapse of the Credit-Anstalt in May 1931, the effect of Dutch monetary policy was not deflationary. On the contrary, the bank rate was reduced on May 16 1931 to a record low of 2 per cent.

In the second half of 1931 this changed. In the critical period between the beginning of July and the end of September 1931, when the financial crisis had spread to Germany and Great Britain, the Nederlandsche Bank's gold reserve increased considerably (figure 6.3). During these weeks Dutch commercial banks liquidated their holdings of foreign securities on a considerable scale, as a result of which gold exports to The Netherlands from first Germany and later Great Britain were relatively large (Hurst 1932). After Germany imposed restrictions on the export of capital on 13 July 1931, thereby *de facto* leaving the gold standard, capital was repatriated from London on an enormous scale, and the Dutch banking system thus made a major contribution to undermining the position of sterling. The Nederlandsche Bank can hardly be accused of having speculated against the pound, and in fact it left the foreign exchange reserve intact until sterling's collapse (Hurst 1932; Joh. de Vries 1989, pp. 442–3). In August 1931 Vissering, the president of the Nederlandsche Bank, did try to get a written guarantee from the Bank of England concerning the gold value of the Nederlandsche Bank's sterling reserves, but, for understandable reasons, the Bank of England declined to give such a guarantee. The Nederlandsche Bank lost almost 30 million guilders on account of the fall in the value of sterling, and, to avoid endangering the functioning of the Nederlandsche Bank, much of this loss had to be covered by the government (Joh. de Vries 1989, p. 478).

On 29 September 1931, eight days after sterling went off gold, the bank rate was raised by a full percentage point. The background to this was probably that the Nederlandsche Bank wanted to demonstrate its commitment to defending the guilder, but at a time when the Nederlandsche Bank's gold reserve was increasing extremely rapidly such a move seemed contrary to the rules of the system. There was no evidence of speculation against the guilder, and the inflow of gold can only have been stimulated as a result of the Nederlandsche Bank's decision to raise interest rates.

The period September 1931 to September 1936 was principally character-ised by the defence of the gold standard. In 1933 and again in 1935 the bank rate was increased to prevent a sharp fall in the gold reserve and to counter-act speculation against the guilder. In 1933, during the dollar crisis, a short-term increase in the bank rate to 4.5 per cent was sufficient to settle the markets. In 1935 considerably more was necessary to avert a crisis after the Belgian franc was devalued. During the course of that year, the bank rate was altered no less than 15 times, a record; at one point it reached 6 per cent, a level unprecedented since 1914 (Keesing 1947, pp. 198–201). But the gold cover continued to remain extremely high, in 1935 it even reached almost 75 per cent, as a result of which in a technical sense the guilder could scarcely have been considered vulnerable. The devaluation of September 1936 was caused then by the fact that the other members of the gold bloc, France and Switzerland, devalued, which left the Dutch position untenable.

In conclusion, there is much evidence that between 1925 and 1936 the Nederlandsche Bank stuck closely to the rules of the game. The most important exception to this concerns the increase in the bank rate in September 1931 and the sterilising of gold inflows during the second half of that year. There is nothing to indicate that bank-rate policy was influenced by domestic political considerations to any great extent; retaining the gold standard continued to be the principal aim of bank-rate policy, despite growing criticism of the gold standard, particularly in 1935 and 1936.

6.3.4 The debate about the gold standard

Despite the financial crisis of the period 1921–4, the 1920s were years of rapid economic growth and relatively low unemployment in The Netherlands. After 1929, and particularly after 1931, this picture changed radically: the depression of the 1930s lasted longer in The Netherlands than in its main trading partners Great Britain and Germany. Unemployment increased up to 1936, whereas in other countries unemployment peaked in 1932–3, and only during 1936, after The Netherlands had left the gold stan-dard, did the economy begin to show serious signs of recovery (Van Zanden and Griffiths 1989, pp. 140–59). Contemporaries claimed that as early as 1933 economic development in The Netherlands and in other gold-bloc countries deviated unfavourably from economic development in those countries that had already left the gold standard by 1931, a claim disputed by those supporting retention of the gold standard (Griffiths 1987, pp. 173–8).

There was thus a political debate from the beginning of 1933 over whether The Netherlands should retain the gold standard or whether it should devalue the guilder. It was the first major debate on monetary policy in Dutch history, and it was characteristic of the tensions that emerged during the interwar period as a result of trying to balance external and internal economic priorities: whether to aim for instance at a stable currency, or whether to aim at stability in the labour market and in levels of production. In the middle of 1934 those supporting devaluation formed their own organisation, the Nederlandsche Vereeniging voor Waardevast Geld, in which well-known economists sat alongside businessmen and politicians, not as representatives of the organisations to which they were affiliated but as individuals. By means of petitions and public discussion the association tried to focus attention on the arguments for devaluation and to put pressure on government policy (Griffiths and Schoorl 1987). They were not very successful. Not a single political party of any significance adopted their arguments for devaluation, even the social-democratic SDAP was anxious to avoid being accused of debasing the currency. There was virtually no political pressure to devalue. The most significant pressure on the cabinet came from the president of the Nederlandsche Bank, Trip, a fiery supporter of the gold standard. The arguments against devaluation varied from moral considerations – devaluation amounted to debasing the currency, or, worse, a breach of promise – to warnings that leaving the anchor offered by gold would lead to inflation. Reference was often made to hyperinflation in Germany in 1923 (Griffiths 1987).

Critics of the policy of the government pointed not only to the disadvantageous effects of retaining the gold standard, but also to the fundamental inconsistencies in the aims being pursued. Officially, after 1931 a policy of adjustment was followed which aimed at lowering wages and prices to bring them to world-market levels as quickly as possible. These adjustments were scuppered by continuing budget deficits, the agricultural crisis policy, introduced in 1931 in order to keep agricultural prices at a reasonable (i.e., high) level, and protectionist measures aimed at protecting certain parts of industry (Keesing 1947, pp. 165 ff.). The gap between the level of prices in The Netherlands and those on the world market did hardly decrease in 1934 and 1935. The economist Goudriaan calculated in 1936 that at this rate it would take at least another twenty years before this process of adjustment was complete. The influence of such criticism on government policy was slight. The devaluation of the guilder in September 1936 was not the result of a well-considered policy but was forced on the government after the collapse of the gold bloc with the devaluation of the French and Swiss francs.

After September 1936 the discussion concerning the influence of the gold standard on the development of the Dutch economy between 1931 and 1936 continued. In 1947, in a remarkable survey of the economic development of The Netherlands during the interwar period, Keesing argued that sticking to the gold standard and the failure to follow a consistent policy of adjustment led to the depression lasting longer in The Netherlands (Keesing 1947). This view has since been challenged. P.W. Klein, for instance, has argued that the length of the depression reflected the structure of the Dutch economy in the 1930s (Klein 1973). Recent research has vindicated the general thrust of Keesing's argument though (Van Zanden 1988a; Drukker 1990).

6.4 Old rules, new conditions, 1914–1940

In a certain sense the interwar period was one of extreme conservatism in the financial history of The Netherlands. The symbols of the liberal world order of the period prior to 1914, i.e., the gold standard and the *gulden financieringsregel*, were restored with tenacity, even frenzy. The large commercial banks, after 1923 even more dominant in the banking system than before World War I, tried to return to the strategies and commercial practices of the nineteenth century, and broke up the intimate bonds with large-scale industry that had come into being during the revolutionary 1910s. The radical break caused by World War I and the changed political, social and economic relationship that resulted were insufficiently recognised. How much things had changed can be seen from the growing interference of the state with almost all aspects of public life, from unemployment insurance and housing to agricultural prices and import quotas for industrial products, leading to a doubling of the share of government in National Income. But policy makers lacked the necessary concepts and ideas to integrate these new relationships with a new approach to financial–economic policy. Instead, they relied on the rhetoric of nineteenth-century liberalism, or what was understood by this during the interwar period, which had serious consequences for the financial and economic policies implemented. The retention of the gold standard is the best known, and most detrimental, example here. The real breakthrough only came after 1945, when the gold standard and the *gulden financieringsregel* were definitively discredited, and during the period of post-war reconstruction the state had to take an active role in economic life. It was supported in this by the ideas of economists such as Keynes and Tinbergen, who formulated a new, strictly national approach to economic policy.

7 Towards a new maturity, 1940–1990

JAAP BARENDREGT AND HANS VISSER

7.1 Introduction

The Second World War led to a complete reversal in the perception of the role of the state in the national economy of The Netherlands. The passive role of laissez-faire which it had adopted in the 1930s had been markedly unsuccessful. After the war, therefore, an active policy was implemented which led to the creation of a welfare state. Before we examine the social and economic policies that resulted in the welfare state, we will look closely at the 1940s, where the story is one of war and reconstruction. Special attention must be paid to the financial consequences of the German occupation, notably to the ballooning public debt and money supply, as well as to the ways in which these major financial problems were handled after liberation.

In the financial sector, the post-war period began with the demarcation lines between the different financial institutions still pretty well intact: the various kinds of financial institutions all had their market segments well defined. The late 1950s saw the beginning of a process of diversification and expansion. We will describe this process, sketch the development of the payments system and end by describing how the Nederlandsche Bank reacted to the changing environment.

7.2 War and peace

7.2.1 The German occupation

The pressure on the Dutch economy mounted throughout the war years. As in other countries, one of the conditions imposed as part of the surrender to Nazi Germany was the recognition of German occupation currency, the so-called *Reichskreditkassenscheine*. The Dutch monetary authorities, the Ministry of Finance and the Nederlandsche Bank, fearing the effects of mixed circulation, agreed to provide the German troops and civil servants stationed in The Netherlands with Dutch money. At least the Germans could then finance their expenditure on the same footing as before the agreement. German demands, however, became increasingly heavy with special tributes towards the war. The total cost of these direct charges eventually reached 9 billion guilders.

Next, there were public expenses caused by the war. These included the organisation of food distribution, the costs of evacuation, compensation for war damage and even the funding of extra policemen and the Nederlandse Landwacht, a police force set up to counter the resistance movement. All in all, expenditure caused solely by the occupation amounted to 11 billion guilders by the end of the war in May 1945.

If we remember that total public expenditure in 1939, a year of increasing defence expenditure in response to the growth of international tension, had barely exceeded 1 billion guilders, it becomes clear that the occupation had a massive effect on both the budget and the public debt. Although normal expenditure was successfully covered by ordinary public income (see table 7.1), increasing expenses forced the government to borrow about 10 billion guilders. Five long-term loans were issued to the tune of 3.5 billion guilders, and the remainder was financed by short-term debt. From the autumn of 1944 onwards, the private sector did not want to lend to the state any more, and the administration was forced to rely on the Nederlandsche Bank. Despite all this lending to the state, private sector liquidity had increased enormously, since of course the government was spending all the money it borrowed. Moreover, the possession of floating debt had given a huge potential lending power to Dutch financial institutions.

Full financial integration of the Dutch into the German economy took place on 1 April 1941, when the German authorities lifted the exchange controls between the two countries. The Dutch guilder virtually became a German mark, with a value of 1.327 Reichsmarks. In this sense The Netherlands were put at a disadvantage *vis-à-vis* countries such as Belgium and France, where exchange controls with Germany had not been abolished. Reichsmarks flooded into The Netherlands, because the German balance-of-payments deficit with The Netherlands could no longer be controlled by the Dutch authorities. A huge transfer of Reichsmark assets into guilder assets also started, because national governments and international investors mistrusted the Reichsmark. Belgium, for example, tried to pay the Dutch with Reichsmarks, whilst refusing to accept Reichsmarks from the Dutch. The country thereby sought to minimise her own Reichsmark possessions and at the same time to burden the Dutch with ever larger quantities of this unwelcome currency (Trip 1946, pp. 47–8). By the end of the war the German balance-of-payments debt to The Netherlands had grown to 6.7 billion guilders. An amount of 2 billion guilders was subtracted as war tribute by the German authorities and the resulting debt of 4.7 million

Table 7.1. *Comparison of Dutch government income and expenditure during World War II (in millions of guilders)*

	All public expenditure (a)	Public expenditure caused by the German occupation (b)	Remainder	Public income (a)	Public deficit
1939	1,051	–	1,051	867	184
Since May 1940	1,411	737	674	671	740
1941	3,574	2,323	1,251	1,750	1,824
1942	3,827	2,196	1,631	1,912	1,915
1943	3,769	2,368	1,401	2,022	1,747
1944	4,418	2,746	1,672	1,884	2,534
1st half of 1945	1,876	700	1,176	478	1,398
Total since May 1940	18,875	11,070	7,804	8,717	10,158

Source: Barendregt 1993, p. 20.

guilders accumulated at the Nederlandsche Bank. The result was that, over the whole period of occupation (1940–5), the total purchasing power of the Dutch private sector increased from 2.3 billion guilders to 8.7 billion (Barendregt 1993, p. 113)

On the production side, however, there was a decline in the quantity and quality of goods and services offered to the Dutch population. Several reasons accounted for this. The Allied blockade of Dutch harbours meant that sea trade was only possible with northern and eastern Europe. The forced migration of many Dutch workers to Germany and elsewhere, and the deportation of Jews and others, were major factors in a marked decline in production. German confiscations of animals, stocks, transport equipment, and other means of production, plus increasing production for the *Reich*, also contributed to the decline. The growing scarcity of goods meant that, from quite soon after the invasion, purchasing power could not fully find its way on to the market. As a result the money supply far exceeded the normal value of the supply of goods and services (money overhang). The export surplus with Germany and the increasing national debt further stimulated this development.

The money overhang manifested itself clearly in the financial sector. The credit accounts of the financial institutions increased by nearly 4 billion guilders during the occupation, i.e., they more than doubled. Mortgages decreased by 200 to 300 million guilders, and life insurance premiums rose by 700 million guilders. State loans became an advantageous investment for the money overhang, especially after the closing of the stock exchange. Private individuals lent approximately 3 billion guilders to the state. The Nederlandsche Bank, private banks and Giro banks lent 4.5 billion guilders (De Jong 1976, pp. 240–1; CBS 1989, p. 145; Herstelbank 1955, p. 49).

Due to the money overhang, price rises were to be expected. The authorities took several measures to counter inflation. They first introduced price controls but could not prevent the development of a black market. Next, in order to hit the black marketeers, who were thought to accumulate their wealth in the highest denominations, all notes of 1,000 and 500 guilders were taken out of circulation (March 1943).

From the beginning of 1944, the increasing supply of Reichmarks and the growing national debt began to be a problem for the Nederlandsche Bank. Its banknote reserves had fallen to 180 million guilders, whereas the banknotes in circulation amounted to 3.5 billion. The response of the National Socialist president of the bank, Rost van Tonningen, was to propose to the German civil service in The Netherlands either to have Dutch money printed abroad or to introduce the Reichsmark as the official currency in The Netherlands (Barendregt 1993, p. 26). Later, serious fuel problems arose for the printers of paper money. Distribution also became very difficult after a major railway strike. A crisis in the supply of paper emerged even, and the authorities of cities such as Rotterdam and The Hague went so far as to print their own emergency money. Rost van Tonningen warned the head of the German civil service, Seyss Inquart, that complete monetary chaos would erupt in the early summer of 1945 (Barendregt 1993, p. 28). If the northern and western parts of The Netherlands had not been liberated in May 1945, the Nederlandsche Bank would probably have had to overprint old bank notes with zeros in order to increase their value and local currencies would indeed have been issued.

7.2.2 The money purge and after

Immediately after the war, one of the first measures taken by the new Minister of Finance, Lieftinck, was to defuse the highly explosive monetary situation. He drastically reduced the money supply in July and in September and October 1945 simply by blocking most of it in a money purge. The pace of deblocking was to be determined by increasing national production. As a touchstone Lieftinck applied a 50 per cent ratio of money supply, i.e., cash and demand deposits, to nominal Net National Income at market prices Y, which in his view would more or less ensure a monetary equilibrium. Such an equilibrium denotes that the amount of money in circulation corresponds with the value of the demand for goods and services, so that the money sphere does not influence absolute prices. The 1938 ratio had been 46 per cent. Recent, adapted figures with new definitions indicate an adapted ratio of about 39 per cent. If we apply Lieftinck's touchstone to the recent figures, then we can assume that he was aiming at a 42 per cent ratio. With this target in mind, the Ministry of Finance managed to direct the allocation of deblocked money through a permit system. Part of it flowed back to the state in the form of tax arrears, part of it was absorbed by new wealth taxes to finance post-war reconstruction. These new taxes ultimately yielded 3.2 billion guilders. Finally, a large proportion of the money in blocked accounts was consolidated. The government 'froze' 2 billion guilders via long-term government bonds and 5-year savings certificates, and it 'captured' 1.6 billion guilders through long-term investment certificates. The last blocked money was only released in June 1952.

The money purge was a necessary step towards economic recovery, but on its own it was far from sufficient. Even more important was the restoration of national production and exports. This demanded the purchase of fuel, raw materials and capital goods, mostly from foreign sources, and shortage of foreign exchange became the main bottleneck in the recovery. The Dutch government tried to control the allocation of foreign currency, endeavouring to ensure that scarce foreign assets were employed in the best possible way. In spite of these efforts, the balance of payments remained a major problem. Foreign credits and the sale of gold and Dutch possessions abroad barely sufficed to finance the deficits of 1946 and 1947, which mainly consisted of dollar shortages. The pressure was further increased because, during these two years, war expenses in Indonesia amounted to 500 million guilders of foreign currency from a total balance-of-payments deficit of 3.7 billion guilders (Van Zanden and Griffiths 1989, p. 193). On the other hand, it must be said that the deficits partly served to drain off the rapidly increasing money supply (see table 7.2).

In 1948 Marshall Aid provided room for manoeuvre. A new industrialisation offensive began to increase the pace of recovery. Dutch competitiveness was improved, especially *vis-à-vis* the United States, by a 30 per cent devaluation of the guilder in 1949. The German market also opened up further in this year. Table 7.2 shows the increase of national production.

On the domestic front, the state controlled prices, wages, dividends, house and ground rents, and regulated scarcity by means of rationing. It also had control over deblockings. Nevertheless, a new money overhang developed. Table 7.2 shows that the ratio of money supply to national income exceeded the 1938 figure for several years, mainly for two reasons. The first was the hoarding of money. The limitations imposed on consumption and investment hindered the spending of income, at least until 1948/9.

Table 7.2. *Ratio of money supply (M; yearly average) to net national income at market prices (Y); balance of payments (B; current account), 1938–1952 (in million guilders)*

	M	Y	M/Y	B
1938	2,075	5,399	38.7	+97
April 1945	8,720	3,000	290.6	
Dec. 1945	3,704	7,490	49.5	
1946	5,274	9,928	53.1	−1,312
1947	7,100	120,066	58.8	−1,667
1948	7,372	13,306	55.4	−1,139
1949	7,338	15,181	48.3	−222
1950	7,044	16,900	41.7	−1,066
1951	6,922	19,279	35.9	−90
1952	7,402	20,092	36.8	+1,870

Sources: Barendregt 1993, pp. 113, 233; Lieftinck 1973, p. 14 (for Y (April 1945)); CBS, 1955, p. 304 (for balance of payments).

After this date, the increased supply of goods more than absorbed the increase in the money supply for the first time since the occupation (see table 7.2). The new abundance also made possible the alleviation of rationing and the lowering of price subsidies. Probably, also some distrust existed of demand deposits. The fact that banking secrecy had been abolished, as well as the knowledge that the tax inspectors had been given a great deal of liberty to locate tax arrears and wealth accumulated during the occupation, no doubt served to increase such doubts.

Money kept at home could not so easily be examined by the fiscal authorities. Consequently, much of the money apparently in circulation did not really circulate at all. Furthermore, not all branches of industry had started at the same time and at the same pace. Slow starters required continual deblocking, while other branches generated more free money than they were able to spend.

The second, and most important, reason for the high ratio of money supply to national income were the serious budget deficits faced by the government, especially in 1945 and 1946. On the income side, public income stagnated due partly to low national income and partly to the disorganisation of the tax collecting system. Public expenses, by contrast, were exceptionally high due to reconstruction and to the war in Indonesia. For example, price subsidies alone ate up the equivalent of the entire annual pre-war public income (Lieftinck 1946, p. 225). These subsidies were designed to contain inflation by compensating for the difference between import prices and domestic prices. However, the government's method of financing deficits by increasing the money supply was inflationary in itself. It merely served to create a new money overhang.

The disastrous financial position of the state becomes very clear when we realise that domestic long-term lending and Marshall Aid was providing the government with substantial additional resources. Minister of Finance Lieftinck tried desperately to keep state expenditure low. Personal bilateral discussions with his Cabinet colleagues frequently lasted through the night. Many ministers were driven to exhaustion to reduce their spending demands. Lieftinck also strove to keep the debt service as low as possible. He consolidated short-term debt only with great reluctance and forced through a reduction in short- and long-term rates of interest. Institutional investors were particularly annoyed by this. However, the main instrument of this cheap money policy was the repeated prolongation of short-term Treasury paper, and the financial institutions were therefore in possession of large quantities of such assets. This effectively prevented the Nederlandsche Bank from applying the traditional pre-war quantitative monetary instruments, such as a discount policy.

Lieftinck's reluctance to consolidate the public debt meant that a large supply of quasi-money was available. This so-called secondary liquidity could be easily transferred into primary liquidity, i.e., cash and demand deposits, simply by not renewing short-term public debt when it matured, which indeed occurred during the Korea boom in 1950. Trade liberalisation in 1950 immediately led to increased imports as the private sector tried to restore commercial supplies and stocks. Later in the year, the war in Korea stimulated a growth in imports in anticipation of shortages and a new round of rationing and import hindrances. These imports were partly the product of speculative demand (Nederlandse Regering 1951, III-2). The resources for the private non-financial sector were provided by bank advances of 450 million guilders, deblocking frozen accounts of 90 million, redemption of Treasury paper, and cash and deposit reserves. The result was a balance-of-payments deficit of 1,066 million guilders on the current account. In 1949 the figure had been only 222 million (see table 7.2). For the first time since the war, the Nederlandsche Bank resumed its policy of using the discount rate. The intention was to convey to the financial institutions the Nederlandsche Bank's attitude towards the monetary situation. In this particular case it considered that bank credit had become excessive. The new policy thus symbolically declared that, as far as the Nederlandsche Bank was concerned, the economic situation was about to return to normal.

7.3 Public finance

7.3.1 The budget as a macro-economic instrument

Economic events between the wars had proved that markets did not function as smoothly as neoclassical economists wanted the politicians to believe. Protective market restraints in the international economy and inflexibilities in various national markets had of course played their part in crippling neoclassical economic tools. After the miseries of the economic crisis and the Second World War a strong desire to build a new society had emerged in leading political circles in several countries. Assisted by the bureaucracies set up during the war, Western European governments began to plan, nationalise and invest in order to reconstruct their national economies. Programmes for the redistribution of wealth and income were initiated, which allowed workers and the elderly a fairer share of national income. Social security improved and taxes were made more progressive. The new economic theory developed by John Maynard Keynes with its emphasis on demand management fitted in perfectly with the general desire for state intervention. In a sense Keynesianism became the post-war legitimisation of government action, although Keynes himself did not prescribe the control systems that were applied during the early years of reconstruction. In The Netherlands many elements of this control system were abolished in the fifties (see below). State intervention, however, continued.

The most theoretically promising development was the Keynesian policy of demand management to try and neutralise cyclical economic processes. The two dominant political parties, the KVP (Catholic) and PvdA (Social Democrat), who controlled from 59 per cent to 66 per cent of parliamentary seats while they were in government (1945–58), agreed on this issue. The Protestant and Liberal parties (27 per cent to 30 per cent of the seats) at first opposed such policies, because they preferred pre-war budget strategy. However, major differences of opinion existed between KVP and PvdA too, notably around the PvdA's preference for using periods of cyclical upswing to create reserves for periods of recession (Ter Heide 1986, pp. 272–3, 292).

The idea of a reserve fund was introduced in 1949 by a non-political committee under the chairmanship of Jan Tinbergen and the vice-chairmanship of Witteveen, both of whom worked at the Central Planning Bureau. The committee proposed the creation of a state-controlled tax-free capital fund, financed by private investment. Its aim was to prevent overinvestment during periods of cyclical upswing and recession. The investment money was to be blocked in accounts at the Nederlandsche Bank on a voluntary basis. It would only be released after receiving government approval, which would be given on the basis of timing and the minimum levels required to guarantee the desired cyclical effects. This proposition bore a close resemblance to the deblocking measures of the money purge and probably originated from Sweden where such policies had some success (Lindbeck 1975, pp. 97–102). The PvdA faction in parliament, on the other hand, proposed a public fund financed by tax revenues. In 1953, a period of cyclical upswing, their spokesman Hofstra advocated early redemption of public debt. He warned against pro-cyclical government proposals to reduce tax rates, mainly because they had a general character. Nevertheless, the government, in which the PvdA was participating, decided to go ahead. It gave priority to a general stimulus for structural development, i.e., industrial growth. A similar design was executed during the next cyclical upward movement in 1956, when new tax-rate reductions stimulated an expansion. When yet another cyclical upswing arrived, it provoked some conflict of views in political circles. This time the Cabinet and especially Hofstra, now the Minister of Finance, wished to anticipate future cyclical developments. He planned to continue to depress demand in 1959 and 1960 by maintaining tax levels. However, the right-wing majority in parliament, including KVP members, only authorised such a policy for one year and Hofstra and his PvdA colleagues resigned in anger from the Cabinet (Ter Heide 1986, pp. 318–21; Zijlstra 1992, p. 74). This government crisis proved that it was virtually impossible for states to create a buffer for periods of recession. Another attempt was made in 1970 by a Liberal Minister of Finance, Witteveen, who introduced the so-called *wiebeltax* or swing tax as a policy instrument against cyclical economic movements. This allowed for a temporary flexibility of tax rates within a range of 5 per cent, combined with reductions or increases of government expenditure that amounted to at least 20 per cent of the fluctuation in tax revenues. The government implemented the *wiebeltax* in 1971 and 1972 during a period of cyclical upswing. Later Cabinets refrained from using it because of the negative effects in other areas of governmental concern. The left-wing dominated Den Uyl Cabinet (1973–7), for example, stressed the indiscriminate and undesirable effects the *wiebeltax* would have on income distribution during the period of recession which was then, they felt, afflicting the economy (Koopmans and Wellink 1978, p. 35 note 1).

Demand management during periods of economic recession faced different problems than during periods of upswing. In the 1950s in particular, Cabinets took serious policy measures to neutralise temporary downward trends in economic activity. However, these measures seem to have been ill-timed, due to delays in the three stages of policy implementation. It was often difficult to recognise the stage the cycle was at. If, let us say, a downward economic movement was noticed (first stage), then countermeasures had to be formulated (second stage). Such steps needed parliamentary approval and they sometimes could only be implemented, for fiscal reasons, on 1 January of the following year (third stage). More often than not, the whole operation took more than a year and the effects of the policy then turned out to be pro-cyclical. For example, in 1951–2, real wage reductions, cuts in government expenditure, early tax collection and tax rate increases stimulated an economic recession after the Korea boom. Another example comes from 1956–7, when it took Finance Minister Hofstra ten months to formulate countercyclical measures and get them through parliament, even though he acted with great vigour throughout. The effects, therefore, were only visible in 1958 when the economy was once more in recession. Countercyclical government policies were generally implemented too late during boom periods and were not implemented at all during upward swings in the economy.

Instability returned in the 1970s, though this time in a more structural way than in the 1950s. During the first years of the decade, a worldwide economic upswing led to a rise in the world price of basics. This in turn stimulated worldwide inflation, which was already well established on the back of high wage and price rises, and was being fuelled by rapid money growth (Annual report De Nederlandsche Bank 1975, pp. 11–12, 19–21). The prices of industrial products valued in American dollars, however, were rising at an even faster rate. The OPEC oil-cartel reacted with oil price increases which created deflationary pressure within the world economy. The OPEC-countries were not able to spend their newly acquired capital in the short term. The Den Uyl Cabinet decided to increase state deficits, enabling The Netherlands to play a part in preventing a serious international recession. The government succeeded in again reducing the deficit, by increasing public income from taxes and from non-taxes, which rose from 2.4 per cent of Y (1973) to 4.9 per cent in 1977 (see table 7.3). This second source was bolstered by revenues from natural gas production, which had been linked to the price of oil. The policy of the Den Uyl Cabinet can be regarded as the last conscious effort to direct economic developments with a Keynesian set of instruments, using the public deficit as the main tool.

According to Keynesian theory the entire budget is itself an economic instrument. Growing budgets or debts increase national spending. Even if the state absorbs this increase completely through raised taxes and social security premiums, there still remains an impulse towards increased spending which has multiplier effects (Haavelmo 1945). Such a view suggests that the high government deficits of the 1980s would still have had a Keynesian effect.

However, by the start of the 1980s deficits had become so high (see table 7.3) that it was now impossible to counteract any further downward eco-

Table 7.3. *Data on public finance (+ = surplus), tax income and social premiums (as percentage of NNImp (=Y)), 1950–1990*

	1950	1957	1965	1973	1975	1977	1983	1990
Public balance (cash basis)	+1[a]	−4.4	−5.1	−1.4	−5.0	−3.8	−9.4	−5.2
Tax burden	30.5	24.0	26.1	28.4	29.1	29.9	28.1	31.9
Soc. premiums	4.7	8.7	12.2	17.4	19.3	18.7	24.3	19.3
Total	35.2	32.7	38.3	45.8	48.4	48.6	52.4	51.2

Note: [a] State budget deficits (CBS 1956, p. 111, minus redemptions of long-term debt; De Nederlandsche Bank 1950, p. 52.
Sources: Van Sinderen 1990, pp. 530–1; Knoester 1989, pp. 96–7, 128–9, 160–1; Messing 1981, p. 19; Centraal Planbureau 1991, p. 171.

nomic movement by more expansive measures. Ever since the 1960s real wages had increased at the expense of profits. Investment aimed at replacing labour had also become more expensive due to the rise in interest rates in the late 1970s and the early 1980s. Company reorganisations and bankruptcies in the private sector were ever more frequent.

The resulting rise in unemployment and a widespread flight into disability allowances boosted public spending from the mid 1970s onwards (see table 7.3). Furthermore, the state was consuming its own resources by increasing the number of civil servants and raising the level of benefits. In addition, it began to subsidise stagnating economic sectors and enterprises, and tried to stimulate investment with tax incentives. As a consequence, state investment itself decreased. Developments in the world economy, trade union demands and an increased tax burden further reduced profits in the private sector. Consequently, investment declined and economic growth virtually stopped. The government was thus unable to use economic growth, as it had done in the past, to finance its growing needs. On the contrary, public sector growth was now self-sustained, based on high interest rates and a growing public debt. Interest payments ballooned (see table 7.4). Thus, the positive Keynesian effects were outweighed by the negative effects of declining profits in the private sector (see also Knoester 1991).

Since the beginning of the 1980s, the reduction of the budget deficit has been the central economic theme, irrespective of economic developments. Some successes have been recorded, as we can see in table 7.3. We will return to this issue in the next section.

Table 7.4. *Interest payments by the Dutch State (in bn guilders) (1) and as percentage of NNImp (2) and of State expenses (3), 1950–1990*

	1950	1960	1965	1970	1975	1980	1983	1985	1990
(1)	0.5	0.6	0.8	1.7	2.9	6.9	4.5	19.6	23.0
(2)	2.9	1.6	1.3	1.6	1.5	2.3	4.2	5.2	6.3
(3)	10.1	6.6	4.9	5.2	4.0	5.3	9.4	11.9	11.0

Sources: Moerman/Vuchelen 1986, p. 28; Staten-Generaal 1988/1989, pp. 15/16. ad (3) Sociaal-Economische Raad 1978, p. 7; Nederlandse Regering 1992, pp. 278, 293, p. 300; Centraal Planbureau 1991, p. 107.

7.3.2 The causes of exploding public expenditure and income

Before the Second World War the Dutch state had taken on the responsibility for the social security of its citizens, but its measures had been far from adequate. In previous periods there had always been some attempts by society to protect its weakest members, but it had never been able to address the task properly. The state had finally created basic provisions such as poor relief, disablement benefits and pensions, but the allowances paid out had been low and there were many who could not afford the premiums. After the Second World War, all kinds of insurance provisions like accident, medical, disability and pension insurances became government priorities, along with improved health care, education and housing. The state frequently offered services at prices well below cost, and in some cases even for free (merit goods). Social security benefits, for example, rose sharply from 10 per cent of national income in 1950 to 33 per cent in 1985 (Van Zanden and Griffiths 1989, p. 70). Table 7.3 sets out the ways in which this growth of the public sector (state and social security) was financed, i.e., largely by raising the levels of social premiums. Tax increases as expressed in per cent of Y (=NNImp) were moderate, a restraint made possible by growth in non-tax income from gas production and the running of increasingly large deficits. Moreover, if we look at the tax and social premium burden expressed in daily wages etc., then we notice a regular growth, due entirely to social premiums: the tax burden actually decreased (see table 7.5). Obviously, the total sum of wages has risen faster than national income. Indirect taxes expressed in daily wages have also shown a tendency to fall, except for the 1980s, but have retained a remarkably constant share of total tax income at approximately 42 per cent from 1946–90. All in all, the state has been unable to cover its expenses sufficiently from income, particularly since 1970. Net public debt had in fact risen to 67 per cent of national income by 1990 (Y(1990) = 454 billion guilders).

Table 7.5. *Tax and social premium burden expressed in daily wages (number of days), 1951–1988*

	Tax on wages, salaries and social benefits[a]	Social premiums[a]	Total	Indirect taxes	Total
1951	75	9	84	108	192
1960	66	32	98	72	170
1970	66	47	113	67	180
1980	65	50	115	60	175
1988	57	66	123	69	192

Notes: [a] Paid by employees and persons on welfare only.
Sources: Calculations from CBS, Nationale Rekeningen 1960, pp. 84, 88; 1972, p. 109; 1975, pp. 113, 116; 1990, pp. 56, 58, 128, 150 and 151.

A second important cause of budget growth was the gradual erosion of the power of Ministers of Finance to control public expenditure. Indeed, changes in the mechanism of this control made it virtually impossible to control public expenditure at all. The situation was further aggravated by economic problems in the 1980s.

During the reconstruction period Minister Lieftinck (1945–52) kept a close watch on every cent spent by the Cabinet by carefully screening ministerial budgets. In fact, it could even be said that Lieftinck's bilateral discussions with the other ministers determined these budgets. He had the backing of his Prime Minister, who turned a deaf ear to complaints from the spending ministers. The Council of Ministers only seldom discussed individual budget items. By 1952 public expenditure had been reduced from more than 47 per cent of National Income in 1946 to well under 30 per cent (Nederlandse Regering 1958, p. 20). Since the beginning of the 1960s, however, the figure has constantly risen again.

During the 1950s the practice of bilateral preparation lost ground. Decisions were more and more taken by the Cabinet. This gave ministers the chance mutually to support each other, thereby undermining the position of the Minister of Finance. Minister A could now claim resources confident that minister B would not object, because he had himself already agreed not to object to B's claims. The same mechanism functioned within political parties: parliamentary specialists could act in the same way as ministers inside the Cabinet. This was, of course, a climate under which pressure groups could flourish, and successful campaigns imposed yet further demands on the budget.

The introduction in 1961 of the so-called structural budget policy was another measure which undermined the position of the Minister of Finance. The aim of its promoter, Minister of Finance Zijlstra, was to create a touchstone for future public expenditure to replace budget policies which repeatedly changed under pressure from cyclical economic movements. Zijlstra's plan was to establish a pattern of expenditure within a medium-term growth path for the national economy. In the longer term the budget balance, i.e., deficits, was to be brought into line with the structure of private sector savings and investment, of which the current account of the balance of payments is one expression. Demand would then keep pace with production capacity (Burger 1975, p. 330). If necessary, countercyclical measures could be taken, such as the delay of planned reductions in the rate of tax, such as in 1961, which could be introduced later at an appropriate time (Zijlstra 1992, p. 124). There was also a built-in countercyclical component because decreases in tax income, or even budget deficits due to recession, would not have great consequences if the state continued to base its spending on the medium-term growth path. For the same reason, increases in tax income and budget surpluses during periods of economic upswing would not matter either. In practice however, the Zijlstra touchstone for budget deficits presented his Cabinet colleagues with more freedom than before, because it allowed them to decide how to divide up the money available within the expenditure norm. Economic growth now implied by definition that there were more public funds to spend. Because national income increased enormously, so did public expenditure. In addition, of course, the climate of growth did not encourage a rigorous evaluation of the necessity for expenditure, nor did it lead to a decrease in the burden laid upon the taxpayer.

One other important change in budget technique was the introduction in 1966/7 of long-term estimates for budget items. This led to the development of the so-called camel noses, which are plans that cost a small amount of money in the beginning but a lot of money in the future. This again gave ministers the chance to claim their share, as previously determined by the long-range estimates.

Reductions in the growth of national income in the 1970s naturally created difficulties. Successive Ministers of Finance took countermeasures to limit the growth of public expenditure. They ended the use of the structural budget policy and demanded that ministries compensate overspending within their own budgets. The importance of bilateral negotiations was emphasised. In addition they introduced periodical evaluations of budget spending and government schemes which formulated targets to reduce the budget deficits. Nevertheless, ministers found many procedures to undermine or even evade cuts in their departmental budgets.

They thus aimed to defend their positions *vis-à-vis* their own civil service and against external pressure groups. For instance, windfalls were used to limit the reductions needed in their budgets, whereas setbacks were seldom compensated (Toirkens 1989, pp. 21–3). During the 1980s public income suddenly increased more than expected due to a cyclical upswing which began in 1983. The government deficit was thereby reduced, but it could be argued that it was not yet being reduced in a structural, non-cyclical way (De Kam *et al.* 1990, p. 619).

7.3.3 A turn in policy

Events in the 1970s and 1980s undermined the belief that the state could freely manipulate the economy, correcting the flaws of the private sector. Keynesianism did not offer a satisfactory solution to the economic problems of the day. There was economic stagnation combined with inflation (stagflation). Expanding the public sector to neutralise this problem was no longer an option. In The Netherlands the high burden on the taxpayer in taxes and social premiums combined with wage increases introduced in the 1960s, which brought Dutch workers into line with international wage levels, had made labour expensive *vis-à-vis* capital by the 1970s. The large public sector had in fact undermined the competitiveness of the Dutch economy. This resulted in a high number of redundancies and a hefty rise in the number of people on unemployment and disability benefit. In such a climate those economic theorists who believed in the ineffectiveness of state intervention became very influential (monetarists and neoclassics) as did theorists who stressed the importance of supply instead of demand (supply siders). There was revival of the classical view of the state under which assistance is only given to the private sector in ways which allow this sector to operate freely, apart from the correction of major flaws. In The Netherlands the government gave up all kinds of intervention, such as wage and price policy. It tried to simplify the fiscal system and reduced individual social allowances. Governments played competitiveness on foreign markets as the trump card in the argument for economic recovery. Low wage demands by trade unions (caused by the economic recession in the beginning of the 1980s) and low inflation rates did indeed have a positive effect when the international economic situation finally improved. Thanks to high profits most of the private sector was back on its feet again. To support the revival the state tried to reduce the burden on the taxpayer, but without much success, as the data in table 7.3 indicate. The reduction of government budget deficits remained the primary concern.

Table 7.6. *Private and semi-private savings, 1951 and 1986 (in billions of guilders and in percentage of National Income)*

	Investment by pension and private insurance funds		Savings at banks		Investment by investment funds		Total
	Guilders	%Y	Guilders	%Y	Guilders	%Y	%Y
1951	8	40	4	20	0	0	60
1986	240	120	150	40	37	10	170

Source: CBS 1989, pp. 145, 149.

7.4 The financial sector

7.4.1 The capital market

The state generally financed its budget deficits on the Dutch capital market. This market could supply sufficient amounts of money, thanks to the growth in savings, especially semi-private or collective savings (pension, social insurance and private insurance funds; see table 7.6).

Consequently, the state has only rarely requested loans expressed in foreign currency, for instance during the first post-war years in order to finance reconstruction through imports. The redemption of foreign currency debt was completed in 1976. The role of the pension funds is especially important in this area. Their investments have grown from 18 per cent of Y in 1951 to 83 per cent in 1986. Large amounts of capital were invested in public debt, partly compulsorily under regulations imposed by the state, as in the case of the large state pension fund, the Algemeen Burgerlijk Pensioenfonds or ABP, and the remainder voluntarily. The other institutional investors, i.e., savings banks, have also invested in low-risk long-term assets expressed in Dutch currency. Partly because of regulations introduced by the Nederlandsche Bank, these assets constitute primarily the public debt and loans to local government. Foreign investors and other private investors have tended to take greater risks and have invested relatively more in shares (Van de Paverd 1982, p. 46). Moreover, the strong guilder has been an extra reason for foreign investors to buy Dutch securities, because it increases their profit margin if expressed in weaker currencies. A change in loan conditions has also encouraged long-term lending to the state by private investors and banks (see table 7.7). First of all, interest rates rose due to growing inflation, increasing uncertainty and the fostering

Table 7.7. *Owners of consolidated public debt (in %), and the debt itself (in billion guilders), 1938–1987*

	1938	1952	1960	1970	1980	1987
Institutional investors[a]	44	63	30	52	63	50
Banks[b]			22	15	11	20
Foreign invest.	56[c]	37[c]			11	12
Private invest.			48[c]	33[c]	14[c]	18[c]
Consolidated Public debt	3.2	8.4	12.5	23.5	78.1	234.5

Note:
[a] for 1938 and 1952: including savings banks; [b] for 1960–1987: including savings banks; [c] remainder.
Sources: Herstelbank 1955, pp. 245, 260 (for 1938 and 1952); De Kam *et al.* 1990, p. 64 (for 1960–1987); CBS 1989, p. 168 (for consolidated public debt).

of tight money policies by central banks. Furthermore, the growing public debt enabled investors to negotiate more favourable conditions, which resulted in shorter redemption periods. They were thereby left free to respond to changing circumstances. Table 7.7 shows the ownership of government bonds over the period 1938–87.

The monetary authorities, i.e., the state and the Nederlandsche Bank, have usually been critical of short-term loans in the period under consideration, because of their money-creating side effects. Nonetheless, in the 1940s, when long-term public borrowing had been halted, in the years 1968–71, and again from 1976 to 1983, short-term financing of state deficits increased. An agreement between the Nederlandsche Bank and the government finally put an end to most forms of inflationary state borrowing. Since 1982, the overall effect of fiscal policy on the total money supply, i.e., primary and secondary liquidity, has been deflationary, although there were still some inflationary effects in 1986, 1987 and 1989 (Annual reports De Nederlandsche Bank, appendices). Nowadays, much of the Dutch public debt is negotiated on the London stock exchange, after issue in The Netherlands, as are many of the shares of the largest Dutch companies. This deflection of trade seriously undermines the position of the Amsterdam stock exchange, a position which has never really been strong since 1940.

Trade on the stock exchange stagnated in the Second World War, due to policy measures adopted by the occupying authorities. The blocking of price rises had the side effect of encouraging investment in public debt rather than shares (De Roos and Wieringa 1953, pp. 219–20). At a later stage, the stock exchange was even closed. After the war, stock trade was severely hindered by various government measures, largely of a legal or fiscal nature, introduced to protect the owners of stocks, especially Jews, who had been dispossessed during the war. An additional factor was the danger of black money and enemy capital being hidden in securities. On top of all this, the government imposed war taxes and capital levies (Joh. de Vries 1976, pp. 202–13). Feeling ran so high that the stock exchange even went on strike for one week in the beginning of the 1950s. The practice of internal financing by companies, then stimulated by the low wage policy of the government, further restricted the number and value of issues for a long time. In the 1960s and 1970s, however, profits were eroded by rising wages and the growing tax and social premium burden on employers. Consequently, the demand for bank credit and bond loans rose, also encouraged by fiscal regulations. Rising interest rates further affected profits. Recovery from the recession of the late 1970s and early 1980s, and a booming stock exchange in the mid 1980s, lured a growing number of companies into applying for official quotation and issuing shares. Nonetheless, the value of the share issues remained small compared to bonds, with 2.5 billion guilders against 25.4 million guilders, including public debt in 1986. The stock exchange is still dominated by a limited number of large companies: Royal Dutch Shell, Unilever, Philips, each with equity of more than 10 billion guilders in 1988, and AKZO. In 1990, the financial merger conglomerates ABN AMRO and Internationale Nederlanden Groep (ING) joined this group of large companies, but the earlier merging of the only two large national issuing houses, Algemene Bank Nederland (ABN) and Amsterdam–Rotterdam Bank (AMRO), has probably affected the international position of the Amsterdam stock exchange. This position has been particularly vulnerable since the 'big bang' on the London stock exchange, which computerised stock trade and reduced transaction costs, notably through the so-called private placements. The result has been the deflection of trade to which the Amsterdam stock exchange became particularly vulnerable, which was mentioned above.

7.4.2 The scramble for savings

The dawn of the post-war period found the commercial banks in an extremely liquid position, which Mr Lieftinck's monetary policy did nothing to reduce. As business firms had little need for trade credit, being quite liquid themselves, and the banks considered medium- and long-term investment credit not their bailiwick, they had no choice but to invest in public debt. It was not until 1954 that the credit supply of the commercial banks was again at the pre-war level in real terms and it was only in 1956 that the private sector overtook the public sector in the banks' credit portfolio (Van der Werf 1988, p. 213).

Dutch banks, apart from Nederlandsche Middenstandsbank (NMB, Netherlands Bank for Small- to Medium-Size Enterprises) and the agricultural cooperative banks, had traditionally only been interested in granting short-term credit. NMB for that matter only granted medium-term credit to small- to medium-size enterprises under government guarantees. In order to fill the need for longer-term investment credit, the government founded the Herstelbank or Recovery Bank in 1945, which also paid out war damage recompense. Its share capital was 300 million guilders, more than the share capital of the then five big commercial banks combined. The state took 151 million guilders and the remaining 149 million was taken up by other investors, including commercial banks and institutional investors, who had to be lured by a state guarantee on dividends. Still, with the memories of an unhappy involvement in long-term credit in the early 1920s still comparatively fresh and fearing that the Herstelbank was one more step on the way to a socialist economy, the banks and the institutional investors participated only reluctantly (Posthuma 1955, p. 25). The Herstelbank demonstrably played a useful role, but as commercial banks became more involved in medium-term credit and restrictions on stock and bond issues were lifted, the need for the services of Herstelbank diminished. Originally set up for a period of 25 years, it was transformed in 1962 into the Nationale Investeringsbank (National Investment Bank, NIB), seeing its capital reduced to only 100 million guilders. In the 1970s the NIB channelled government aid to ailing business firms and in the 1980s it developed into an investment bank (Scholtens 1991). The Herstelbank and other banks in 1951 founded the Export Financieringsmaatschappij (Export Finance Company), which provided longer-term export loans. It was quite a success, because export credit could be insured against risks with the Nederlandsche Credietverzekerings-Maatschappij (Dutch Credit Insurance Company), also established in 1951.

The steadily increasing demand for investment credit and export credit was not fully met by the Herstelbank and the Export-Financieringsmaatschappij. Banks began in the early 1950s to provide this kind of credit, at first through specialised daughter companies, but as these had to fund themselves with relatively expensive bonds, the banks took over medium-term lending themselves, using their cheaper term deposits. In order to keep any mismatch between assets and liabilities resulting from increased medium-term lending within manageable proportions, the commercial banks in the late 1950s became interested in attracting private savings, which were relatively cheap compared with bonds. A squeeze on the banks' liquidity ratio also contributed to the banks' need for savings

Table 7.8. *Shares of different groups of banks in the market for savings, 1950–1988 (in percentages.)*

	1950	1960	1970	1980	1988
Rijkspostspaarbank	32	24	18	14	16
Savings banks	29	28	25	17	16
Agricultural banks	37	39	42	41	40
Commercial banks	1	8	16	28	28
Total	100	100	100	100	100

Source: Bosman 1989, p. 42.

deposits. Firstly, net receipts from abroad, an important source of liquidity creation during the 1950s, dried up in the 1960s, as did inflationary finance by the government, and, secondly, nominal national income started to rise steeply after the 1964 wage explosion. This made for an increase in the circulation of note and coin, putting the banks' balances with the Nederlandsche Bank under pressure. But there were additional reasons for the banks to try actively to attract savings. Credit control that only allowed increased lending if it was matched with increased funding through longer-term borrowings or share capital also fanned the banks' thirst for savings. For another thing, the fast and continuing increase in real per capita income for the first time made the great mass of private individuals interesting as potential clientele for the commercial banks.

The quest for savings deposits spurred the banks on to develop an extensive branch network and generally to move into retail banking, which some had already done on a small scale in the 1950s, providing consumer credit. If the banks were to succeed in attracting savings deposits, they had to offer other services as well, which they began doing on a large scale in the mid 1960s. Prominent amongst these was the provision of salary payments into bank accounts, which absolved employers from the need to pay out their work force in note and coin. The banks also entered the market for mortgage loans, and in 1967 offered interest on demand deposits and provided cheques which were guaranteed up to a certain sum, in an attempt to draw clients away from the postal giro system or prevent them switching allegiance. Also, these services helped to keep the money within the bank circuit and prevent it leaking away through withdrawals of note and coin. A further service was the introduction of Eurocheques in 1974, which could be used for payments abroad.

Not surprisingly, the ones to suffer from this decision of the commercial banks to tap the savings market were the savings banks, including

Rijkspostspaarbank (RPS), the postal savings bank (see table 7.8). These banks could be seen as institutional investors, because their *raison d'être* was to provide opportunities to save and their investment or credit activities were subordinate to the liabilities side of the balance sheet. Savings banks usually were small outfits whose scope was local or at the most regional and who hardly competed amongst each other. The RPS was another matter, being part of the Ministry of Transport and having the counters of the post offices at its disposal. Being non-profit institutions, usually in the guise of foundations, the savings banks were not subject to profit taxes. As against this, they were restricted as to the kind of activities they were allowed to engage in. In particular, loans to business enterprises were forbidden territory.

Thanks to the aggressive behaviour of the commercial banks, the quiet in this cozy market niche was disturbed around 1960, never to return. The savings banks now had to compete head-on with the commercial banks for the savings of the non-rich. The consequences for the savings banks were far-reaching. For one thing, given the penchant of consumers for one-stop shopping, in financial markets no less than in other markets, the savings banks had to broaden the variety of financial services they offered. Also, this meant that the commercial banks in effect dictated the interest rates that the savings banks could offer, which forced them to revise their invest- ment policy. As for the increased variety of financial services, savings banks first offered their clients the opportunity to use their savings deposits to pay rent, taxes, electricity bills etc. but soon offered full-fledged payments services. Forced by the competition from the commercial banks and the postal giro system, they became in effect money-creating banks. Earlier the high cost of frequent currency payments had made big institu- tions come to an agreement with the Nederlandse Spaarbankbond (Savings Banks Union) to pay pensions into people's savings accounts. A government department offered this option in 1949, the Dutch railways followed in 1951 and when old age pensions for all over 65 were introduced in 1957, recipients could opt for receiving these through their savings bank (Buning 1957, p. 99).

Savings banks traditionally invested in bonds and granted credit to the government. With the increased competition for savings, coupled with an increased volatility of interest rates in general, the savings banks were con- fronted with the need to adjust credit interest rates with increasing fre- quency, while debit rates were fixed for considerable periods of time. This situation called for investments with a more variable rate of interest. As the way to business credit was blocked, mortgages offered an attractive alterna- tive. Even if interest rates on mortgage credit could not be adjusted as fre- quently and as easily as the rates on overdrafts, they were not, like the interest rates on government bonds, fixed for 25 or even 40 years. For the members of the Nederlandse Spaarbankbond collectively the percentage of total assets invested in mortgage loans increased from 16.1 in 1950 to 16.7 in 1960, 22.0 in 1970 and 44.2 in 1980 (Eizenga 1985, pp. 18–19). Given the steadily increasing public-sector borrowing requirement, this was not for want of new government issues. Even the reduction in the maturity of government bonds to as short as seven years in the inflationary climate of the 1970s was not sufficient to stem this movement. Probably it was not interest rate risk in the first place which led savings banks to invest so much in mortgage loans, but customer relations.

To sidestep the ban on commercial bank activities and in order to provide their clients with a number of services they could not themselves separately provide at a reasonable price, a number of savings banks jointly with the German Westdeutsche Landesbank Girozentrale and the commercial bank Mees & Hope, who opted out after two years, founded the Bank der Bondsspaarbanken (BdB) in 1971. This was registered as a commercial bank and did foreign business and stock trading, partly on behalf of the savings banks. It also granted credit to business firms and acted as a kind of central bank for the savings banks. In particular, it acted as the clearing institute for payments between clients of savings banks and also as a broker in the market for private placements.

7.5 Increase of scale in banking

7.5.1 The survivors

Although the number of banks had been declining slowly but surely after the war, the only important merger before 1964 was the one between Amsterdamsche Bank and Incasso-Bank in 1948. Then the European Common Market was launched in 1958. This led to mergers between business firms and in their wake to a huge increase in the demand for medium-term credit by big customers. The banks were more or less forced to follow developments in the non-bank business sector, just as they had been around World War I. Medium-term credit outstanding grew from 114 million guilders in 1960 to 5,513 million in 1970 (Hoffmann 1971, p. 481; monetary policy played a role as well, see below). So Amsterdamsche Bank in 1964 joined forces with Rotterdamsche Bank to form AMRO Bank and Nederlandsche Handel-Maatschappij or NHM and Twentsche Bank merged into Algemene Bank Nederland (ABN), which in 1967 again was joined by Hollandsche Bankunie or HBU. This merger wave culminated in the takeover in 1975 of the merchant bank Pierson, Heldring & Pierson by AMRO and the merchant bank Bank Mees & Hope by ABN, though both banks continued operating as separate entities. Of the 126 provincial banks, that is banks whose head office was not in Amsterdam or Rotterdam, that existed in 1946 only 17 were left in 1985, and few were still independent (Van der Werf 1988, p. 229). For the big banks takeovers were a means to penetrate the urbanising countryside. The process was accelerated by the failure of the small Teixeira de Mattos bank in 1966, which led to a flight of deposits from small banks to the bigger banks, which were seen as more safe.

Meanwhile, international activities had been gaining importance. Although a number of Dutch banks traditionally had had a large overseas business, in particular the ABN forerunners NHM (in Asia) and HBU (in Latin America), internationalisation entered a new phase after the European currencies had been made convertible at the end of 1958. The banks became more and more involved in activities in international money and capital markets. In the 1960s and early 1970s international cooperation in banking consortia and in syndicates which extended loans to multinational enterprises and less-developed countries, became quite popular. The 1973 oil crisis, which led to huge amounts of money in the hands of oil-exporting countries seeking employment, provided a boost to this kind of international lending but at the same time planted the seeds of its decline, which was sparked off by the debt crisis of the early 1980s. The banking consortia were not very successful anyway. A consortium could, for instance, open an office in some country, where all participating banks could serve their own clients. But what if such an office succeeded in attracting new customers; how to divide the spoils? Furthermore, the participating banks in a loan syndicate perhaps too easily expected the syndicate leader to take care of investigating the soundness of a loan (Frentrop 1987). The disappointing experience with loose cooperation constructs led internationally to a shift in interest from consortia to mergers and takeovers. It may be noted that the Dutch banks were to all appearances not unduly hurt by the debt crisis. First of all, they were not heavily involved in the countries experiencing payments difficulties and their portfolios were well diversified anyway, and secondly, the Nederlandsche Bank kept tabs on the exposure of the banks in LDCs. The banks had to report their LDC exposure semi-annually as from May, 1981. This had already been agreed upon in 1980, well before the crisis broke out (Coljé 1988 pp. 97–101).

With the increasing openness of financial markets in the world, and most of all the rapidly approaching integrated European financial market, the Dutch financial world became convinced that Dutch banks, even the big ones, were too small to hold their own against international competition. A few of the smaller banks were taken over by foreign banks (Slavenburg's by Credit Lyonnais and Nederlandsche Crediet Bank by Chase Manhattan) but the experience has not been an entirely happy one for the buyers, as the banks in question had been on the brink of collapse. This will not have whetted the appetite of foreign bankers for a takeover of a Dutch bank. Attempts at cross-border mergers (between AMRO and the Belgian Generale Bank in the late 1980s) proved abortive, and so the Dutch banks turned to each other and to the financially powerful insurance companies. This was made possible by the lifting of the ban on close cooperation between banks and insurance companies as of the first of January 1990 and by the monetary authorities' attitude towards bank mergers becoming significantly more lenient.

In October 1989 NMB merged with Postbank, though both banks retained their own separate branch networks. Postbank was the result of a merger between the postal giro system or Postcheque- en Girodienst (PCGD) and Rijkspostspaarbank (RPS) in 1986 after PCGD already had absorbed the Gemeentegiro (Amsterdam Municipal Giro System) in 1979. Though PCGD had stolen a march on the banks by introducing computers and offering attractive payment facilities around 1962/3, the banks caught up and made inroads into PCGD's and RPS's territory. PCGD and RPS were not free to offer similar services to the banks when the latter developed retail banking. Legal impediments stood in the way, and for any policy change the Minister had to give his consent, or even laws had to be changed. Slowly but surely, though, PCGD and RPS broadened their product variety, intensifying their cooperation in the process until in 1972 they presented themselves to the public as one integrated financial institution. But till 1970 they were, for instance, not allowed to follow the banks and offer interest on demand deposits, and not until 1982 were they able to buy and sell foreign exchange and sell holiday packages or offer overdraft facilities to business firms. It had been clear for some time that PCGD and RPS had to evolve into a full-fledged bank if they were not to perish. After years of discussion, the second bill to establish Postbank as an independent firm was introduced in 1984 and Postbank started work in 1986. The first bill, introduced in 1977, had been based on the idea that a privatised Postbank was necessary to increase competition in the banking industry, an idea which did not go down well with that industry. Now the forerunners of Postbank had traditionally invested in public debt and had difficulty in entering the more lucrative market for business loans, whilst NMB was interested in Postbank's large share of the market for savings deposits and also in growth for its own sake, in order to be better able to survive in the post-1992 world. Postbank could make use of NMB's expertise in a number of fields, including stock investment. Its investment fund, launched in 1990, succeeded in attracting quite a few people who had never invested in stocks before. In 1991 NMB Postbank merged with the Nationale-Nederlanden insurance group into ING (Internationale Nederlanden Groep) and became ING-Bank (Internationale Nederlanden Groep Bank) in 1992. This was amongst other things in order to be able to become a global player, NMB Bank having entered the international market in the mid 1970s. The state, which during the war had taken an 86 per cent share in NMB's capital, had been gradually divesting, but after the merger of NMB and the fully state-owned Postbank it had a 50 per cent stake in the new combine and continued divesting after. The merger between NMB Postbank and Nationale-Nederlanden resulted in the state holding a 7 per cent stake in ING, which in 1993 was sold to a pension fund. At the time of the merger between NMB Postbank and Nationale Nederlanden in 1991 it was stipulated that the shares held by the state would be sold as a whole, in order to prevent unfriendly parties becoming owners. In September 1991 AMRO and ABN merged in order to be able to hold their own on global markets, and in the process cut costs by reducing the number of branch offices. Their affiliated merchant banks, Pierson, Heldring & Pierson and Bank Mees & Hope respectively, followed suit in 1992 to become Bank Mees Pierson. The Dutch banking scene is now dominated by three giants, the third one being Rabobank. This is the central organisation of the agricultural cooperative banks, formed in 1972 through a merger of the two then existing central organisations. These two, one of them strongly Roman Catholic, had more or less carved up the country between them but were increasingly unable to avoid serving the same neighbourhoods. Consequently, they had come under pressure from local banks, which saw themselves pitted against each other, to merge. Also, a merger was called for in order to cut costs and still retain the dense branch network necessary for attracting savings (De Vries 1973, pp. 207, 223–4). As the agricultural population has been shrinking over the decades, the agricultural cooperative banks have also turned to the urban market and have extended their services to non-agricultural firms, in particular small- and medium-size enterprises. Rabobank in 1990 took a 100 per cent interest in the Interpolis insurance company, which in 1991 merged with another insurance company, Avéro Centraal Beheer Groep.

One may wonder what made mergers between banks and insurance companies so appealing to those involved. For banks, insurance companies are attractive because they have large amounts of money available, so that funding will become cheaper and more funds become available for large-scale medium- and long-term investments. Moreover, an alliance with a wealthy insurance company may help to improve a bank's standing on the capital market, again making for lower funding costs. For another thing, it was felt that bank share prices were relatively low. Mergers with insurance companies were seen as a means to avert raiders. Finally, teaming up with insurance companies would give the bank access to a large range of insurance products, which could be offered to a bank's clients in order to make available a full range of financial products and keep its work force busy. For insurance companies, alliances with banks mean that a large number of sales outlets become available, with costs lower than with independent intermediaries or own agents (Böttcher 1990). As insurance policies become more standardised and fierce competition eats into profit margins, the importance of a large number of outlets, even if not all staffed with insurance specialists, has been increasing. Also, there was a well-founded fear that banks might develop their own insurance products.

The problematic standing of some banks' shares on the capital market and the related low share prices were a legacy of the difficult times experienced in the early 1980s, when the banks were saddled with bad debt resulting from the post-second-oil-crisis slump. This contributed to disintermediation. First-class borrowers were able to attract funds directly from investors at lower interest rates than the banks and therefore bypassed the banks (cf. Eijgenhuijsen *et al.* 1987, p. 52). The banks reacted to this loss by introducing new services, generating commission instead of interest income.

7.5.2 Still struggling

For the savings banks life has become difficult. Savings banks have traditionally been quite small. When they became exposed to the chill winds of competition small-sized operations no longer were viable and a process of concentration set in. One-stop shopping meant that savings banks had to develop into financial supermarkets and in order to help their clients satisfactorily they had to resort to automation. The high set-up costs of automation and the scale economies involved are one reason for concentration. A related reason was, and is, that new technical developments work against banks with only a local or regional presence. Bank clients wish to have access to cash dispensers all over the country, for example. As a result, out of the hundreds of savings banks that even in 1960 still existed, 266 in fact, few remain. Through mergers, two large-scale operations have been formed, Verenigde Spaarbank (VSB) and SNS Bank. VSB teamed up with the AMEV insurance company in 1990 and jointly with the Belgian insurance company AG Groep formed Fortis Groep. AMEV had been feeling a need for its branches abroad to cooperate with banks and the lack of know-how in this area had made itself felt. For VSB a merger was attractive because it would enable the bank to broaden its product range and, perhaps more important, because it was seen as a fast way to expand to regions of the country not previously covered (Gerards and Schipper 1989). In 1992 it started a joint venture with the Spanish insurer Caixa, as part of a strategy

to become a European player with several 'home markets'. With two relatively big organisations and only a handful of smaller savings banks left, no
separate role was left for BdB. SNS Bank, which had a majority share to
start with, absorbed it in 1991. In 1994 it also took over the relatively small
NOG insurance company.

The savings banks have lost their role as the principal refuge for nickel-
and-dime savers. They have to compete on equal terms with other financial
institutions, which implies that they should not be given special privileges.
Savings banks had been exempt from profit tax. As from 1969 a new law
restricted the exemption and a 1984 law altogether abolished it, albeit with a
transition period of 13 years. Against this, they have entered the commercial
overdraft loan market, however cagily. Their natural habitat is made up of
small- and medium-sized enterprises, non-profit organisations and the pro-
fessions, but it has proved far from easy to wrest a slice of this market from
well-established competitors with more know-how. Mortgage loans may
help to reduce interest rate risk; overdraft loans are much better in this
respect of course. Also, overdraft loans may help prevent extreme fluctuations in a bank's liquidity position. If salaries are paid into the accounts of a
bank's customers at the end of every month it is better to have the business
firms that pay the salaries and are the beneficiaries of return flows of money
during the next monthly period as clients as well. Over a month total liabilities of a bank are much more stable in such a situation, and on average a
smaller fraction of assets has to be held in liquid form. The savings banks
face an additional disadvantage *vis-à-vis* the commercial banks in that
private clients are as yet hardly charged for the costs of running the payments system (though changes are in the air) and savings banks have a disproportionate percentage of private clients as against business clients. The
end result is a sorry tale of steadily declining market shares. While the
savings banks have been trying to develop into full-fledged commercial
banks, others launched new attacks on their (and the other banks') savings
reservoir, making life even more difficult for them. The Robeco investment
company founded its Roparco subsidiary in 1981. Roparco offers a relatively high interest rate whilst savers can dispose quite freely of their money
instead of giving up disposability for a certain period or having to pay a
penalty in case of withdrawing money. Roparco has been able to offer such
favourable terms because, though registered as a commercial bank, it only
accepts payments into its accounts or withdrawals from its accounts
through accounts that people hold with other banks. Its operating costs are
consequently low. Insurers, such as AEGON with its daughter Spaarbeleg,
also have entered that market.

One way to survive is to offer products that others do not. An interesting
phenomenon in this respect is the development of ethical banking.

Algemene Spaarbank voor Nederland (ASN) distinguishes itself by the ethical norms it applies in its investments (bonds and private placements). It does not invest in firms doing trade with countries with a poor human rights record or in firms that produce weaponry. ASN is one of three banks connected with the trade union movement who in 1990 combined with two insurance companies to form the Reaal Groep, a group that lacks coherence and was left again in 1992 by one of the banks. Another ideological bank is Triodos Bank,which bases itself on anthroposophic ideas and aims at stimulating new kinds of initiatives, such as ecologically sound investments.

7.5.3 The victims

If savings banks have been reduced in number and fight a bitter battle for survival and commercial banks have merged and combined with insurance companies, mortgage banks had no choice but to throw in the towel in the early 1980s. Mortgage banks specialise in granting credit with mortgages as security. Apart from own funds, they initially funded themselves exclusively by issuing mortgage bonds, from the 1950s on supplemented by private placements. Mortgage bonds used to differ from other bonds in that they were issued on tap, which enabled the mortgage banks immediately to adjust their credit interest rates to changes in market conditions and the volume of their borrowing to the volume of their lending. They were not subject to the so-called *calendrier* or calendar, a kind of waiting list for bond issuers administered by the Nederlandsche Bank with a view to preventing disruptions of the bond market which was in force from 1946 till the deregulation of the Dutch capital market in 1986. Furthermore, in contrast to other bonds, under an agreement with the Vereniging voor de Effectenhandel (Stock Brokers Association) mortgage bonds can be sold directly by the issuers to the public through their own branches or through commercial banks, bypassing the stock exchange. Against this, mortgage banks were not allowed to attract funds from the public for periods shorter than two years.

The first ten years or so after the war were disappointing for the mortgage banks, as the housing market was subject to rent controls and dominated by government financed housing corporations and local councils. Things brightened up when the government, in an effort to stimulate home-ownership, as of 1 June 1956 began to grant subsidies to owner-occupiers of newly built houses and enabled local authorities to provide mortgage guarantees. This last measure made it possible for financiers to lend up to 90 per cent, instead of 65 or 70 per cent, of the building costs. Though providing a fillip to the activities of the mortgage banks, this measure sowed the seed of later difficulties. The availability of government guarantees meant that specialised knowledge of the housing market was no longer a prerequisite for survival in the mortgage loan business. Home owners who defaulted on their debt payments would be bailed out by the state and nothing was gained by the financier if he had an accurate idea of the value of a house in the case of foreclosure. As it happened, this made it attractive for other banks to enter the home loan market and so contributed to the ultimate foundering of the independent mortgage banks. It should be noted that, apart from mortgage banks operating in the real estate sector, there have been ship mortgage banks, which in 1971 were accepted as members of the Association.

With their loan business to home owners thriving, in the 1960s some of the big mortgage banks, to wit Friesch-Groningse Hypotheekbank (FGH) and the Westland and Utrecht mortgage banks, after their merger in 1969 known as the Westland-Utrecht Hypotheekbank (WUH), started to branch out into various real-estate activities, including property development, investment for their own account and, in the case of FGH, real-estate agency. Such activities could not be financed through mortgage bonds, as these had to be backed by mortgages. It was hoped that this diversification would bring a measure of risk-spreading, but these hopes were dashed when the real-estate crunch came around 1980. This followed after a boom which had started in 1975 and was fuelled by high inflation, lagging interest rates and high inflation expectations. All this had made real estate look like a safe investment and made prices soar. When the boom burst and both demand for and prices of real estate fell precipitously in 1979 and the following years, mortgage banks felt the crunch of increased competition. Commercial banks and savings banks had the edge on interest rates, as they could fund themselves with relatively cheap savings deposits. Life insurance companies and pension funds, also active in housing finance, did not have to pay high interest rates to attract funds either. To pile on the agony, the mortgage banks lost their monopoly of issues on tap. As from 1981, commercial banks have been allowed to issue *bankbrieven*, which are bonds issued on tap by banks. Initially these were restricted to a total of 500 million guilders a year for all the commercial banks together, but as from 1987 no restrictions apply. The commercial banks naturally have been more interested in selling their own product than in selling a similar product issued by mortgage banks. Worst of all, the mortgage banks got bad publicity as it emerged that they had overexpanded and had to shed personnel and reduce the number of branch offices. Mortgage bonds could only be sold at increasingly higher yields as compared with other bonds, if indeed they could be sold at all. The Westland Utrecht Hypotheekbank (WUH) attempted to safeguard funding by selling mortgage loans to the Algemeen Burgerlijk Pensioenfonds (ABP), the civil servants' pension fund, which would bring in slightly over 3 billion guilders over the period 1981 through 1983. A high supply of WUH mortgage bonds in the secondary market depressed prices in 1981, increasing effective yields to dizzying levels so that funding, i.e., attracting investors, became well-nigh impossible. The Nederlandsche Bank initiated a safety net in order to maintain orderly market conditions, but the syndicate providing the safety net did not prevent the yield on WUH mortgage bonds rising to as high as 15 per cent (Gerards and Schipper 1994, p. 9). Meanwhile, losses, in large part from the property development sector, continued accumulating and in 1982 the Nederlandsche Bank lifted its ban on banks and insurance companies buying into mortgage banks. ABP supplied subordinated loans and, more important, the Nationale-Nederlanden insurance company acquired preference shares. The Nederlandsche Bank helped finance a foundation specially set up in 1983 to take over bad loans from WUH. Nonetheless, further aid proved necessary and in 1986 WUH became a wholly owned daughter of Nationale-Nederlanden. Similarly, the Friesch-Groningse Hypotheekbank (FGH) had to be rescued by a financial injection from the Rijkspostspaarbank (RPS) in 1983 and by further participations in 1986 from Postbank and the AEGON insurance company. After new losses had been run up in 1986, AEGON took over FGH in 1987. Postbank opted out because it still was a government agency and was not allowed by the Minister of Finance to become heavily involved in a private mortgage bank: the Conservative Liberal party and the Christian Democrats in parliament feared that foreign investors would react negatively to a takeover by a state bank (Mulder 1987, p. 64).

The big two among the independent mortgage banks found a safe haven with insurance companies. No such luck befell Tilburgsche Hypotheekbank, a small outfit that had made big loans to borrowers of dubious reputation and had taken recourse to counterfeit surveys of real estate in order to justify its loans. As a collapse of Tilburgsche would severely damage the whole industry, the big three, FGH, WUH and Rabohypotheekbank after some prodding by the Nederlandsche Bank furnished Tilburgsche with an 18 million guilders subordinated convertible loan. But to no avail. Nobody was interested in taking over the Tilburgsche and in August 1983 it was declared bankrupt. The healthy parts of the estate were then bought by the ENNIA insurance company, which later became part of AEGON.

The biggest mortgage bank, Rabohypotheekbank, which came into being in 1975 through a merger of Boerenhypotheekbank and Raiffeisenhypotheekbank, was little affected by the trials and tribulations of other mortgage banks. For one thing, they had restricted themselves to the core business of mortgage banks. Also, they had less difficulty selling their mortgage bonds and attracting private placements than other mortgage banks, because of the high repute of the Rabobank group of which they were a part and which guaranteed their liabilities. They took over Nederlandse Scheepshypotheekbank or Dutch Ship Mortgage Bank, which with mortgage bonds in disrepute faced insurmountable difficulties in funding themselves, in 1986. As the other remaining independent mortgage bank, Friesch-Hollandsche Hypotheekbank, had already been taken over by the AMEV for the same reason, this marked the end of the era of independent mortgage banks.

None of the independent mortgage banks proved able to weather the storms of the early 1980s. Even without the shocks in the real-estate market around 1980 it is doubtful whether the independent mortgage banks could have survived much longer than they actually did (cf. Koelewijn 1987; Voûte 1989). In a capital market where the government left increasingly less opportunities for other borrowers, funding became increasingly harder and more expensive. There is little reason to believe that the mortgage banks would have been able to hold their own not only against the government as a big borrower, but also against the commercial banks, cooperative banks and savings banks, which had the advantage of cheap funding through savings deposits, while the commercial banks also intruded into the territory of tap-issued bonds. The loss of their sheltered niche on the capital market combined with increased competition on the home loan market, in particular from other banks and RPS with their extensive branch networks, could hardly have failed to turn their profits into losses.

7.5.4 The payments mechanism

In the passage on the concentration movement among savings banks the importance of technological developments in the payments mechanism was already hinted at. The payments mechanism was for a long time a subject on which the banks and PCGD carefully avoided coming to an agreement. Already before the war attempts had been made by the banks to introduce a payments system that would provide a cheaper alternative to payments by cheque, which were subject to stamp duty. On a small scale this Bankiersgiro or Bankers' Giro started functioning in December 1937, but it did not really take off. The system was cumbersome and payments took quite a time to effect, because there were no less than 25 clearing banks in the system. Participating banks channelled payments through these banks. They, in turn, cleared any remaining balances via the Nederlandsche Bank, once a day. In 1944 Kas-Vereeniging started another system, and so The Netherlands entered the post-war period with no less than five separate payments systems, each using their own forms, and run respectively by the Nederlandsche Bank, PCGD, the Amsterdam Municipal Giro System,

Bankiersgiro and the Kas-Vereeniging's giro. Attempts at holding consultations between PCGD and the Bankers' Association on unifying the forms had something of a ritual dance, a very slow one at that, and came to grief. The banks were not very forthcoming and PCGD for its part wished to retain the system where banks, in order to be able to make payments on behalf of their clients, had to keep balances on accounts with PCGD (Wolf 1983, p. 42). In the meantime business firms started to make increased use of PCGD, because automation had made it possible for them to send large numbers of payment orders on punch cards or magnetic tapes. On top of that, PCGD had introduced pre-punched giro credit slips, which clients of firms and other organisations only had to sign and which simplified book-keeping a great deal. Especially after a number of municipal services had strongly advised the public to shift to this method of payment, the banks started to make haste (Wolf 1983, p. 43). After all, the number of accounts held with PCGD increased threefold between 1960 and 1970, from less than 800,000 to 2.25 million, doubling again over the next decade (Peekel and Veluwenkamp 1984, p. 14).

The year 1967 saw the establishment of Bankgirocentrale (BGC), the bank giro centre, by the commercial banks and the agricultural cooperative banks, who were in 1969 joined by the savings banks. BGC processes all giro payments between the several banks and those between the participating banks and Postbank. After payments have been effected, remaining claims of banks on each other are settled via the banks' accounts held with the Nederlandsche Bank. This clearing takes place once a day. At the time, such a system only existed in Sweden. At last progress was also made in making life for the public easier. After eight years of laborious negotiations, the banks and PCGD came to an agreement to introduce pre-punched giro credit slips that could be used for either payments system (Wolf 1983, p. 63).

Remittances were made without charge. The banks initially even provided stamp-free envelopes, if only because the postal giro system had been traditionally doing the same. Against the costs of running the payments mechanism the banks received the interest returns on loans outstanding, but, as the paper work is quite labour intensive and interest on loans is uncertain and fluctuating, the costs were more and more felt as a burden. This was a major reason for some of the smaller banks to pull out of the retail market around 1990. As from 1990 the banks have been introducing charges for their payment services, but ever so slowly because of the concerted opposition from both consumer and business organisations, even if charges on payment accounts are low in comparison with other European countries (cf. Jongepier 1991). The Nederlandsche Bank by contrast strongly supports the banks in this respect, out of concern for their financial health.

Even if PCGD via Postbank has become part of a commercial bank, the postal giro system and BGC have not yet been integrated. Payments from accounts held in one system to accounts held in the other are possible, but time-consuming. One integrated system would of course be preferable. The then Minister of Finance, Dr Duisenberg, in 1975 gave orders to investigate how to integrate the two payment systems. Integration takes place by steps and it will probably take till the turn of the century before it will be completed.

The developments described all served to increase the attractiveness of bank money *vis-à-vis* currency. A further step along this road has been the introduction of EFTPOS (Electronic Fund Transfer at Point of Sale). This was only spreading slowly at first, because business firms tended to consider the costs charged them too high, but in the early 1990s the system really took off.

7.6 Functions and development of the Nederlandsche Bank

7.6.1 Supervision

Unlike some other countries, such as Belgium and Germany, in The Netherlands the central bank is charged not only with monetary policy but also with prudential supervision. Monetary policy is concerned with keeping the value of the guilder steady, both in terms of other currencies, in practice the Deutschmark, and in terms of purchasing power. Prudential supervision is concerned with protecting the banks' creditors. After the war, supervision was still based on a 1932 regulation, which did not give the Nederlandsche Bank much hold over the banks. This changed after the Wet Toezicht Kredietwezen (WTK for short), based on the 1948 Bank Act, came into force in 1952. It authorised the Nederlandsche Bank to issue rules on capital–asset ratios and liquidity ratios. A third branch of policy was so-called structure policy, aimed at preventing financial combines coming into existence that would be too powerful. In particular, banks and insurance companies were not allowed to hold significant amounts of each other's shares. The difficulties in the mortgage bank sector in the early 1980s led to the first weakening of this principle, and with the approach of the integrated European financial market it was to all practical purposes discarded in January 1990. The only restriction now is that banks and insurance companies should remain separate legal entities, but there are no objections from the monetary authorities to banks and insurance companies being in one holding. With both banks and insurance companies in the same holding, the Nederlandsche Bank remains responsible for prudential supervision of the banking leg and the Verzekeringskamer (Insurance Chamber) for supervision of the insurance leg. This is quite different from prudential supervision of banks. With insurance companies, it is not capital–asset ratios that count, but the relationship between income and future obligations, on the one hand, and own capital, on the other. It is to be expected that the Nederlandsche Bank and the Verzekeringskamer will have to cooperate ever closer in the future in order to redress or prevent unfair competition, as banks sell insurance policies and insurance companies sell banking products, in particular mortgage loans.

National rules as to supervision are more and more shaped or even superseded by those of international agencies. In 1989 the EC passed the Second Banking Directive, to which national laws had to be adapted by 1 January, 1993, at the latest. This guideline opens up all national financial markets of the member states to the financial institutions of all member states. A credit institution from a member state after that date will be able to open a branch office or provide cross-border services in any other member state. It will be able to offer the same kind of services abroad as it is entitled to offer in its home market. Each EC country is responsible for the prudential supervision of those banks that have their headquarters in that country, applying the common capital-adequacy standards, whilst monetary supervision is the province of the country where a subsidiary is active.

International developments forced the Dutch monetary authorities to give up their opposition against close ties between banks and insurance companies, after they had opened the door a crack at the time of the mortgage bank crisis. They had also been opposed to *banques d'affaires*, i.e., banks heavily involved in non-bank firms through share ownership, again out of a concern about concentration of power. WTK 1978 stipulated that banks should not hold more than 5 per cent of the share capital of another firm, and then only temporarily, unless given special permission. Also, a bank is not allowed to invest more than 20 per cent of its own capital in non-financial firms. The Nederlandsche Bank had already made an exception in order to enable the banks providing capital to small- and medium-sized enterprises. In 1980 the banks received general permission to take a minority share in such firms, to a maximum of 2.5 million guilders and in principle for no longer than five years, in 1986 extended to 4 million and ten years respectively. The provisions of the Second Banking Directive forced the Dutch monetary authorities to soften their stance further. In WTK 1992, effective as of the 1 January 1993, the time limit on share holdings by banks in non-financial firms was dropped. Also, the Nederlandsche Bank routinely agrees with investments that do not exceed 10 per cent of a bank's own capital and stay within 30 per cent of own capital for the aggregate of such investments, with a possibility of increasing these ceilings to 15 per cent and 60 per cent respectively.

Prudential supervision cannot mean that the central bank guarantees creditors that banks will never fail. That would put a premium on irresponsible behaviour by bank managers: if a risky venture succeeds, the spoils are for the bank shareholders and managers, if a venture goes sour, the central bank and ultimately the tax payer has to pay up. There is thus a moral hazard problem in prudential supervision. The Dutch solution, introduced in 1979 with the revised WTK, is that deposits or other registered claims of individuals, foundations and associations are guaranteed up to an amount that is reviewed every three years, in the 1989–91 period 40,000 guilders per individual or institute, and the same for the next three years. Unlike the American system, this is a mutual guarantee system. If a bank fails to redeem claims on it, the rest of the Dutch banking system will compensate the victims. Again, unlike the American system, the Dutch solution appears to avoid the moral hazard problem while at the same time providing full protection to small depositors. Big depositors and business firms should be able to avoid risky banks and if they are lured by high credit interest rates offered by little-known financial institutions, they must suffer themselves if such a bank fails. This fate befell a few Dutch municipalities when the obscure Amsterdam American Bank closed its doors in 1981. Prudential supervision does not imply a guarantee by the Nederlandsche Bank to creditors of financial institutions. Legal action by creditors of failed financial institutions (Amsterdam American and Tilburgsche) against the Nederlandsche Bank therefore was bound to come to grief.

Though the system is satisfactory from the point of view of moral hazard and protection to depositors, the distribution of the burden is perhaps not entirely fair. First of all, cautious banks have to pay for the careless ones, which can hardly be avoided without changing to another system (for instance, an insurance system with premiums dependent on the perceived risk of assets). More seriously, Dutch banks suffer if a Dutch subsidiary, even if itself perfectly sound, of a foreign bank has to close its doors as a result of the failure of the parent (De Leeuw 1992). And of course, the system would fall apart if any of the big three were to fail.

Over the years, the Nederlandsche Bank has extended its supervision to other sectors, in addition to the commercial banks. WTK 1952 charged the Nederlandsche Bank with the task of supervising the savings banks and prudential supervision was introduced in 1954, when the Nederlandsche Bank issued directions on required liquidity, followed in 1958 by directions on capital–asset ratios. Before 1954 there had already been a degree of self-regulation by the Spaarbankbond. This apparently was up to the standards required by the Nederlandsche Bank, for it was agreed that the Spaarbankbond would henceforth supervise the savings banks on behalf of the Nederlandsche Bank. The Nederlandsche Bank did not take over until 1

January 1990.WTK 1978 brought the mortgage banks within the compass of the Nederlandsche Bank's control, effective from 1 January, 1980. From 1936 onwards they had exercised a form of self-regulation, over and above supervision from RPS. When in 1928 the Centrale Beleggingsraad or Central Investment Council was formed in order to supervise investments on behalf of a number of government agencies, RPS was charged by this council with supervision on mortgage bonds, which they had already done since 1905 on their own initiative. This state of affairs formally ended only in 1952 (De Knocke van der Meulen 1981, p. 36). In 1991 investment funds were brought under the Nederlandsche Bank's supervision.

7.6.2 Monetary policy

Minister of Finance Pieter Lieftinck opted for a rather dirigiste policy immediately after the war, aimed at keeping interest rates, and with it the cost of investing and the burden of the government debt, low. This policy could succeed because the capital market was strictly controlled. Monitoring went so far that all bank loans over 50,000 guilders had to be okayed by the Nederlandsche Bank. The Nederlandsche Bank's status itself was to be changed shortly. Firstly, in 1948 it was nationalised, even if it retained the legal guise of a limited liability company. Secondly, the 1948 Bank Act, which defined the tasks and the powers of the Nederlandsche Bank, was passed, with the instruments at its disposal to be spelled out later in the WTK (1952, revised in 1956, 1978 and 1992). Article 9 charges the Nederlandsche Bank with safeguarding, as far as possible, the value of the guilder, both in terms of purchasing power – i.e., the internal value of the guilder – and in terms of its price expressed in foreign exchange – i.e., the external value of the guilder. But how should it go about fulfilling these tasks? Traditionally, central banks tried to defend the internal and/or the external value of their currency by influencing the money supply or credit conditions through the discount window and open-market operations. WTK 1952 gave the Nederlandsche Bank additional instruments, such as the imposition of minimum liquidity ratios, credit ceilings and selective credit control, all of which had been deployed prior to WTK 1952 coming into effect, on the basis of special arrangements. Directly after the war there was little scope for discount policy. The banks were superliquid, awash with Treasury bills, as Mr. Lieftinck in his concern for low interest rates made no haste in consolidating the public floating debt. In the period 1952–4 the state took measures to decrease the liquidity of the banks, through length-ening the term of the bills to a maximum of twelve years. The year 1954 saw the introduction of cash ratios. The Nederlandsche Bank could compel the banks to keep an interest-free deposit with the Nederlandsche Bank as a percentage of their liquid liabilities, to be revised every month. In this way, credit expansion by the banks could be kept within bounds. Later on, in 1956 and 1957, with balance-of-payments deficits and a continuing increase in bank note circulation, both of which were a drain on the banks' liquid assets, the banks became more dependent on the Nederlandsche Bank, and from the mid 1970s it has been customary for them to be in the red with the Nederlandsche Bank, even if during the 1960s the banks' liquidity position was improving through inflationary finance by the government and private-sector balance-of-payments surpluses (Van der Werf 1988, pp. 211, 215; Den Dunnen and De Wilde 1991, p. 23). If the banks are in the red the Nederlandsche Bank has a handle on them. In 1958–60, though, the balance of payments on the money account was comfortably in the black. The Nederlandsche Bank did not want to impose higher cash ratios, because that would induce the banks, which had built up a considerable volume of foreign assets, to repatriate these assets, i.e., sell them to the Nederlandsche Bank. In the circumstances, the Nederlandsche Bank pre-ferred the banks to hold foreign assets, rather than see its own foreign cur-rency reserves grow, for reasons of international monetary cooperation. This meant the Nederlandsche Bank had to give up exclusive reliance on indirect measures, i.e., manipulation of the discount rate and the cash ratio, for direct measures, such as credit ceilings and moral suasion (De Haan *et al.* 1981, pp. 78–81).[1] Without abandoning the discount rate as an instru-ment of monetary policy, during the 1961–72 period the Nederlandsche Bank relied mostly on various forms of direct credit control. By and large these implied ceilings on short-term credit expansion, overdraft loans and loans for periods shorter than two years, complemented in 1965 by a rule for the expansion of the volume of longer-term loans (two years and over) not to exceed the growth of longer-term liabilities (De Roos and Renooij 1980, pp. 181 ff.). This meant that the creation of broad money through medium- and long-term credit would be neutralised by a fall in the money supply through shifts of money and near-monies into savings deposits, longer-term time deposits and bonds.

The problem with direct controls is that they do not conform with market forces. In particular, it was felt that credit ceilings, limiting credit expansion by individual banks to some percentage increase over the credit volume of a previous period, stifled competition. It proved difficult to accommodate the rapidly increasing number of foreign banks into the system (Renooij 1979, p. 11). Also, near-banking – i.e., short-term credit between non-banks – was in this way stimulated, reducing the impact of monetary policy measures. WTK 1978 therefore created the opportunity for the Nederlandsche Bank to extend its monetary supervision to the liquidity-creating activities of non-banks – i.e., the issue of short-term debt – but not without a government ordinance. Furthermore, as the dividing lines between the various financial institutions became blurred, the Nederlandsche Bank extended its grip over those institutions whose debt had been assuming a more liquid character: the savings banks in 1969, PCGD in 1970 and RPS in 1973. Note that this concerns monetary policy, not prudential supervision.

Required liquidity ratios were re-introduced in 1973 but phased out again in 1977 in favour of credit ceilings. These ceilings differed from the earlier ones in that the Nederlandsche Bank did not fix an upper limit to the volume of credit, but to the volume of liquidity creation through credit granting, be it short term or long term. If a bank hit the ceiling, it could always increase its lending, provided it also managed to attract new long-term funds, such as savings deposits. Any increase in the volume of broad money was in that way compensated for by the fall brought about by converting broad money into less liquid forms. The end result would be an increase in long-term interest rates.

The shift from salary payments in hard cash to payments into giro and bank accounts that took place in the 1960s led to changes in the composition of the (narrow) money supply (see table 7.9). (Coins are issued by the Ministry of Finance but brought into circulation by the Nederlandsche Bank, before 1993, for small denominations, by the post offices; shifts by the public from bank money into coins involve payments by the banks into the account which the government holds with the Nederlandsche Bank.) Consequently, any increase in the currency supply makes the banks more dependent on the Nederlandsche Bank for if the public wants notes or coin, the banks have to buy these on their behalf from the Nederlandsche Bank and their balances held with the Nederlandsche Bank fall. A falling share of currency in the money supply eases the pressure on the banks' balances with the Nederlandsche Bank and so lessens the Nederlandsche Bank's hold on them. This is what the banks were achieving in the 1960s. Various cash reserve instruments are available, though, to keep them in the red and enable the Nederlandsche Bank to control short interest rates.

For a large part of the post-war period, the Nederlandsche Bank attempted to control the domestic price level through manipulation of the broad money supply and the rate of exchange through manipulation of the short interest rate. It was thought that the control of the money supply would have a greater impact on long-term rates of interest than on short-term rates. The credit ceilings were indeed aimed at influencing long rates, so that spending could be controlled. Short rates then remained available for regulating short-term international capital movements and consequently could be used for weakening or strengthening the guilder in foreign-exchange markets. To these ends, the Nederlandsche Bank maintained, or even created, a strict division between short-term credit markets and long-

Table 7.9. *Bank money and currency, 1955–1993*

Year	Currency as per cent of national income	Bank money	Currency as per cent of the narrow money supply	Bank money
1955	14.4	19.2	43	57
1960	12.8	15.7	45	55
1965	12.0	14.0	43	57
1970	9.0	14.5	38	62
1975	7.5	16.8	31	69
1980	7.2	14.3	33	67
1985	7.5	16.3	32	68
1990	7.8	18.7	29	71
1993	7.4	22.1	25	75

Source: The Nederlandsche Bank, Annual reports.

term capital markets. Developments in either market should not in any appreciable degree spill over into the other one. Short-term bond issues therefore were forbidden, as were bullet loans, loans that are fully redeemed at one fixed date, and which, when the redemption date draws close, tend to be used as money market paper. Nor could commercial paper and negotiable certificates of deposit find favour with the Nederlandsche Bank.

After the final breakdown of the Bretton Woods system of fixed but adjustable parities in 1973, which had tottered and been patched up in 1971, the rate of exchange more and more assumed pride of place in monetary policy. Besides, international capital movements exploded, increasing the interest elasticity of capital flows to very high values indeed. All this meant that the use of the interest-rate instrument in the attempt to stabilise exchange rates elicited increasingly large capital inflows and outflows, which were manifested in notable rises and falls of the domestic money supply and made an independent money-supply policy illusory. On top of that, the liberalisation of financial markets in the world marched on. The Netherlands, with its large sector of international firms, its important financial community and its concern for the future of Amsterdam as a financial centre, could not afford to remain in slow lane. The year 1986 saw the abolition of the restrictions on the issues of debt instruments. The artificial separation between the short-term credit market and the capital market is a thing of the past and the Nederlandsche Bank has effectively given up its attempts to control the money supply. Exchange-rate policy now occupies centre stage and a stable price level is largely dependent on price develop-

Table 7.10. *Inflation rates, 1950–1990 (averages)*

	1950–60	1960–70	1970–80	1980–90
Netherlands	3.3	5.4	8.4	1.9
Belgium	2.4	3.6	7.6	4.4
France	6.4	4.2	9.7	6.1
Germany (FRG)	3.2	3.2	5.1	2.7
United Kingdom	4.0	4.1	14.4	5.8
United States	2.5	2.8	7.1	3.7

Sources: 1950–60 calculated as cumulative growth rates from OECD GNP price indexes taken from Maddison 1964, p. 45. Other periods GDP deflators, source *World Development Report* 1982, 1992.

ments in the countries whose currencies are pegged to each other and to the guilder in the European Monetary System. Nonetheless, a money-supply or credit-supply policy cannot entirely be dispensed with, because too high a rate of domestic credit creation would cause capital exports, either direct or via a fall in interest rates, leading to a drop in the foreign-exchange reserves of the central bank and the commercial banks. Ultimately confidence in the stability of the guilder would be damaged and investors would launch an attack on the guilder. As an aside, maintaining confidence has also been the reason for the Nederlandsche Bank to prefer the short-term interest rate as an instrument for exchange-rate policy to direct interventions in the foreign-exchange market, which are thought to be more apt to make the market nervous, i.e., make it expect exchange-rate changes (Den Dunnen and De Wilde 1991, p. 13).

Over the years, the Nederlandsche Bank's monetary policy, supported by a largely non-inflationary fiscal policy and, some would add, by incomes policy, has been quite successful in maintaining the external value of the guilder, even if the inflation record has been less impressive (see table 7.10). True, in September 1949, when the pound sterling was devalued by 30.5 per cent *vis-à-vis* the American dollar, The Netherlands followed suit with a devaluation of 30.2 per cent, upping the par value of the dollar from 2.65 guilders to 3.80. It is a moot point whether this large devaluation was really necessary, and the Nederlandsche Bank would indeed have settled for a devaluation of about 24 per cent (Bakker and Van Lent 1989, p. 170), but Mr Lieftinck's policy was to keep Dutch prices low relative to other countries. Pressure from the Minister of Agriculture, S. Mansholt, seems to have played a role as well (Van Lennep and Schoorl 1991, pp. 45, 144). The liberalisation of European trade in 1950 helped to translate the devaluation into increased exports, at the cost of some upward pressure on the domestic price level. Moderate inflation rates and mounting current account surpluses in Germany and The Netherlands together with the wish to keep imported inflation at bay led to a revaluation of the mark and the guilder by 5 per cent in March 1961 (Yeager 1966, p. 418). This caused protests by exporters and a general stir hard to imagine for those accustomed to the violent exchange-rate changes of the post-1973 period. Nevertheless, the appreciation proved too small to offset the inflation differentials *vis-à-vis* other countries and so contributed, through high profits and overemployment, to the 1964 wage explosion. In the post-Bretton Woods era, a number of European countries cooperated in order to narrow exchange-rate fluctuations, culminating in the European Monetary System (EMS) in 1979. Within the EMS, which for all practical purposes is a system of fixed-but-adjustable parities, the Dutch policy has been to follow parity changes of the Deutschmark, though the Minister of Finance, H.O.C.R. Ruding, snubbed the Nederlandsche Bank by only partially following the revaluation of the Deutschmark in March 1983. The poor inflation record of the 1970s was a result of downward real wage rigidity. Wages were fully compensated for the rise of energy prices resulting from the 1973–4 oil crisis, at the cost of falling profits and rapidly rising unemployment. Here incomes policy, or the lack of it, made the Nederlandsche Bank's task in fighting inflation a hopeless one.

Article 26 of the 1948 Bank Act gives the Nederlandsche Bank a very high degree of independence from government interference in the field of monetary policy, as apart from the pegging of exchange rates. If the Minister and the Nederlandsche Bank disagree and do not succeed in patching up their differences, the Bank Act provides for a lengthy procedure to bring the Nederlandsche Bank on its knees. So far, this procedure has not been used. The independence of the Nederlandsche Bank is jealously guarded, and not without reason for, as former Bank President Dr. Jelle Zijlstra tells us in his memoirs, politicians and civil servants every now and then attempt to undermine Article 26 (Zijlstra 1992, pp. 212 ff.). This independence meant, inter alia, that the Nederlandsche Bank could not be forced by the government to finance its deficits. The 1948 Bank Act stipulates that the government has the right to demand interest-free loans from the Nederlandsche Bank, subject, though, to a ceiling of only 150 million guilders. If the government wanted more, it had to try to conclude an agreement with the Nederlandsche Bank. Such agreements typically restricted borrowing by the state from the Nederlandsche Bank, i.e., selling Treasury bills to them, to a small percentage of the total state budget, basically to bridge seasonal fluctuations in the financing needs of the government. Of course, the second stage of European Monetary Integration, which came into effect on 1 January 1994, changed all this: no direct financing of the state by the central bank is allowed at all.

The aims of stabilising both the internal and the external value of the guilder are not necessarily always compatible. Maintaining stable exchange rates when foreign countries suffer from high inflation inevitably leads to imported inflation, and, if one wants to give priority to stable prices, a float-ing rate system or periodic revaluations are inevitable. The Netherlands have been lucky in that its main trading partner, the German Federal Republic, still haunted by the memory of the hyperinflation of the early 1920s, made price stability one of its overriding policy objectives. Linking the guilder to the mark has therefore been a convenient way to fulfil the tasks set by the Bank Act.

If and when the European Central Bank becomes a reality, the Nederlandsche Bank will lose its sway over monetary policy. The loss of autonomy is more nominal than real, though, as the leeway available for conducting an independent monetary policy has steadily narrowed with the increasing openness of the economy and in particular with the explosive growth of actual and potential capital flows over the last two decades or so. The Nederlandsche Bank cannot do much else than follow the Bundesbank. What will remain is its task in prudential supervision.

7.7 Summary

When the reconstruction had been completed in the beginning of the 1950s, the new Keynesian ideas on government spending as an instrument for eco-nomic policies could be put into practical effect. Successive governments aimed at stabilising the economy by means of the budget but, partly due to lengthy procedures, this policy proved to intensify cyclical swings instead.

The creation of an unprecedented social security and welfare system also led to a high tax and social premium burden that undermined the competitiveness of the business sector. Moreover, the building up of the welfare state and the weakened position in the Cabinet of the Minister of Finance undermined budget discipline, so that large deficits developed which led to a dominating role by the government as a borrowing party on financial markets. Yet, the growth of semi-private or collective savings enabled the state to cover its deficits entirely on the Dutch market.

Dutch banking developed stormily. The demarcation lines between the financial institutions in the different market segments were broken up under the increasing competition for deposits. This led to a first wave of diversification and mergers in the 1960s. A second one, stimulated by the prospect of a united Europe, followed after the Nederlandsche Bank lifted its ban on mergers between banks and insurance companies. As a result, a few powerful combines offering a wide array of services, loom in the financial markets.

Amidst these changes the Nederlandsche Bank had to adapt its supervision as well as its policy instruments, which are primarily aimed at protecting the value of the guilder. The economic and monetary cooperation within Europe gradually limited the scope of these instruments. The Nederlandsche Bank has successfully pegged the Dutch currency to the Deutschmark, a situation that resembles the 1930s when the guilder had been pegged to gold.

Notes

1 The credit ceilings that were in place during 1957–8 were ineffective because of a cyclical downswing.

8 Conclusion

MARJOLEIN 'T HART, JOOST JONKER, AND JAN LUITEN VAN ZANDEN

Over the last 25 years, financial history has travelled the familiar road towards specialisation. Rondo Cameron's twin path-breaking volumes used finance and banking to focus on details about the origins of modern economic growth (Cameron 1967, 1972). Since then, the focus seems to have turned, as financial history became more introspective. Monographs, and journals on as well as associations of financial history proliferated, but the subject itself fragmented further into specialisms with the broader questions of economic and political development receding into the background. As a result, the main topics of banking, public finance, and currency have become isolated from each other, each confined to separate textbooks or at best separate chapters, such as in Kindleberger's classic and courageous attempt at a synthesis (Kindleberger 1984).

In this book, we have attempted to bridge some of these faults by exploring the relationship between banking, currency and public finance in The Netherlands over a period of nearly five centuries. Our main aim was to show how since the mid sixteenth century the gradual evolution of very different regions into a single national state with a firmly integrated economy largely depended on progress in the financial sphere. The preceding chapters all demonstrate the importance of the links between the three ostensibly separate fields of banking, currency and public finance, bottlenecks in any one of them slowing down progress in all. Once a particular obstacle is out of the way, banking, currency and public finance mesh to produce a new phase of growth, only to be halted again by economic, political or technical constraints cropping up elsewhere. After the broad analytical outline of the changing relationships between government, the economy and the financial system in the Introduction, we want to summarise the key aspects of the three financial economic phases which may be distinguished from the late sixteenth century: (1) provincial primacy, roughly 1570–1800; (2) the coming of the nation-state, from 1800 to 1914; and finally (3) from nation-state to wider monetary integration, from 1914 until today. Each started with a period of innovation and renewal, and ended with one of the constituent elements reaching its limits and thus checking the others.

8.1 Provincial primacy, 1570–1800

Around 1550, The Netherlands were fragmented into numerous regions and cities with a high degree of political and economic autonomy, though loosely grouped into provinces (*gewesten*). During the sixteenth century, the political focus gradually shifted towards the provinces under the centralising policies of the Habsburg Empire, culminating in the joint revolt against Spain and the ensuing creation of the Republic of the United Provinces (1579).

The principle of representative government by the consent of its constituent provinces enabled the Republic to pioneer a financial revolution. The cost of the war against Spain was met by establishing a long-term public debt subscribed by the same elites that ran the provinces. This political unity of sorts was, however, seriously impaired by continuing fiscal, financial and institutional fragmentation. Each of the provinces jealously guarded its autonomy enshrined in an independent fiscal system, tailored by the Habsburg Empire to its particular social and economic structure. While allowing wide regional differences in levels of taxation to persist, this attitude undermined the Republic through financial starvation and denied it the benefits of integration.

The monetary system of the Republic underwent a strikingly similar partial modernisation. The money circulation was in complete disorder, consisting of a wide variety of debased and foreign coins. To counter the confusion and thereby promote trade, the Amsterdam city council established the Bank of Amsterdam (1609), which exchanged any currency against the going rate for a credit on its books expressed in a unit of account, the *gulden* (bank guilder). The unique stability of the guilder and the girosystem of the Bank provided a basis of rapid and reliable settlement from which Amsterdam grew into the commercial capital of the world. Within The Netherlands however, banking remained a purely local affair. A number of cities followed the Amsterdam example and set up their own Bank of Exchange, but as these limited themselves to promoting local interests a system of interregional settlement failed to materialise.

These two features, the growing debt and the stable guilder, spurred the Dutch Golden Age. Both operated satisfactorily until about 1620, signalling the switch from innovation to consolidation in the phase of provincial primacy. The regular funded debt paid for the frequent wars which crippled countries dependent on less efficient ways of raising revenue, and was exported as so-called Dutch finance to the United Kingdom after the

Glorious Revolution. At the same time the rock-solid guilder underpinned a rapid expansion of trade and allied services, turning Amsterdam into the commercial hub of Europe.

However, because of continuing political fragmentation, blessings and handicaps went hand in hand. Firstly, the decentralised government which ensured the support of regional elites for successive loans prevented drastic measures to cut the deficit. With the need for revenue outstripping the capacity of the existing fiscal structure, regional autonomy asserted itself most strongly over taxation, thus causing any attempt at fiscal reform to be doomed. The Republic became caught between high yet insufficient taxes and a spiralling public debt, causing the economic arteries to harden at a time when increasing competition put a premium on flexibility. Secondly, local autonomy enabled merchants to fashion economic institutions best suited to their needs, but limited the scope of institutional expansion to the city and its immediate vicinity. The Bank of Amsterdam wallowed in a proud sclerosis, firmly clinging to the limited role of hoarding gold and running the giro circulation at a time when elsewhere banks set up in its image, like the Bank of England, had been offering regular credit and bank-notes for a long time. The crises of 1763 and 1773 painfully revealed both the inadequacy of the system of the Bank of Amsterdam and the urgent need for some central bank to shore up trade with credit. Moreover, the guilder had long run its course. It served well in European trade, but did nothing for the chaotic circulation at home. As a unit of account bank money provided a yardstick, but no suitable replacement, for the bewildering varieties of coin produced by the several autonomous mints. Thus, the regional pride which inspired the Dutch revolt came home to roost as fiscal and monetary fragmentation. Consequently a political and economic stalemate set in during the last quarter of the eighteenth century, followed by a slow collapse before the French invasion of 1795.

8.2 The coming of the nation-state, 1800–1914

The breakthrough came with the Batavian Revolution and the ensuing French occupation (1795–1813). In just under 20 years regional autonomy disappeared, to be replaced by centralised government. Even so, financial and economic integration was far from complete. The new Kingdom of The Netherlands (1813) started with a shattered economy, a crushing public debt and a currency uniform only in theory. Tax revenue continuously fell short of expenditure, forcing the autocratic King William I to bypass parliament with ever more ingenious financial constructions. As a consequence political suspicion frustrated initiatives to bring the state deficit back under control after the disastrous escalation during the Belgian secession. Tax harmonisation and currency reform had to be postponed, so economic integration stalled, and banking thus remained tied to local and regional niches.

The fiscal, monetary and constitutional reforms of the 1840s completed the political breakthrough begun 50 years earlier, creating the necessary preconditions for further financial growth. Within 20 years a national financial system came into being, channelling deposits to the Amsterdam stock exchange, and extending advances through the agency network of the Nederlandsche Bank. This system had the great advantage of being uniform, flexible and secure, but at the cost of bolstering the financial centre and denying commercial banking a firm deposit base. As a result, commercial banking developed late, while provincial banking remained conspicuously weak.

Even so, the financial system as a whole proved resilient enough to withstand shocks like the hesitant change from a silver to gold standard and the neighbouring *Gründerkrise* in the 1870s, and provided a sound basis for the economic growth and budding industrialisation from the 1890s onwards.

8.3 From nation-state to wider monetary integration, 1914–

The international upward economic trend after 1895 brought the first signs of a new phase. It was characterised, on the one hand, by increasingly interventionist government policies and the continuing integration between different sectors of the economy. On the other hand, one can discern a shifting focus, from national points of reference for economic and financial policies towards an international framework. This caused a certain disorientation. During the 1920s and 1930s, the limitations of the national cadre became increasingly obvious, but, except for the budding coordination and cooperation between central banks, no substitutes were as yet available. Reinforced by the economic crisis and the war, a certain parochialism thus survived until in the 1950s when alternatives underpinning the international orientation sprang up.

Successive governments found themselves forced to move away from the ideal of the caretaker state towards active control over the economy, first during World War I and again during the economic crisis of the thirties. At the same time, the growing strength with which pressure groups and lobbies advanced their rival claims on public spending led to the abandonment of balanced budgets and creative accounting to camouflage deficits. State intervention was haphazard, however; only in the late thirties did the debate on public finance move towards deliberately using the budget as an instrument of economic and social policy.

Dutch banking traditionally kept to itself and steered clear of active involvement with other sectors of the economy. World War I proved to be a turning point here as well, stimulating developments towards greater integration. Attracted by sudden expansion due to import substitution, banks moved into industrial finance by granting long-term credits on a wide scale. Cooperative banking spread rapidly in the countryside with the growing demands of agriculture, its success boosting a similar chain of banks for city shopkeepers and traders. Finally, the increased economic activity stimulated the substitution of cash payments by bank transfers.

The banking system lacked the experience to cope with the forced pace of change, however, and the economic downturn of 1920 precipitated a prolonged crisis from which it had to be rescued by the combined action of the Nederlandsche Bank and the government. This shock inspired the banks to excessive concern with liquidity. They abandoned industrial finance for time honoured short-term commercial credit; sectoral economic integration thus slowed down, though it did not come to a halt.

The strain on public finance, increasing economic integration and the banking crisis pushed the Nederlandsche Bank centre stage. Its pivotal role in managing the currency through the international financial upheaval added political weight to its economic influence. From this position the bank went out of its way to promote a return to the pre-war situation of balanced budgets, strict adherence to the gold standard and sound banking based on short-term credit only. This policy appeared to be successful with the economic upturn after 1924, but it became more and more out of touch in the crisis climate of the thirties. However, working in close conjunction with the government, the bank adhered rigidly to its outdated convictions, thereby preventing an early recovery.

The conclusions of the public debate in the thirties on government spending as an instrument for social and economic policies were put into practical effect after World War II. As a result, the traditions of laissez-faire were finally dumped in favour of active intervention, and the state moved from the sidelines to the heart of the economy. Successive governments aimed to stabilise the economy by means of the budget but, partly due to delays in procedures, this policy proved to intensify cyclical swings instead. Moreover, it further undermined a budget discipline already under severe pressure from interest groups. The government came to dominate the financial markets by borrowing to cover the large deficits.

Boosted by the prosperity of the late fifties and sixties, the Dutch financial sector developed very rapidly and, helped by the breakdown of exchange controls built up since 1914, started to look outward again. The segmentation into different markets each catered for by separate banks was broken up by mergers that accelerated after the sixties. Consequently, a limited number of financial institutions tend to remain, offering a wide assortment of services. Meanwhile, the Nederlandsche Bank faced a decline of its national policy instruments, which more or less forced the bank to follow German monetary policies.

From the perspective presented in this book, the apparent collapse of the Exchange Rate Mechanism and the subsequent stalling of the European Monetary Union spells the advent of just the sort of bottleneck which characterised the development of the Dutch financial system over the past centuries. With that in mind, the one lesson to be learnt from the preceding chapters should be that a mustering of political will towards further unity makes sense only if it can be built on the underlying economic and financial realities.

Glossary

agio	premium levied by Bank of Amsterdam on the sale of solid coins
ARA	Algemeen Rijksarchief, The Hague
bankbrieven	bonds issued on tap by banks
Banken van Leening	banks of loans, modelled after the Lombards
bankgulden	bank money, money of account, bank guilder
Bankiersgiro	Bankers' Giro, girosystem between banks
Bankwet	Banking Act
banques d'affaires	banks heavily involved in non-bank firms through share ownership
Batavian Revolution	change of the political system due to French invasion of 1795
bede	provincial tax on request by king during Habsburg domination
bullet loans	loans fully redeemed at one fixed date
commissionairs	commission traders
convooien and licenten	customs during time of the Republic
Council of State	executive body of the States General during time of the Republic
crédit foncier	mortgage banking activities
Cultuurstelsel	system of exploitation of colonial fields and plantations
customs/custom duties	import and export duties
daalder, thaler	major coin in early modern Europe
De Nederlandsche Bank	the Dutch national (central) bank in the nineteenth and twentieth centuries
deferred debt	debt with no interest payments (due to Napoleon's tiёrcering), but gradually converted by King William I as interest bearing debt
direct taxes	taxes upon persons or personal property
dukaat, ducaton	major coin in early modern Europe
excises	indirect taxes on consumption
farmed taxes	taxes collected by a private entrepreneur, paying a lump sum for the right of collection to the state

financial revolution	development of funded debt in public finances
funded debt	public debt safeguarded by regular taxation
generality lands	reconquered areas during the time of the Republic, administered by the Council of State
gewesten	provinces (or counties) in the Dutch Republic and in the Habsburg Empire
Girodienst	Giro system
gouden tientje	gold coin of ten guilders
gulden financieringsregel	golden rule of accumulation in government finance
gulden	guilder
honderste penningen	taxes on property of stocks and bonds at 1 per cent
incidence of taxation	tax burden
indirect taxes	taxes upon trade or consumption
issues on tap	bonds offered for sale continuously (and not in one single bunch, as bonds usually are)
kassier	cashier
kassierspapier	cashier's paper, tender notes
kredietvereniging	mutual credit association
LDC	less-developed countries
merit goods	services offered by the state at prices well below cost, and in some cases even for free
monetary equilibrium	a situation in which the amount of money in circulation corresponds with the value of the demand for goods and services, so that the money sphere does not influence absolute prices
money overhang	a situation of the money supply exceeding the normal value of the supply of goods and services
money purge	process of enforced deflation through the blocking and controlled deblocking of money in circulation
muntbiljetten	temporary paper money as coin replacements
Nederlandse Landwacht	police force set up to counter the resistance movement during World War II
NEHA	Nederlandsch Economisch Historisch Archief (Amsterdam)
negotiepenningen	coins specifically used for trade during time of Republic
Patriots	political movement with democratic tendencies in the 1780s, partly revived with the Batavian Revolution of 1795
petitie	request
pillarisation	specific development of the Dutch political system along with the clusters of organisations according to denomination or ideology
polder	land reclaimed from the sea
prolongatie	on call money market

promessen	promissory notes, IOUs
quota	system of distribution (of tax burden for example)
Reichskreditkassenscheine	German occupation currency during World War II
redemption	buying off with a lump sum
semi-direct duties	taxes regarded as excises but levied either according to produce or to expected consumption
Staat van Oorlog	list of expenses of the United Provinces
Stadhouder	highest dignitary of the United Provinces during time of Republic, at the same time commander of the military forces; previously governor for the king; position held by the Princes of Orange and Nassau.
stagflation	a situation of economic stagnation combined with inflation
States General	highest authority during time of the Republic, made up from provincial delegates; parliament since establishment of kingdom of The Netherlands
stuiver	stiver
tax farmer	private entrepreneur, collecting taxes for the government
tiërcering	reduction of state debt by two-thirds enacted during Napoleonic period
wiebeltax or swing tax	temporary flexibility of tax rates within a range of 5 percent
Wisselbank	bank of exchange, generally Bank of Amsterdam during 1609–1820
wisselruiterij	setting up a chain of finance – or accommodation bills
zeehandelaren	(lit. sea traders) big merchants
zilverbon	silver certificate, a 'promissory note backed by silver yet to be issued', in practice a type of banknote

Bibliography

Attman, A., 1983b. 'The bullion flow from the Netherlands to the Baltic and the Arctic, 1500–1800', in *The interactions of Amsterdam and Antwerp with the Baltic region, 1400–1800. Papers presented at the third conference of the 'Association Internationale d'histoire des Mers Nordiques de l'Europe', Utrecht, August 30th–September 3rd 1982*. Amsterdam: NEHA, pp. 19–21.

Aylmer, G.E., 1987. *Rebellion or revolution? England 1640–1660*. Oxford: Oxford University Press.

Baelde, M., 1963. 'Financiële politiek en domaniale evolutie in de Nederlanden onder Karel V en Filips II (1530–1560)', *Tijdschrift voor Geschiedenis* 76: 14–33.

Bakker, A. and M.M.P. van Lent, 1989. *Pieter Lieftinck 1902–1989*. Utrecht/Antwerp: Veen.

Bakker, G.P. den and C.D. van Bochove, 1988. 'Discussie: Nederland in het interbellum', *Economische Statistische Berichten* 73: 341–3.

Barbour, V., 1950. *Capitalism in Amsterdam in the seventeenth century*. Baltimore: Johns Hopkins University Press.

Barendregt, J., 1993. *The Dutch money purge. The monetary consequences of German occupation and their redress after liberation, 1940–1952*. Amsterdam: Thesis Publishers.

Becht, H.E., 1908. *Statistische gegevens betreffende den handelsomzet van de Republiek der Vereenigde Nederlanden gedurende de 17e eeuw (1579–1715)*. The Hague: Boucher.

Berge, L.G. van den, 1939. *Giroverkeer in Nederland*. Den Haag: Uleman.

Bernanke, B. and H. James, 1991. 'The Gold Standard, deflation and financial crisis in the great depression: an international comparison', in R.G. Hubbard (ed.), *Financial markets and financial crises*. Chicago: University of Chicago Press, pp. 33–68.

Blockmans, W.P., 1988. 'Princes conquérants et bourgeois calculateurs. Le poids des réseaux urbains dans la formation des états', in *La ville, la bourgeoisie et la genèse de l'état moderne*. Bielefeld/Paris: CNRS, pp. 167–81.

Boer, M.G. de, 1921. *Geschiedenis der Amsterdamsche stoomvaart*. Amsterdam: Scheltema en Holkema.

Boeschoten, W.C., 1992. *Hoofdlijnen van de economische geschiedenis van Nederland 1900–1990*. Amsterdam: NIBE.

Bogucka, M., 1990. 'Dutch merchants' activities in Gdansk in the first half of the 17th century', in J.Ph.S. Lemmink and J.S.A.M. van Koningsbrugge (eds.), *Baltic affairs. Relations between the Netherlands and north-eastern Europe, 1500–1800.* Nijmegen: Instituut voor Noord- en Oosteuropese Studies, pp. 19–32.

Boissevain, G.M., 1902. *Prae-advies over de vraag: Behoeft onze bankwet herziening, hetzij in haar stelsel, hetzij in haar onderdelen?* Amsterdam: Miller.

Bonney, R., 1995. 'Revenues', in R. Bonney (ed.), *Economic systems and state finance.* Oxford: Clarendon Press, pp. 423–506.

Boone, M., 1989. 'Triomferend privé-initiatief versus haperend overheidsoptreden? Over pachters van indirecte belastingen in laatmiddeleeuwse steden', *Tijdschrift voor Sociale Geschiedenis* 15: 113–38.

Bos, N.J.P.M., 1990. 'Vermogensbezitters en bevoorrechte belastingbetalers in de negentiende eeuw', *Bijdragen en Mededelingen betreffende de Geschiedenis der Nederlanden* 105(4): 553–78.

Bos-Rops, J.A.M.Y., 1993. *Graven op zoek naar geld. De inkomsten van de graven van Holland en Zeeland, 1389–1433.* Hilversum: Verloren.

Bosher, J.F., 1970. *French finances, 1770–1795: From business to bureaucracy.* Cambridge: Cambridge University Press.

Bosman, H.W.J., 1989. *Het Nederlandse bankwezen.* Amsterdam: NIBE.

Böttcher, F.M.J., 1990. 'Fusie tussen bank en verzekeraar: mode of noodzaak?', *De Spaarbank* no. 7/8.

Brandes de Roos, R., 1928. *Industrie, Kapitalmarkt und industrielle Effekten in den Niederlanden, ein Beitrag zur Kenntnis der niederländischen Industrie und der Faktoren, welche die Beschaffung ihrer Anlage-Kapitalien beeinflüssen.* The Hague: Nijhoff.

Brood, Paul, 1991. *Belastingheffing in Drenthe, 1600–1822.* Meppel: Boom.

Brugmans, I.J., 1961. *Paardenkracht en mensenmacht. Sociaal-economische geschiedenis van Nederland, 1795–1940.* The Hague: Nijhoff.

1963. *Begin van twee banken, 1863.* Rotterdam: Rotterdamsche Bank.

Bruijn, J.R., 1970. *De admiraliteit van Amsterdam in rustige jaren, 1713–1751.* Amsterdam: Scheltema en Holkema.

Bruijn, J.R., F.S. Gaastra and I. Schöffer (eds.), 1987. *Dutch Asiatic shipping in the 17th and 18th centuries,* 3 vols. The Hague: Rijks Geschiedkundige Publicatiën.

Buist, M.G., 1974. *At spes non fracta, Hope & Co. 1770–1815, merchant bankers and diplomats at work.* Amsterdam: Nijhoff.

1977. 'The sinews of war: the role of Dutch finance in European politics', in A.C. Duke and C.A. Tamse (eds.), *Britain and the Netherlands* VI. The Hague: Nijhoff, pp. 124–40.

1979. 'Russia's entry on the Dutch capital market, 1770–1815', *Fifth international economic history conference Leningrad 1970* IV, vol. 3. The Hague: Mouton, pp. 151–64.

Buning, J.R.A., 1957. *Nederlandse Spaarbankbond 1907–1957.* Amersfoort: Nederlandsche Spaarbankbond.

Burger, H., 1975. 'Structural budget policy in the Netherlands', *De Economist* 123(3).

Burke, Peter, 1974. *Venice and Amsterdam. A study of seventeenth-century elites.* London: Temple Smith.

Cameron, R.E. (ed.), 1967. *Banking in the early stages of industrialization, a study in comparative economic history.* Oxford: Oxford University Press.

1972. *Banking and economic development, some lessons of history.* Oxford: Oxford University Press.

Camijn, A.J.W., 1987. *Samen effectief, opkomst, bloei en overgang van de Vereeniging van Effectenhandelaren te Rotterdam.* Rotterdam: Stichting Historische Publicaties Roterodamum.

Carter, A.C., 1975. *Getting, spending and investing in early modern times. Essays on Dutch, English and Huguenot economic history.* Assen: Van Gorcum.

Cauwenberghe, E.H.G. van, 1983. 'Inflation in the Southern Low Countries, from the fourteenth to the seventeenth century: a record of some significant periods of high prices', in N. Schmukler and E. Marcus (eds.), *Inflation through the ages: economic, social, psychological and historical aspects.* New York: Brooklyn College Press, pp. 147–56.

CBS (Centraal Bureau voor de Statistiek) 1924–39. *Maandstatistiek.* Utrecht: CBS.

Nationale Rekeningen, several years (1960, 1972, 1975, 1990). The Hague: CBS.

1955. *De Nederlandse volkshuishouding in de periode 1945–1955, Maandschrift.* Utrecht: CBS.

1956. *Statistisch Zakboek 1955.* Utrecht: CBS.

1969. *Zeventig jaren statistiek in tijdreeksen.* The Hague: CBS.

1987a. *Macro-economische ontwikkelingen 1921–1939 en 1969–1985.* The Hague: CBS.

1987b. 'Main National Account Series 1900–1986'. Occasional paper NA–017. The Hague: CBS.

1989. *Negentig jaren statistiek in tijdreeksen, 1899–1989.* The Hague: CBS.

Centraal Planbureau 1991. *Macro-economische verkenningen 1992.* The Hague: CPB.

Chapman, S.D., 1984. *The rise of merchant banking.* London: Allan & Unwin.

Cieslak, E., 1983. 'Amsterdam als Bankier von Gdansk im 18. Jahrhundert', in *The interactions of Amsterdam and Antwerp with the Baltic region, 1400–1800. Papers presented at the third conference of the 'Association Internationale d'histoire des Mers Nordiques de l'Europe', Utrecht, August 30th–September 3rd, 1982.* Leiden: Nijhoff, pp. 123–31.

Coljé, H., 1988. *Het toezicht op de banken in Nederland.* Amsterdam: NIBE.

Collins, M., 1984. 'The business of banking: English bank balance sheets, 1840–1880', *Business History* 26: 43–58.

Coppens, H., 1992. *De financiën van de centrale regering van de Zuidelijke Nederlanden aan het einde van het Spaanse en onder Oostenrijks bewind (ca. 1680–1788).* Brussels: Verhandelingen Koninklijke Academie van Wetenschappen.

Davis, R., 1966. 'The rise of protection in England, 1689–1786', *Economic History Review* 19: 306–17.

DNB (De Nederlandsche Bank). *Jaarverslag,* several years. Amsterdam: DNB.

Dehing, P.W.N.M., 1991. 'De Amsterdamse Wisselbank en Venetië in de zeventiende eeuw', in M. de Roever (ed.), *Amsterdam: Venetië van het Noorden*. The Hague: SDU, pp. 120–36.

1995. 'Geld als water? Amsterdam en de internationale kapitaalstromen (1600–1730)', in C.A. Davids, M. 't Hart, H. Kleijer and J. Lucassen (eds.), *De Republiek tussen zee en vasteland. Buitenlandse invloeden op cultuur, economie en politiek in Nederlands, 1580–1800*. Louvain: Garant, pp. 229–48.

Deursen, A. Th. van, 1976. 'Staat van oorlog en generale petitie in de jonge Republiek', *Bijdragen en Mededelingen betreffende de Geschiedenis der Nederlanden* 90: 44–55.

1979. *Het kopergeld van de Gouden Eeuw*, vol. III. Assen: Van Gorcum.

1981. 'De Raad van State onder de Republiek, 1588–1795', in *450 jaar Raad van State*. The Hague: Staatsuitgeverij.

Dickson, P.G.M., 1967. *The financial revolution in England: a study in the development of public credit, 1688–1756*. New York: St. Martin's Press.

Dillen, J.G. van (ed.), 1925. *Bronnen tot de geschiedenis der wisselbanken van Amsterdam, Middelburg, Delft en Rotterdam*, 2 vols. The Hague: Rijks Geschiedkundige Publicatiën.

1931. 'Effectenkoersen aan de Amsterdamsche beurs, 1723–1794', *Economisch-historisch jaarboek* 17: 1–46.

1964. *Mensen en achtergronden. Studies uitgegeven ter gelegenheid van de tachtigste jaardag van de schrijver*. Groningen: Wolters.

1965. 'La banque de change et les banquiers privés à Amsterdam aux XVIIe et XVIIIe siècles', in *Troisième conférence internationale d'histoire économique* V. Paris: Mouton, pp. 177–85.

1970. *Van rijkdom en regenten. Handboek tot de economische en sociale geschiedenis van Nederland tijdens de Republiek*. The Hague: Nijhoff.

Doorman, H.J., 1866. *Financieele beschouwingen, het op beleening of prolongatie uitzetten van gelden*. The Hague: s.n.

Dormans, E.H.M., 1991. *Het tekort. Staatsschuld in de tijd der Republiek*. Amsterdam: NEHA.

Drukker, J.W., 1990. *Waarom de crisis hier langer duurde*. Amsterdam: NEHA.

Dunnen, E. den and S. de Wilde, 1991. *Instrumenten van het geld- en valutamarktbeleid in Nederland*. Amsterdam: NIBE.

Durand, Yves, 1971. *Les fermiers généraux au XVIIIe siècle*. Paris: Université, Faculté des Lettres.

Eagly, R.V. and V.K. Smith, 1976. 'Domestic and international integration of the London money market, 1731–1789', *The Journal of Economic History* 36: 198–216.

Eeghen, C.P. van, 1943. 'Het faillisement der firma Coenraad & Hendrick van Son in 1762', *Economisch-historisch Jaarboek* 22: 82–187.

Eerenbeemt, H.F.J.M. van den, 1959. *Van Lanschot en het Tilburgse bedrijfsleven 150 jaar geleden*. The Hague.

Eichengreen, B.J., 1990. *Elusive stability*. Cambridge: Cambridge University Press.

Eijgenhuijsen, H.G., J. Koelewijn and H. Visser, 1987. *Investeringen en de financiële infrastructuur*. The Hague: Staatsuitgeverij.

208   Bibliography

Eisfeld, C., 1916. *Das nederländische Bankwesen*. The Hague: Nijhoff.

Eizenga, W., 1985. *De ontwikkeling van de spaarbanken na de Tweede Wereldoorlog*. Amsterdam/Deventer: Kluwer.

Elias, J.E., 1903/5. *De vroedschap van Amsterdam*, 2 vols. Haarlem: Loosjes.

Engels, P.H., 1862. *De belastingen en de geldmiddelen van den aanvang der Republiek tot op heden*. Utrecht: Kemink en Zoon.

Ent, L. van der, W. Fritschy, E. Horling and R. Liesker, 1996 (forthcoming). 'Public finance in the United Provinces of the Netherlands in the 17th and 18th centuries', paper presented at the international conference on State Finance: the European Experience, c. 1200–1800, Colchester, July 1995.

Faber, J.A., 1971. *Drie eeuwen Friesland. Economische en sociale ontwikkelingen van 1500 tot 1800*. Wageningen: Landbouwhogeschool.

Fasseur, C., 1975. *Kultuurstelsel en Koloniale Baten*. Leiden: University Press.

Financiële instellingen, 1987. *Financiële instellingen in Nederland 1900–1985, balansreeksen en naamlijst van handelsbanken*. Amsterdam: De Nederlandsche Bank.

Frentrop, P., 1987. 'Nederlandse banken denken na over internationale samenwerking'. *NRC-Handelsblad*, 10 October.

Friedman, M. and A.J. Schwartz, 1963. *A monetary history of the United States 1867–1960*. Princeton: Princeton University Press.

1982. *Monetary trends in the United States and the United Kingdom*. Chicago: University of Chicago Press.

Fritschy, J.M.F., 1986. 'De Generale Beleenbank' en de financiële problemen in de beginjaren van de Bataafsche Republiek', *Jaarboek voor de Geschiedenis van Bedrijf en Techniek* 3: 109–34.

1988. *De patriotten en de financiën van de Bataafsche Republiek. Hollands krediet en de smalle marges voor een nieuw beleid (1795–1801)* The Hague: Hollandse Historische Reeks.

Fritschy, W., 1983. 'Overheidsfinanciën als uiting van het "institutioneel onvermogen" van de achttiende eeuwse Republiek?', *Economisch en Sociaal Historisch Jaarboek* 46: 180–228.

1989. 'Financiele unificatie en natievorming. Een onderzoek in Overijssel', *Bijdragen en Mededelingen betreffende de Geschiedenis der Nederlanden* 104: 665–83.

1990. 'Taxation in Britain, France and the Netherlands in the eighteenth century', *Economic and Social History in the Netherlands* 2: 57–79.

1992. 'Staatsvorming en financieel beleid onder Willem I', in C.A. Tamse and E. Witte (eds.), *Staats- en natievorming in Willem I's Koninkrijk (1815–1830)*. Brussels: Vub Press, pp. 215–37.

1994b. 'Financieel beleid onder – of ondanks? – Colijn', in J. de Bruijn and H.J. Langeveld (eds.), *Colijn, bouwstenen voor een biografie*. Kampen: Kok, pp. 199–234.

1995. 'Geld en oorlog. Financieel beleid in Holland en Overijssel vergeleken met Groot-Brittannië en Oostenrijk (1740–1785)', in C.A. Davids *et al.*, *De Republiek tussen zee en vasteland*. Louvain: Garant, pp. 207–29.

1996. *Gewestelijke financiën ten tijde van de Republiek der Verenigde Nederlanden. Deel I. Overijssel 1604–1795*. The Hague: Instituut voor Nederlandse geschiedenis.

Fritschy, W. and E. Bloemen, 1997 (forthcoming). *The first Benelux, 1815–1830*.

Fritschy, W. and R.H. van der Voort, 1994a. *De Nederlandse staatsbegrotingen 1798–1914*, in *Broncommentaren* XII. The Hague: Instituut voor Nederlandse Geschiedenis.

Fruin, R., 1980. *Geschiedenis der staatsinstellingen in Nederland tot den val der Republiek*. The Hague: Nijhoff.

GAA = Gemeente Archief Amsterdam (Municipal Archives Amsterdam), several archives.

Gaastra, F.S., 1976. 'Geld tegen goederen: een structurele verandering in het Nederlands-Aziatisch handelsverkeer', *Bijdragen en Mededelingen betreffende de Geschiedenis der Nederlanden* 89: 249–72.

1982. *De geschiedenis van de VOC*. Haarlem: Fibula.

1983. 'The exports of precious metal from Europe to Asia by the Dutch East India Company, 1602–1795', in J.F. Richards (ed.), *Precious metals in the later medieval and early modern worlds*. Durham: Carolina Academic Press, pp. 447–75.

1989. *Bewind en beleid bij de VOC. De financiële en commerciële politiek van de bewindhebbers, 1672–1702*. Zutphen: Walburg Pers.

Gales, B.P.A. and K.E. Sluyterman, 1993. 'Outward bound. The rise of Dutch multinationals', in G. Jones and H.G. Schröter (eds.), *The rise of multinationals in continental Europe*. Aldershot: Elgar, pp. 65–99.

Gelder, H. Enno van, 1978/79. 'De Nederlandse manualen 1586–1630', *Jaarboek voor Munt- en Penningkunde* 65/66: 39–79.

1980. *De Nederlandse munten*. Antwerp and Utrecht: Aula.

Gerards, J.L. and J.J.M. Schipper, 1989. Interview with J.L.M. Bartelds and B.J.H.S. Feilzer, *Bank- en Effectenbedrijf* 38(10).

1994. Interview with J.F. Visser, *Bank- en Effectenbedrijf* 43(3).

Glamann, K., 1958. *Dutch Asiatic trade 1620–1740*. The Hague: Nijhoff.

Goey, F. de and P. van de Laar, 1995. 'Scheepsfinanciering: een comparatief perspectief', *Tijdschrift voor Zeegeschiedenis* 14: 23–62.

Goldsmith, R.W., 1987. *Premodern financial systems. A historical comparative study*. Cambridge: Cambridge University Press.

Govers, F.G.G., 1972. *Het geslacht en de firma Van Lanschot, 1737–1901*. Tilburg: Stichting Zuidelijk Historisch Contact.

Graaf, T. de and J.J. Modrow, 1995. 'Bankiers en reders: belangen en invloeden van banken op maritiem gebied', *Tijdschrift voor Zeegeschiedenis* 14: 63–108.

Grapperhaus, F.H.M., 1982. *Alva en de tiende penning*. Zutphen: Walburg Pers.

Griffiths, R.T., 1979. *Industrial retardation in the Netherlands 1830–1850*. The Hague: Nijhoff.

1987. 'The Policy Makers', in R.T. Griffiths (ed.), *The Netherlands and the Gold Standard, 1931–1936*. Amsterdam: NEHA, pp. 165–92.

Griffiths, R.T. and J. Schoorl, 1987. 'The Single Issue Pressure Groups', in R.T.

Griffiths (ed.), *The Netherlands and the Gold Standard, 1931–1936.* Amsterdam: NEHA, pp. 139–64.

Haan, H. den, 1977. *Moedernegotie en grote vaart. Een studie over de expansie van het Hollandse handelskapitaal in de 16e en 17e eeuw.* Amsterdam: SUN.

Haan, H. den, S. Korteweg, S.K. Kuipers and J.K.T. Postma, 1981. *Het moderne geldwezen,* vol. IV. Amsterdam: Hollandse Uitgeversmaatschappij.

Hall, F.A. van, 1840. *Proeve van een onderzoek naar de schuld van het Koninkrijk der Nederlanden.* Amsterdam: Diedericks.

Hart, M. 't, 1989a. *In quest for funds. Warfare and state formation in the Netherlands, 1620–1650.* Leiden: University Dissertation.

1989b. 'Cities and state making in the Dutch Republic, 1580–1680', *Theory and Society* 18: 663–88.

1990. 'Staatsvorming, sociale relaties en oorlogsfinanciering in de Nederlandse Republiek', *Tijdschrift voor Sociale Geschiedenis* 16: 61–85.

1993. *The making of a bourgeois state. War, politics and finance during the Dutch revolt.* Manchester: Manchester University Press.

1994. 'Tussen kapitaal en belastingmonopolie. Interne grenzen aan staatsvorming in Nederland, 1580–1850', in H. Flap en M. van Leeuwen, *Op lange termijn. Verklaringen van trends in de geschiedenis van samenlevingen.* Hilversum: Verloren, pp. 129–46.

1995a. 'The emergence and consolidation of the tax state', in R. Bonney (ed.), *Economic systems and state finance.* Oxford: Clarendon Press, pp. 281–94.

1995b. 'The Dutch Republic: the urban impact upon politics', in C.A. Davids and J. Lucassen (eds.), *A miracle mirrored. The Dutch Republic in European perspective.* Cambridge: Cambridge University Press, pp. 57–98.

Hart, S. and J. McCusker, 1979. 'The rate of exchange on Amsterdam in London: 1590–1660', *The Journal of European Economic History* 8(3): 689–705.

Harthoorn, P.C., 1928. *Hoofdlijnen uit de ontwikkeling van het moderne bankwezen voor de concentratie.* Rotterdam: NV Drukkerij Strömberg & Co.

Hauser, H., 1936. *L'histoire des prix en France de 1500 à 1800.* Paris: Les Presses Modernes.

Haavelmo, T., 1945. 'Multiplier effects of a balanced budget', *Econometrica* 13: 311–18.

Heckscher, E.F., 1934. 'The Bank of Sweden in its connection with the Bank of Amsterdam', in J.G. van Dillen (ed.), *History of the principal public banks.* The Hague: Nijhoff, pp. 161–99.

Heerding, A., 1986. *Geschiedenis van de NV Philips' Gloeilampenfabrieken, II, Een onderneming van vele markten thuis.* The Hague: Nijhoff.

Heide, F.J. ter, 1986. *Ordening en verdeling. Besluitvorming over sociaal-economisch beleid in Nederland 1949–1958.* Kampen: Kok Agora.

Hen, P.E. de, 1980. *Actieve en re-actieve industriepolitiek in Nederland.* Amsterdam: De Arbeiderspers.

Herstelbank, 1955. *Tien jaar economisch leven in Nederland. Herstelbank 1945–1955.* The Hague: Nijhoff.

Hirschfeld, H.M., 1922. *Het ontstaan van het moderne bankwezen in Nederland.* Rotterdam: Nijgh & Van Ditmar.

Hoffmann, H., 1971. Het Nederlandse bankwezen 1960–1970, *Bank-en Effectenbedrijf* 20(12): 477–8

Hofstee, E.W., 1981. *Korte demografische geschiedenis van Nederland van 1800 tot heden*. Bussum: Fibula.

Homer, S., 1963. *A history of interest rates*. New Brunswick, NJ: Rutgers University Press.

Horlings, E., 1995. *The economic development of the Dutch service sector 1800–1850*. Amsterdam: NEHA.

Houtzager, D., 1950. *Hollands lijf- en losrenteleningen voor 1672*. Schiedam: Roelands.

Houwink, A., 1940. 'Een halve eeuw Nederlandsche staatsschuld, 1798–1848', *De Economist* 90: 585–607.

Hovy, J., 1966. *Het voorstel van 1751 tot instelling van een beperkt vrijhavenstelsel in de Republiek (Propositie tot een gelimiteerd Porto-franco)*. Groningen: Wolters.

Howard, M., 1978. *War in European history*. Oxford: Oxford University Press.

Hurst, W., 1932. 'Holland, Switzerland and Belgium and the English gold crisis of 1931', *Journal of Political Economy* 40: 638–60.

Israel, J.I., 1989. *Dutch primacy in world trade, 1585–1740*. Oxford: Oxford University Press.

1990. 'The Amsterdam stock exchange and the English revolution of 1688', *Tijdschrift voor Geschiedenis* 103: 412–40.

Jaarcijfers 1900, 1915. *Jaarcijfers voor het Koninkrijk der Nederlanden* 1900, 1915. The Hague: CBS.

Jacobsen Jensen, J.N., 1918. 'Moryson's reis door en zijn karakteristiek van de Nederlanden', *Bijdragen en Mededeelingen van het Historisch Genootschap* 39: 214–305.

Janssens, V., 1955. 'Het ontstaan van de dubbele koers courantgeld-wisselgeld in het geldwezen van de Zuidelijke Nederlanden', *Bijdragen voor de Geschiedenis der Nederlanden* 9: 1–18.

1959. 'De goud- en zilverwaarde der geldeenheid/Les équivalences en or et en argent de l'unité de compte', in C. Verlinden (ed.), *Documenten voor de geschiedenis van prijzen en lonen in Vlaanderen en Brabant, XVe–XVIIIe eeuw* I. Bruges, pp. 16–29.

Jong, A.M. de, 1967a. *Geschiedenis van de Nederlandsche Bank*, vols. I–III. Haarlem: Joh. Enschedé.

1967b. 'De economische conjunctuur in Nederland tijdens de jaren 1848–1860', in W.J. Wieringa *et al.* (eds.), *Bedrijf en samenleving, economisch-historische studies over Nederland in de negentiende en twintigste eeuw aangeboden aan prof.dr. I.J. Brugmans bij zijn aftreden als hoogleraar aan de Universiteit van Amsterdam*. Alphen aan den Rijn: Samson, pp. 87–106.

Jong, L. de, 1976. *Het Koninkrijk der Nederlanden in de tweede wereldoorlog*, vol. VII. The Hague: Nijhoff.

Jonge, J.A. de, 1968. *De industrialisatie in Nederland tussen 1850 en 1914*. Amsterdam: SUN.

1977. 'Overheidsfinancien', *Algemene Geschiedenis der Nederlanden* XII. Bussum: Unieboek, pp. 55–8.

1978. 'Tabellen over het economische leven in Nederland 1840–1914', in *Algemene Geschiedenis der Nederlanden* XIII. Haarlem: Fibula, pp. 281–4.

Jongepier, P., 1991. 'Ontwikkelingen rondom de kosten van het betalingsverkeer', *Bank- en Effectenbedrijf* 40(3): 27–31.

Jonker, J.P.B., 1988. Welbegrepen eigenbelang, ontstaan en functie van boerenleenbanken in Noord-Brabant, 1900–1920', *Jaarboek voor de Geschiedenis van Bedrijf en Techniek* 5: 188–208.

1991a. 'Lachspiegel van de voortuitgang, het historiografische beeld van de Nederlandse industriefinanciering in de negentiende eeuw', *NEHA-Bulletin* 5: 5–23.

1991b. 'Sinecures or sinews of power? Interlocking directorships and bank-industry relations in the Netherlands, 1910–1940', *Economic and Social History in the Netherlands* 3: 119–32.

1992. 'Kassierspapier', in J. Lucassen (ed.), *Gids van de papiergeldverzameling van het Nederlandsch Economisch-Historisch Archief*. Amsterdam: NEHA, pp. 107–20.

1994. 'In het middelpunt en toch aan de rand, joodse bankiers en effectenhandelaren 1815–1940', in H. Berg, T. Wijsenbeek and E.J. Fischer (eds.), *Venter, fabriqueur, fabrikant, joodse ondernemers en ondernemingen in Nederland 1796–1940*. Amsterdam: NEHA, pp. 92–113.

1995. 'Spoilt for choice? Statistical speculations on banking concentration and the structure of the Dutch money market, 1900–1940', in Y. Cassis, G.D. Feldman and U. Olsson (eds.), *The evolution of financial institutions and markets in twentieth century Europe*. Aldershot: Scolar Press.

1996a. 'From private responsibility and public duty, the origins of bank monitoring in the Netherlands', *Financial History Review*, 3: pp. 139–52

1996b. *Merchants, bankers, middlemen, the Amsterdam money market during the first half of the nineteenth century*. Amsterdam: NEHA.

Jonker, J.P.B. and J.L. van Zanden, 1996. 'Method in the madness? Banking crisis between the wars, an international comparison', in Ch. Feinstein (ed.), *Banking, currency and finance between the wars*. Oxford: Clarendon Press, pp. 77–93.

Kam, F. de, J. de Haan and C. Sterks 1990. *De kerfstok van Nederland*. Schoonhoven: Academic Service.

Kämper-Attema M. and H.H. Vleesenbeek (eds.) 1986. *Twee kassiers te Rotterdam, een bijdrage tot de geschiedenis van de financiële infrastructuur van Rotterdam, 1850–1914*. Rotterdam: Erasmus Universiteit.

Kappelhof, A.C.M., 1986. *De belastingheffing in de Meijerij van Den Bosch gedurende de Generaliteitsperiode (1648–1730)*. Tilburg: Stichting Zuidelijk Historisch Contact.

Keesing, F.A.G., 1947. *De conjuncturele ontwikkeling van Nederland en de evolutie van de economische overheidspolitiek 1918–1939*. Utrecht: Het Spectrum.

Kesler, C.K., 1982. 'Amsterdam bankers and the West in the 18th century', in M.A.P. Meilink-Roelofsz, M.E. van Opstall and G.J. Schutte (eds.), *Dutch authors on West-Indian history*. The Hague: Nijhoff, pp. 300–14.

Kindleberger, C.P., 1984. *A financial history of Western Europe*. London: Allan & Unwin.

1989. *Manias, panics and crashes. A history of financial crises*. 2nd edn. New York: Basic Books.

Klein, P.W., 1965. *De Trippen in de 17ᵉ eeuw: een studie over ondernemersgedrag op de Hollandse stapelmarkt*. Assen: Van Gorcum.

1973. 'Depressie en beleid tijdens de jaren dertig', in J. van Herwaarden (ed.), *Lof der historie*. Rotterdam: Universitaire Pers Rotterdam.

1980. 'Het sociaal-economische leven 1650–1800. Handel, geld-en bankwezen in de Noordelijke Nederlanden 1650–1795', in *Algemene Geschiedenis der Nederlanden* VIII. Bussum: Unieboek, pp. 160–84.

1982. 'Dutch capitalism and the European world-economy', in M. Aymard (ed.), *Dutch capitalism and world capitalism. Capitalisme hollandais et capitalisme mondial*. Cambridge: Cambridge University Press.

1987. 'De wereldhandel in edele metalen 1500–1800: centraliteit of polycentrisme?', *Tijdschrift voor Geschiedenis* 100: 185–97.

Klein, P.W. and H.H. Vleesenbeek, 1981. 'De geschiedenis van het hypotheekbankwezen', in R. Burgert, J.C. Bouma and H. Visser (eds.), *75 jaar Nederlandse Vereniging van Hypotheekbanken*. S.l., s.n. 1981.

Klompmaker, H., 1979. 'Handel, geld-en bankwezen in de Noordelijke Nederlanden', in *Algemene Geschiedenis der Nederlanden* VI. Bussum: Unieboek, pp. 58–74.

1980. 'Handel, geld- en bankwezen in de Noordelijke Nederlanden 1580–1650', in *Algemene Geschiedenis der Nederlanden* VII. Bussum: Unieboek, pp. 98–127.

Knippenberg, H. and B. de Pater, 1988. *De eenwording van Nederland, schaalvergroting en integratie sinds 1800*. Nijmegen: SUN.

Knocke van der Meulen, J.A.E. de, 1981. 'De geschiedenis van de vereniging', in R. Burgert *et al.* (eds.), *75 jaar Nederlandse Vereniging van Hypotheekbanken*. Nijmegen: Thieme, pp. 31–54.

Knoester, A., 1989. *Economische politiek in Nederland*. Leiden: Stenfert Kroese.

1991. *The inverted Haavelmo effect and the economic consequences of fiscal policies in the 1970s and 1980s*. Research Memorandum 9103, Nijmegen: Catholic University Department Economics.

Knoester, A. (ed.), 1987. *Lessen uit het verleden. 125 jaar Vereniging voor de Staathuishoudkunde*. Leiden: Stenfert Kroese.

Koelewijn, J., 1987. *Het einde der zelfstandige hypotheekbanken*. Amsterdam: Research Memo Vrije Universiteit, Faculteit Economische Wetenschappen, No. 1987/14.

Koopmans, L., A.H.E.M. Wellink, 1978⁴. *Overheidsfinanciën*. Leiden: Stenfert Kroese.

Körner, Martin, 1995a. 'Expenditure', in R. Bonney (ed.), *Economic systems and state finance*. Oxford: Clarendon Press, pp. 393–422.

1995b. 'Public Credit', in R. Bonney (ed.), *Economic systems and state finance*. Oxford: Clarendon Press, pp. 507–38.

Kors, M., 1988. 'De bewindhebbers van de kamer Rotterdam', in *Rotterdam en de VOC. Bulletin Historisch Museum Rotterdam* 2: 12–25.

Korthals Altes, W., 1996. *Van Pond Hollands tot Nederlandse Gulden.* Amsterdam: NEHA.

Kossmann, E.H., 1978. *The Low Countries, 1780–1940.* Oxford: Clarendon Press.

Krans, R.H., 1977. 'Het bedrijf van de Rotterdamse kassiers en makelaars Chabot, 1769–1921', in Joh. de Vries *et al.* (eds.), *Ondernemende geschiedenis, 22 opstellen geschreven bij het afscheid van mr. H. van Riel als voorzitter van de Vereniging het Nederlandsch Economisch-Historisch Archief.* The Hague: Nijhoff, pp. 140–82.

Kuné, J.B. and M. van Nieuwkerk, 1974. 'De ontwikkeling van de geldquote in Nederland, 1900–1970', *Maandschrift economie* 39 (1974–1975): 1–15.

Kymmell, J., 1992. *Geschiedenis van de algemene banken in Nederland, 1860–1914,* I. Amsterdam: NIBE.

Laar, P.Th. van de and H.H. Vleesenbeek, 1990. *Van oude naar nieuwe Hoofdpoort, de geschiedenis van het assurantie-concern Stad Rotterdam anno 1720 NV, 1720–1990.* Rotterdam: Stad Rotterdam Verzekeringen.

Ladewig Petersen, E., 1983. 'War, finance and the growth of absolutism. Some aspects of the European integration of 17th century Denmark', *Europe and Scandinavia. Aspects of the process of integration in the 17th century,* ed. by G. Rystad. Lund: Scandinavian University Books, pp. 33–50.

Lamens, H., 1979. 'De Unie van Utrecht en de landelijke heffingen', *Fiskaal* 6: 440–500.

Landbouw en landbouwcrediet 1948. *Landbouw en landbouwcrediet 1898–1948. Vijftig jaar geschiedenis van de coöperatieve boerenleenbank Eindhoven.* Eindhoven: Centrale Coöperatieve Boerenleenbank.

League of Nations 1929. *Commercial banks 1913–1929.* Geneva: League of Nations.

Leeuw, J. de, 1992. 'Functioneert de Collectieve Garantieregeling nog naar behoren?', *Bank- en Effectenbedrijf* 41(3): 24–8.

Lennep, E. van and E. Schoorl, 1991. *Emile van Lennep in de wereldeconomie.* Leiden: Stenfert Kroese.

Lieftinck, P., 1946. *Witboek betreffende de maatregelen tot zuivering van het geldwezen.* The Hague: Nijhoff.

1973. *The Post-War Financial Rehabilitation of the Netherlands.* The Hague: Nijhoff.

1987. Het Nederlandse financiële herstel 1945–1952; een terugblik, in A. Knoester (ed.), *Lessen uit het verleden.* Leiden: Stenfert Kroese.

Lindbeck, A., 1975. *Swedish economic policy.* London: Macmillan.

Louwerens, M.M., 1993. *Honderdvijftig jaar NV Crediet- en Depositokas, van kredietvereniging naar algemene bank.* Amsterdam: NIBE.

Maassen, H.A.J., 1994. *Tussen commercieel en sociaal krediet. De ontwikkeling van de Bank van Lening in Nederland van Lombard tot Gemeentelijke kredietbank, 1260–1940.* Hilversum: Verloren.

Malsen, H. van, 1934. *Geschiedenis van het makelaarsgild te Amsterdam, 1578–1933.* Amsterdam: Boekhandel Ten Have.

Mansvelt, W.M.F., 1924. *Geschiedenis van de Nederlandsche Handelmaatschappij*. Haarlem: Joh. Enschedé.

McCusker, J.J. and C. Gravesteijn, 1991. *The beginnings of commercial and financial journalism. The commodity price currents, exchange rate currents and money currents of early modern Europe*. Amsterdam: NEHA.

Meere, J.M.M. de, 1980. 'Daglonen in België en Nederland in 1918 – een aanvulling', *Tijdschrift voor Sociale Geschiedenis* 20: 357–84.

Mees, R., 1920. *Gedenkschrift van de firma R. Mees & Zoonen ter gelegenheid van haar tweehonderd-jarig bestaan 1720–1920*. Rotterdam: s.n.

Mees, W.C., 1838. *Proeve eener geschiedenis van het bankwezen in Nederland gedurende den tijd der Republiek*. Rotterdam: Messchert.

Meijer, J.F., 1995. 'Voorstellen tot herziening van de heffing van de convooien en licenten in de jaren 1714–1720', in W. Fritschy, J.K.T. Postma and J. Roelevink (eds.), *Doel en middel. Aspecten van financieel overheidsbeleid in de Nederlanden van de zestiende eeuw tot heden*. Amsterdam: NEHA, pp. 96–114.

Messing, F., 1981. *De Nederlandse economie 1945–1980*. Haarlem: Fibula/Van Dishoeck.

Mitchell, B.R., 1975. *European historical statistics*. London: Macmillan.

1992. *International historical statistics: Europe 1750–1988*. Basingstoke: Macmillan.

Moerman, W.L. and J. Vuchelen, 1986. *Staatsschuld in de Lage Landen*, *Rotterdamse Monetaire Studies*, no. 20. Rotterdam: Stichting Rotterdamse Monetaire Studies.

Mousnier, R., 1980. *Les institutions de la France sous la monarchie absolue*, II. Paris: Presses Universitaires de France.

Mulder, H., 1987. De slag om de laatste hypotheekbank. *Quote*, April.

1977. *Een Rotterdams zeehandelaar, Hendrik Muller Szn., (1819–1898)*. Schiedam: Interbook.

Neal, L., 1985. 'Integration of international capital markets: quantitative evidence from the eighteenth to twentieth centuries', *The Journal of Economic History* 45: 219–26.

1987. 'The integration and efficiency of the London and Amsterdam stock markets in the eighteenth century', *The Journal of Economic History* 47: 97–115.

1990. *The rise of financial capitalism. International capital markets in the Age of Reason*. Cambridge: Cambridge University Press.

Nederlandse Regering 1951. *Elfde verslag van de Nederlandse Regering aangaande de werking van het EHP*. The Hague, 18 July.

Miljoenennota's (Nota's over de toestand van 's Rijks financiën), several years. The Hague.

Nederlandse Waterschapsbank N.V., 1979. *De begroting als instrument van het financieel-economisch beleid*. The Hague: Nederlandse Waterschapsbank.

Noordegraaf, L., 1985. *Hollands welvaren? Levensstandaard in Holland 1450–1650*. Bergen: Octavo.

Noordegraaf, L. and J.T. Schoenmakers, 1984. *Daglonen in Holland*. Amsterdam: Historisch Seminarium.

Nurkse, R., 1944. *International currency experience*. Den Haag: Nijhoff.

Nusteling, H.P.H., 1974. *De Rijnvaart in het tijdperk van stoom en steenkool 1813–1914*. Amsterdam: Holland Universiteits Pers.

1985. *Welvaart en werkgelegenheid in Amsterdam, 1540–1860*. Amsterdam: De Bataafsche Leeuw.

Oosterwijk, A.J., 1983. *Koning van de koopvaart, Anthony van Hoboken (1756–1850)*. Rotterdam: Stichting Historische Publicaties, Roterodamum.

1989. *Reder in Rotterdam, Willem Ruys 1803–1889*. Rotterdam: Stichting Historische Publicaties, Roterodamum.

Overhagen, J.W.B. van and P. de Wolff, 1969. 'De financien van de Nederlandse Rijksoverheid in de periode 1850–1914', *Economisch Historisch Jaarboek* 32: 206–37.

Parker, G., 1974. 'The emergence of modern finance in Europe', in C.M. Cipolla (ed), *The Fontana economic history of Europe* II. Glasgow: Collins, pp. 527–94.

1977. *The Dutch revolt*. London: Allan Lane.

Pas, W. van de, 1995. 'Gelre's eigen gelden. De financiële zelfstandigheid van een niet-patrimoniaal gewest in de Habsburgse Nederlanden in de aanloop naar de opstand', in W. Fritschy, J.K.T. Postma and J. Roelevink (eds.), *Doel en middel. Aspecten van het financieel overheidsbeleid in de Nederlanden van de zestiende eeuw tot heden*. Amsterdam: NEHA, pp. 11–58.

Paverd, P.A. van de, 1982. De beleggingspolitiek van institutionele beleggers onder andere ten aanzien van risicodragend vermogen, *Risicodragend vermogen – is het aanbod hiervan voldoende of is de vraag te klein?* Amsterdam: NIBE.

Peacock, A.T. and J. Wiseman, 1967. *The growth of public expenditure in the United Kingdom*. London: Allan and Unwin.

Peekel, M. and J.W. Veluwenkamp, 1984. *Het girale betalingsverkeer in Nederland*. Deventer: Kluwer.

Peters, L.F., 1994. 'Der Handel Nürnbergs am Anfang des dreissigjährigen Krieges. Strukturkomponenten, Unternehmen und Unternehmer; eine quantitative Analyse'. *Vierteljahrschrift für Sozial- und Wirtschaftsgeschichte*, Beihefte 112. Stuttgart: Steiner.

Phelps Brown, H. and S.V. Hopkins, 1981. *A perspective of wages and prices*. London: Methuen.

Platt, D.C.M., 1984. *Foreign finance in continental Europe and the USA, 1815–1870: quantities, origins, functions and distribution*. London: Allan & Unwin.

Pol, A., 1985. 'Tot gerieff van India. Geldexport door de VOC en de muntproduktie in Nederland, 1720–1740', *Jaarboek voor munt- en penningkunde* 72: 65–197.

1989. *Schepen met geld. De handelsmunten van de Verenigde Oostindische Compagnie, 1602–1799*. The Hague: SDU.

Posthuma, J.F., 1955. Tien jaar Herstelbank, in *Tien jaar economisch leven in Nederland; Herstelbank 1945–1955*. The Hague: Nijhoff.

Posthumus, N.W., 1929. 'The tulip mania in Holland in the years 1636–'37', *Journal of Economic and Business History* 1(3): 434–66.

1943–64. *Nederlandsche prijsgeschiedenis*, 2 vols. Leiden: Brill.

Pot, J.E. van der, 1957. *Abram, Huibert en Elie van Rijckevorsel*. Rotterdam: Donder.

Reitsma, R., 1982. *Centrifugal and centripetal forces in the early Dutch Republic. The States of Overijssel.* Amsterdam: Rodopi.

Rekeningen van de inkomsten en uitgaven van het Koninkrijk der Nederlanden 1824–1850, in *Bijlagen tot de Handelingen der Staten Generaal.* The Hague: SDU.

Renooij, D.C., 1947. 'De Nederlandsche Handel-Maatschappij en het emissiebedrijf', in *Economisch-historische opstellen, geschreven voor prof.dr. Z.W. Sneller.* Amsterdam: Paris, pp. 153–66.

1979. *Structuurveranderingen in het Nederlandse bankwezen en de monetaire politiek.* Amsterdam: NIBE.

Reynen, W.B., 1949. Conjunctuurpolitiek, *Maatschappij-Belangen* 103.

Riemens, H., 1935. *Het Amortisatiesyndicaat. Een studie over de staatsfinanciën onder Willem I.* Amsterdam: Paris.

1937. 'De finantiële politiek onder koning Willem I', *De Gids* 101(3): 144–67.

1949. *De financiele ontwikkeling van Nederland.* Amsterdam: Noord-Hollandsche Uitgevers Maatschappij.

Riley, J.C., 1980. *International government finance and the Amsterdam capital market, 1740–1815.* Cambridge: Cambridge University Press.

1984. 'Dutch economy after 1650: decline or growth?', *The Journal of European Economic history* 13: 521–69.

Roos, F. de and W.J. Wieringa, 1953. *Een halve eeuw rente in Nederland.* Schiedam: NV Levensverzekering-Maatschappij HAV Bank.

Roos, F. de and D.C. Renooij, 1980[8]. *De algemene banken in Nederland.* Leiden: Stenfert Kroese.

Roover, R. de, 1974. 'New interpretations of the history of banking', in J. Kirshner (ed.), *Business, banking and economic thought in late medieval and early modern Europe. Selected studies of Raymond de Roover.* Chicago: University of Chicago Press, pp. 200–38.

Roovers, J.J., 1932. *De plaatselijke belastingen en financiën in den loop der tijden. Een historische schets.* Alphen aan de Rijn: Samson.

Schama, S., 1977. *Patriots and liberators: revolution in the Netherlands, 1780–1813.* New York: Knopf.

Schimmel, W.F., 1882. *Geschiedkundig overzicht van het muntwezen in Nederland.* Amsterdam: s.n.

Schimmelpenninck, G., 1845. 'Etat approximatif des sommes payées par la Republique Batave, tant par suite de l'entrée des armées françaises sur le territoire Batave, qu'en vertu de ses traités avec le Gouvernement Français pour l'entretien des troupes Françaises comme aussi a titre d'avances pour ce Gouvernement, depuis de la dite entrée jusqu'au Decembre 1804', in G. Schimmelpenninck, *Rutger Jan Schimmelpenninck en eenige gebeurtenissen van zijn tijd.* The Hague: s.n., vol. II, pp. 312–14.

Schneider, J. and O. Schwarzer, 1986. 'International rates of exchange: structures and trends of payments mechanism in Europe, 17th to 19th century', in W. Fischer, R. Marvin McInnes and J. Schneider (eds.), *The emergence of a world economy 1500–1914. I Papers of the IX International Congress of Economic*

History. Beiträge zur Wirtschafts- und Sozialgeschichte. Wiesbaden: Steiner, pp. 143–70.

Scholtens, L.J.R., 1991. *Ontwikkelingen en activiteiten van de Nederlandse overheidsbanken.* Amsterdam: NIBE.

Schremmer, D.E., 1989. 'Taxation and public finance: Britain, France and Germany', in *The Cambridge Economic History* VIII. Cambridge: Cambridge University Press, pp. 315–495.

Schubert, E.S., 1988. 'Innovations, debts and bubbles: international integration of financial markets in Western Europe, 1688–1720', *The Journal of Economic History* 48: 299–306.

Sickenga, F.N., 1864. *Bijdrage tot de geschiedenis der belastingen in Nederland.* Leiden: Engels.

Sinderen, J. van (ed.), 1990. *Het sociaal-economisch beleid in de tweede helft van de twintigste eeuw.* Groningen: Wolters-Noordhof.

Slechte, C.H., 1982. *'Een noodlottig jaar voor veel zotte en wijze'. De Rotterdamse windhandel van 1720.* The Hague: Nijhoff.

Smith, M.F.J., 1919. *Tijdaffaires aan de Amsterdamsche beurs.* The Hague: Nijhoff.

Smits, J.P., 1990. 'The size and structure of the Dutch service sector in internationalperspective, 1850–1914', *Economic and social history in the Netherlands* II: 81–99.

1995. *Economische groei en structuurveranderingen in de Nederlandse dienstensector, 1850–1913. De bijdrage van handel en transport aan het proces van 'moderne economische groei'.* Amsterdam: s.n.

Sneller, Z.W., 1940. *Rotterdams bedrijfsleven in het verleden.* Amsterdam: Paris.

Sociaal-Economische Raad 1978. *Advies inzake de omvang en groei van de collectieve sector,* no 11. The Hague.

Spooner, F.C., 1980. 'On the road to industrial precision: the case of coinage in the Netherlands (1672–1791)', *Economisch- en Sociaal-Historisch jaarboek* 43: 1–18.

Spooner, F.C., 1983. *Risks at sea: Amsterdam insurance and maritime Europe, 1776–1780.* Cambridge: Cambridge University Press.

Spufford, P., 1995. 'Access to credit and capital in the commercial centres of Europe', in C.A. Davids and J. Lucassen (eds.), *A miracle mirrored. The Dutch Republic in European perspective.* Cambridge: Cambridge University Press, pp. 303–37.

Staten-Generaal 1988–1989. *Handelingen der Tweede Kamer,* 20995, no. 1. The Hague.

Statistiek van het Koningrijk der Nederlanden. Bescheiden betreffende de geldmiddelen. (1911): 'Aperçu du montant des impôts et de quelques autres revenus pour les exercises 1831–1910'. The Hague: Staatsdrukkerij.

Sterks, C.G.M., J. de Haan and C.A. de Kam, 1989. De erfenis van Ruding, *Economisch Statistische Berichten* 74.

Stevens, Th., 1970. 'De familie Kann en haar financiële activiteiten gedurende vier eeuwen', *Studia Rosenthaliana* 4: 43–95.

1976. 'Begrotingsnormering 1814–1939', *Economisch- en Sociaal-Historisch jaarboek* 39: 101–47.

Stipriaan, A. van, 1993. *Surinaams contrast. Roofbouw en overleven in een Caraïbische plantage kolonie 1750–1863.* Leiden: KITLV Uitgeverij.

Stoffer, J., 1986. *Het ontstaan van de NMB.* Deventer: Kluwer.

Tegenwoordige Staat der Vereenigde Nederlanden 1739. XVIII: Overijssel. Amsterdam: Tirion.

Thompson, I.A.A., 1976. *War and government in Habsburg Spain, 1560–1620.* London: Athlone Press.

Tienhoven, J.P. van, 1917. *Industrie en banken (de handel volgt de banken).* Amsterdam: s.n.

Tijn, Th. van, 1965. *Twintig jaren Amsterdam, de maatschappelijke ontwikkeling van de hoofdstad van de jaren '50 der vorige eeuw tot 1876.* Amsterdam: Scheltema & Holkema.

Tilly, C., 1990. *Coercion, capital and European states, AD 990–1990.* Oxford: Basil Blackwell.

Toirkens, S.J., 1989. *Ministers en bezuinigen.* Stichting Rotterdamse Monetaire Studies.

Tracy, J.D., 1985a. *A financial revolution in the Habsburg Netherlands. Renten and renteniers in the County of Holland, 1515–1565.* Berkeley, Los Angeles and London.

1985b. 'The taxation system in the county of Holland during the reigns of Charles V and Philip II, 1519–1566', *Economisch en Sociaal-Historisch Jaarboek* 48: 71–118.

Trip, L.J.A., 1946. *De Duitsche bezetting van Nederland en de financieele ontwikkeling van het land gedurende de jaren der bezetting.* The Hague: Nijhoff.

Veenendaal Jr., A.J., 1996. *Slow trains to Paradise, how Dutch investment helped to build American railroads.* Stanford: Stanford University Press.

Veluwenkamp, J.W., 1981. *Ondernemersgedrag op de Hollandse stapelmarkt in de tijd van de Republiek: de Amsterdamse handelsfirma Jan Isaac de Neufville & Comp., 1730–1764.* Meppel: Urips. Repro.

Veragtert, K., 1981. 'Geld, bankwezen en handel in de Zuidelijke Nederlanden 1792–1844', in *Algemene Geschiedenis der Nederlanden X.* Bussum: Unieboek, pp. 323–60.

Vermaas, A., 1995. 'Real industrial wages in the Netherlands, 1850–1913', in P. Scholliers and V. Zamagni (eds.), *Labours' rewards. Real wages and economic change in 19th and 20th century Europe.* Aldershot: Elgar, pp. 138–50.

Verrijn Stuart, G.M., 1935³. *Bankpolitiek.* Wassenaar.

Verstegen, S.W., 1982. 'De familie van Isendoorn à Blois en de verpachting van de Vaassense watermolens', in *Bijdragen en Mededelingen. Gelre.*

1996. 'Capital income in the Netherlands in the nineteenth century', *Economic and Social History in the Netherlands* 7.

Visser, H., 1980². *Monetaire theorie.* Leiden: Stenfert Kroese.

Vlis, D. van der, 1981. 'Daglonen in en rond Kampen van 1526 tot 1810', *Overijssels Historische Bijdragen* 96: 77–99.

Voort, J.P. van der, 1981. 'Dutch capital in the West Indies during the eighteenth century', *Acta Historiae Neerlandicae. The Low Countries history yearbook* 14: 85–105.

Voort, R.A. van der, 1994. *Overheidsbeleid en overheidsfinanciën in Nederland 1850–1913.* Amsterdam: NEHA.

Voort, R.H. van der, C.A. van Heijningen, 1988. *Sparen in de negentiende eeuw.* The Hague: Stichting Nutsspaarbank.

Voorthuysen, W.D., 1965. *De Republiek der Verenigde Nederlanden en het mercantilisme.* The Hague: Nijhoff.

1989. *Stads-bank van lening, 1614–1989.* Amsterdam: Stads-Bank van Lening.

Voûte, J.R., 1989. *Hypotheekbanken vroeger en nu.* Amsterdam: NIBE.

Vrankrijker, A.C.J. de, 1969. *Geschiedenis van de belastingen.* Bussum: Fibula/Van Dishoeck.

Vries, B. de, 1986. 'Amsterdamse vermogens en vermogensbezitters, 1855–75', *AAG-Bijdragen* 28: 199–216.

Vries, D.P. de, 1989. *Inventaris van de archieven van de bewoners van het huis annex kantoor van de firma M.H. Kingma te Makkum 1726–1932.* Leeuwarden.

Vries, Joh. de, 1958. 'De ontduiking der convoyen en licenten in de Republiek tijdens de 18e eeuw', *Tijdschrift voor Geschiedenis* 71: 349–61.

1959. *De economische achteruitgang der Republiek in de achttiende eeuw.* Amsterdam: Ellerman Harms.

1968. *Hoogovens IJmuiden 1918–1968.* Amsterdam: Meijer Pers.

1973. *De Coöperatieve Raiffeisen- en Boerenleenbanken in Nederland 1948–1973.* Utrecht: Centrale Coöperatieve Raiffeisen-Boerenleenbank.

1976. *Een eeuw vol effecten.* Vereniging voor de Effectenhandel Amsterdam.

1983⁴. *De Nederlandse economie tijdens de 20e eeuw.* Bussum: Fibula/Van Dishoeck.

1989. *Geschiedenis van de Nederlandsche Bank, V, Visserings tijdvak 1914–1931.* Amsterdam: NIBE.

Vries, J. de, 1976. *The economy of Europe an Age of crisis, 1600–1750.* Cambridge: Cambridge University Press.

Vries, J. de and A. van der Woude, 1995. *Nederlands 1500–1815. De eerste ronde van moderne economische groei.* Amsterdam: Balans.

Vries, M. de, 1921. *Tien jaren geschiedenis van het Nederlandsche bankwezen en de Nederlandsche conjunctuur 1866–1876.* The Hague: Nijhoff.

Webber, C. and A. Wildavsky, 1986. *A history of taxation and expenditure in the western world.* New York: Simon & Schuster.

Wee, H. van der, 1977. 'Monetary, credit and banking systems', E.E. Rich and Ch. Wilson (eds.), *The Cambridge Economic History of Europe* V. Cambridge: Cambridge University Press, pp. 240–392.

1983. 'Money and economic interdependence between the Northern and Southern Netherlands and the Baltic (15th–17th centuries)', *The interactions of Amsterdam and Antwerp with the Baltic region, 1400–1800. Papers presented at the third conference of the 'Association Internationale d'histoire des Mers Nordiques de l'Europe', Utrecht, August 30th–September 3rd 1982.* Amsterdam: NEHA, pp. 11–18.

Wee, H. van der and K. Tavernier, 1975. *De Nationale Bank van Belgie en het monetaire gebeuren tussen de twee wereldoorlogen.* Brussels: s.n.

Weeveringh, J.J., 1852. *Handleiding tot de geschiedenis der staatsschulden. Eerste Deel. Nederlandsche Staatsschuld*. Haarlem: Kruseman.

Werf, D.C.J. van der, 1988. *De Bond, de bank en de beurzen*. Amsterdam: NIBE.

Westerman, W.M., 1919. *De concentratie in het bankwezen; een bijdrage tot de kennis der economische ontwikkeling van onzen tijd*. The Hague: Nijhoff.

Westermann, J.C., 1948. 'Statistische gegevens over den handel van Amsterdam in de zeventiende eeuw', *Tijdschrift voor Geschiedenis* 61: 3–15.

Wijtvliet, C.A.M., 1993. *Expansie en dynamiek, de ontwikkeling van het Nederlandse handelsbankwezen 1860–1914*. Amsterdam: NIBE.

Wilson, C.H., 1942. *Anglo-Dutch commerce and finance in the eighteenth century*. 1st edn. 1942; 2nd impr. Cambridge: Cambridge University Press.

1963. 'Taxation and the decline of empires. An unfashionable theme', *Bijdragen en Mededelingen van het Historisch Genootschap* 77: 10–23.

1970. *The history of Unilever, a study in economic growth and social change*. London: Cassell.

Wilterdink, N., 1984. *Vermogensverhoudingen in Nederland. Ontwikkelingen sinds de negentiende eeuw*. Amsterdam: Arbeiderspers.

Winter, P.J. van, 1933. *Het aandeel van den Amsterdamschen handel aan de opbouw van het Amerikaansche Gemeenebest*. The Hague: Nijhoff.

Wolf, H., 1983. *Betalen via de bank – van verleden tot heden*. Deventer: Kluwer.

World Development Report 1982, 1992.

Woud, J. van der, 1947. *De hypotheekbank, haar wezen en hare waarde*. Amsterdam: H.A. van Bottersburg.

Yeager, L.B., 1966. *International Monetary Relations*. New York: Harper & Row.

Zamagni, V., 1989. 'An international comparison of real industrial wages, 1890–1913: methodological issues and results', in *Real wages in 19th and 20th century Europe, historical and comparative perspectives*, P. Scholliers (ed.). Oxford: Berg, pp. 107–40.

Zanden, J.L. van, 1984. 'De opkomst van de eigenerfde boerenklasse in Overijssel, 1750–1830', *AAG-Bijdragen*, 24: 105–30.

1985. *De economische ontwikkeling van de Nederlandse landbouw in de negentiende eeuw, 1800–1914*. Utrecht: Hes.

1985. 'Kosten van levensonderhoud en loonvorming in Holland en Oost Nederland 1600–1850', *Tijdschrift voor Sociale Geschiedenis* 11(4): 309–23.

1987. 'De economie van Holland in de periode 1650–1805: groei of achteruitgang? Een overzicht van bronnen, problemen en resultaten', *Bijdragen en Mededelingen betreffende de Geschiedenis der Nederlanden* 102(4): 562–609.

1988a. *De dans om de gouden standaard*. Amsterdam: Vrije Universiteit.

1988b. 'De economie van Holland in de periode 1650–1850: groei of achteruitgang', *Bijdragen en Mededelingen betreffende de Geschiedenis der Nederlanden* 102: 562–609.

1988c. 'Nederland in het interbellum', *Economisch-Statistische Berichten* 73: 172–86.

1991. 'De introductie van stoom in de Amsterdamse meelfabricage 1828–1855', *Jaarboek voor de geschiedenis van bedrijf en techniek* 8: 63–80.

1993. 'Economic growth in the Golden Age: the development of the economy of Holland, 1500–1650', in C.A. Davids and L. Noordegraaf (eds), *The Dutch Economy in the Golden Age*. Amsterdam: NEHA, pp. 5–26.

(forthcoming). 'Government finances 1807–1850', *Economic and social history in the Netherlands*.

Zanden, J.L. van and R.T. Griffiths, 1989. *Economische geschiedenis van Nederland in de 20e eeuw*. Utrecht: Het Spectrum.

Zeventig jaren statistiek in tijdreeksen. The Hague: CBS, 1970.

Zijlstra, J., 1992. *Per slot van rekening*. Amsterdam: Contact.

Zijlstra, S., 1983. '*Des lieven geldes isser an alle oorten gebreck*', Drentse Historische Studiën VII. Assen: s.n.

Zwitzer, H., 1991. '*De militie van den staat*'. *Het leger van de republiek der Verenigde Nederlanden*. Amsterdam: Van Soeren.

Index

Heterick Memorial Library
Ohio Northern University

	DUE	RETURNED		DUE	RETURNED
1.			13.		
2.			14.		
3.			15.		
4.			16.		
5.			17.		
6.			18.		
7.			19.		
8.			20.		
9.			21.		
10.			22.		
11.			23.		
12.			24.